THE RISING REVIVAL

FIRSTHAND ACCOUNTS OF THE INCREDIBLE ARGENTINE REVIVAL—AND HOW IT CAN SPREAD THROUGHOUT THE WORLD

THE RISING REVIVAL

FIRSTHAND ACCOUNTS OF THE INCREDIBLE ARGENTINE REVIVAL—AND HOW IT CAN SPREAD THROUGHOUT THE WORLD

Edited by C. Peter Wagner and Pablo Deiros

Renew

A Division of Gospel Light
Ventura, California, U.S.A.

Published by Renew Books
A Division of Gospel Light
Ventura, California, U.S.A.
Printed in U.S.A.

Renew Books is a ministry of Gospel Light, an evangelical Christian publisher dedicated to serving the local church. We believe God's vision for Gospel Light is to provide church leaders with biblical, user-friendly materials that will help them evangelize, disciple and minister to children, youth and families.

It is our prayer that this Renew book will help you discover biblical truth for your own life and help you meet the needs of others. May God richly bless you.

For a free catalog of resources from Renew Books/Gospel Light please contact your Christian supplier or call 1-800-4-GOSPEL.

Cover Design by Barbara LeVan Fisher
Interior Design by Britt Rocchio
Edited by Pablo Deiros, C. Peter Wagner and David Webb

Library of Congress Cataloging-in-Publication Data
(Applied for)

Rights for publishing this book in other languages are contracted by Gospel Literature International (GLINT). GLINT also provides technical help for the adaptation, translation and publishing of Bible study resources and books in scores of languages worldwide. For further information, contact GLINT, P.O. Box 4060, Ontario, CA 91761-1003, U.S.A., or visit their website at glint.org, or contact the publisher.

CONTENTS

one

REVIVAL POWER: GOD HAS SET HIS PEOPLE "A-PRAYING"

BY C. PETER WAGNER

C. Peter Wagner is professor of church growth at Fuller Theological Seminary and is president of Global Harvest Ministries. He lives in Colorado Springs, Colorado, with his wife, Doris, where they are involved in establishing the World Prayer Center, designed to link together intercessors from all continents. The author of more than 40 books on missions, church growth, prayer and spiritual warfare, Wagner has served, under Ed Silvoso, as dean of the Harvest Evangelism Institute for several years. Previous to their call to Fuller, the Wagners served as field missionaries to Bolivia for 16 years.

One of the foremost historians and advocates of revival in the twentieth century was the late J. Edwin Orr. I had the privilege of serving with him on the faculty of the Fuller Seminary School of World Mission for two decades. Hardly a faculty meeting went by in which Edwin Orr did not remind us of how dear revival is to the heart of God. One of Orr's more colorful phrases, which he repeated time and again, was: *"Whenever God gets ready to do a great work, He always sets His people a-praying."*

For years and years, whenever Orr would say this, I would respond, sometimes silently and sometimes verbally, "We haven't seen this in our generation as yet, but I dearly hope that we do." I am now glad to report that our hope has become reality, and that God's people are now praying with both quantity and intensity that I have not seen reported in the whole history of the Christian church. Consider this statement by David Bryant: "We may be standing in the vortex of the most significant prayer movement in the history of the church....No generation has ever seen such an acceleration and intensification of prayer worldwide."[1] I don't know a single recognized prayer leader who would disagree with Bryant.

REPORTS OF REVIVAL ARE MULTIPLYING

If we are truly in the midst of an unprecedented global prayer movement, we can expect that tangible signs of revival will be appearing, and this is the case. My guess would be that more reports of revival activity have come forth in the 1990s than in the last eight decades combined. And the frequency of revival reports is accelerating dramatically year after year. Most of the books on revival in bookstores and on library shelves today were written in the 1990s. Given current trends, as well as words frequently being heard through intercessors and prophets, it is not unrealistic to look for a worldwide outpouring of the Holy Spirit, on a magnitude never before experienced, in the very near future.

I am aware of the fact that "revival" is not a strictly technical term used uniformly in Christian circles as are such terms as "justification" or "holy communion" or "eternal life" or "Sunday School." Authors of books on revival who have a more scholarly bent openly recognize this and discuss it. Pablo Deiros, a recognized scholar and church historian, deals with the subject in the next chapter, and the semantic ambiguity makes him cautious about declaring categorically that Argentina is in "revival."

Some say that the term "revival" should apply to what God does to those who are already Christians, and that another term like "awakening" might better be used to describe what He does in bringing unbelievers to Himself or in changing society for the better. Others use revival as more of an umbrella term, arguing there is no true revival without a noticeable increase in evangelistic fruit. Still others use these and similar terms somewhat interchangeably. I find myself in the latter category, but I also like the term "outpouring of the Holy Spirit."

To further complicate the issue, some have developed checklists of criteria against which they evaluate whether a certain occurrence is or is not to be considered a true revival. Predictably, these lists will vary from one observer to another. This means that when a report on

> **Our generation will soon experience such a vast global divine initiative that virtually no one will question whether it is true revival.**

revival is announced, there will almost always be those who say, "That cannot be true revival because [fill in the blank]." This is true of the Argentine revival, especially among some Argentine leaders who have chosen to be spectators (and critics) rather than participants. My own inclination is to accept revival reports more or less at face value without subjecting them to my own critical evaluation. Of course, there are exceptions, but this is the rule. Having said this, I do expect that our generation will soon experience such a vast global divine initiative that virtually no one at all will question whether it is true revival.

Some contemporary revivals are led by "nameless and faceless" believers, while others are led by highly visible figures such as Oral Roberts, Rodney Howard-Browne, Benny Hinn, Karl Strader, John Arnott, Cindy Jacobs, Kenneth Copeland, Henry Blackaby, Sandy Millar, Charles and Frances Hunter, Colin Dye, Randy Clark, John Kilpatrick and the Argentine leaders featured in this book. Many of them, however, were "nameless and faceless" before God chose to set them apart as revival leaders.

TORONTO AND PENSACOLA

The two revival manifestations which have had the most far-reaching international impact to date in the 1990s are those centered in Toronto, Canada, and Brownsville, Florida. The spark was lit in Toronto at John Arnott's Airport Vineyard in January 1994 by Randy

Clark of St. Louis, at that time a relatively unknown Vineyard pastor. By May of that year, it had spread to England through Eleanor Mumford of the South West London Vineyard, who had visited Toronto and been touched by the Holy Spirit. She was invited by Sandy Millar, vicar of the prestigious Anglican church, Holy Trinity Brompton, already a center of renewal in the United Kingdom, to speak at the morning and evening services one Sunday. Here is another example of a "nameless, faceless" person being an instrument of revival in God's hands. After each service, she simply asked the Holy Spirit to come, as she had seen John Arnott do in the Airport Vineyard. What happened? Here is one report:

> There was a time of silence. Then slowly, members of the congregation began to cry quietly, and some to laugh. As the Holy Spirit came, Eleanor asked people to come forward if they wanted prayer. Many did so. As Eleanor's team and members of the church ministry team started to pray, people began to fall in the power of the Spirit. Soon the whole church was affected. There were scenes few had ever seen before.[2]

Cassette tapes of the visitation of the Holy Spirit in Holy Trinity Brompton were widely circulated, and thousands of churches—a large proportion of them Anglican churches—were impacted by the "Toronto Blessing," as it came to be called.

Christian leaders from Japan, Australia, South Africa, Singapore, as well as from England and Scotland, began to flock to Toronto and carried the blessing back to their churches and nations. At one point it was reported that Air Canada had to add extra daily flights from London to Toronto in order to accommodate the enormous volume of passengers.

On Father's Day 1995, the spark of revival was lit in the Brownsville Assembly of God in the suburbs of Pensacola. There God had "set His people a-praying," because for the previous two and one-half years Pastor John Kilpatrick had developed an exceptionally strong local church prayer ministry. On Sunday nights the congregation would gather for prayer around 12 banners set up around the sanctuary in order to identify specific areas of need. They fervently prayed for revival and for many other things.

Another "nameless, faceless" evangelist, Steve Hill, was invited to preach that Father's Day. When he called people forward for prayer after the message, the Pensacola revival began. John Kilpatrick reports, "As I stepped down from the platform to pray with people, I felt a current around my legs and ankles. I first thought it was the wind but then I realized it was more like a river. I could feel the actual current. I went back to the platform and had to have help because I could barely stand up. I told the church, 'This is what we have been praying for. Get in!' People began to go down all over the sanctuary. I went down on the platform and was there until four in the afternoon."[3]

Since then hundreds of thousands from across America and from the nations of the world have flooded to the ongoing revival meetings in Pensacola. Some begin lining up in the early morning in order to be assured of a seat in the evening meeting. Over 100,000 at this writing have either accepted Christ into their lives for the first time or rededicated their lives to His service.

UPSTREAM TO ARGENTINA

When historians analyze the origins of the revival phenomena in Toronto and Pensacola, undoubtedly many contributing factors will surface. One of them, however, will be that both revivals can eventually be traced upstream to Argentina.

John Arnott of Toronto deeply desired to move into a new level of spiritual power. For a year and a half before the Toronto Blessing ignited, Arnott and his wife, Carol, would give their entire mornings to enjoy the presence of the Lord in worship, reading and prayer. They did whatever they could. They invited outside speakers to their church. They attended Benny Hinn's meetings. They sought after God with all their hearts.

When they heard about the revival in Argentina, they learned that Ed Silvoso's annual Harvest Evangelism Institute had been designed to introduce Christian leaders from other nations to the leaders of the Argentine revival. They signed up for the institute in November 1993, the third year of the series. I remember it well because Silvoso had asked me to be the dean of the institute and the master of ceremonies. As was our custom, we prayed specifically that the anointing of the Argentine revival would be imparted to those who came for the week, including our new friends, John and Carol Arnott.

John reports, "We were powerfully touched in meetings led by Claudio Freidzon, a leader of the Assemblies of God in Argentina. Claudio prayed for Carol and me. I fell down, then started analyzing the event as I usually did. *Lord, was this really You? Or did I just fall because I want You so badly?* Carol receives from God so easily, but I have always had a difficult time.

"After I stood up," Arnott continues, "Claudio came over to me and said, 'Do you want the anointing?'

'Oh yes, I want it all right,' I answered.

'Then take it!' He slapped my outstretched hands.

'I will. I will take it,' I said. Something clicked in my heart at the moment. It was as though I heard the Lord say, 'For goodness sake, will you take this? Take it, it's yours.' And I received by faith."[4]

The rest is history.

Steve Hill of Pensacola was a missionary church planter in Argentina when he drank of the waters of the Argentine revival. He says, "I had been prayed for by 15 or 20 people prior to [Pensacola] including evangelists from the great Argentine revival."[5] One of the Argentines who most influenced Hill was evangelist Carlos Annacondia, who also prayed for John and Carol Arnott when they were there.

Another spiritual stream flowed into Steve Hill at Holy Trinity Brompton, where the Toronto Blessing had first taken root in England. He had read of the move of God there in *Time* magazine. He scheduled a visit to England and was strongly touched by the Lord there when vicar Sandy Millar laid on hands and prayed for him. This impartation in England could be traced upstream to Toronto and then to Argentina.

My purpose in this section is not to argue that there is a singular cause-and-effect relationship between Argentina and the revivals in Toronto and Pensacola. Causes of important historical events are invariably much more complex than that. But the purpose is to point out that, when all is said and done, the spiritual anointing being released by God in Argentina has borne major fruit here in North America and around the world. In passing, it is also worthy of mention that, in all probability, the foreign Christian leader who has had the most influence on the nation of Japan in the past four years is none other than Argentine evangelist Carlos Annacondia.

WHY ARGENTINA?

Argentina must be considered among the chief headwaters of the rivers of revival that God is now sending into many parts of the world. My expectation is that this influence will increase significantly in the days to come.

> Argentina is an ordinary
> nation that has come under
> an extraordinary outpouring
> of the grace of God.

Arguably, Argentina as a nation has more to say to the world about revival at this point in time than any other single country. Why is this? Why would God choose Argentina and not Venezuela or the Philippines or Australia or Nigeria or one of many other places? This is a good question, but it is like asking why God chose Martin Luther or John Wesley or Dwight Moody or Billy Graham. None of them was born into Christian royalty, so to speak. The same is true of Argentina. Argentina is an ordinary nation that has come under an extraordinary outpouring of the grace of God.

Revivals usually last two or three years, give or take. Some last longer, such as the East African Revival, which went on for thirty years. Others last only a few months, such as the January 1995 revival at Howard Payne University in Brownwood, Texas. Revival waters spread rapidly from Brownwood to schools like Wheaton College, Gordon College, Asbury College, Eastern Nazarene College, Southwestern Baptist Theological Seminary and others, but petered out by the end of that academic year.

REVIVALS OF HISTORY

Check out the more famous revivals of history. Granting that histori-

ans of revival are not in agreement as to the exact dates of the beginning and end of specific revivals, at least they would agree that most
revivals are relatively short-lived. If we could call the initiating event
the "revival fire" and the ongoing ripple effects the "afterglow," it
might help us achieve more precision in dating revivals. My hypothesis of two or three years applies to the revival *fire*, not to the *afterglow*, which invites a considerable amount of subjectivity when historians look back on it.

For example, the great revival in Florence, Italy, under Savonarola
began in 1496 and ended in 1498. The Protestant Reformation itself
could be considered part of the afterglow of that movement, since
Luther was strongly influenced by Savonarola. The Great Awakening
in the American colonies began in 1739 and ended in 1741. The
Second Great Awakening may have lasted longer, some say from 1800
to 1830; although others date the fire by James McGready's meetings
on the banks of Kentucky's Gasper River from 1800 to 1804, and consider the rest afterglow.

The Third Great Awakening of 1857-1858 lasted only nine months.
The revival in Ulster, Ireland, took place in 1859. The famous Welsh
revival started in 1904 and finished in 1905, leaving a powerful afterglow in many different places around the world. The entire
Pentecostal movement could be considered as the afterglow of the
Azusa Street revival from 1906 to 1909. The Korean revival occurred
in the year 1907. The Tommy Hicks revival in Argentina took place in
1954, and it was preceded by revival of several months in City Bell
under Edward Miller in 1951. The Indonesia revival lasted more than
four years, from 1965 to 1970.

The current Argentine revival is still in the fire stage, although
parts of the afterglow, such as Toronto and Pensacola, have already
begun to surface. Revival ignited in Argentina in 1982 and, at the time
of this writing, it is entering its fifteenth year.

This raises another important question. Why is it that the blessing
of God has tarried for so long in Argentina, while in most instances of
revival it has passed much sooner? As I have observed the development of Christianity and the growth of churches around the world
over the past few decades, I have reached some conclusions. While I
cannot claim that I have final answers to the question, I do think that
I now have developed some reasonable hypotheses.

WHAT THE SPIRIT HAS BEEN
SAYING TO THE CHURCHES

My first hypothesis relates to the times in which we find ourselves. Looking at the past and the present, there is reason to believe we are the first generation in centuries to live in a time ripe for the greatest manifestation of the Holy Spirit ever poured out across the earth. Possibly God has not allowed previous revivals to be extended because it was not yet time. What is it, then, that the Holy Spirit has been saying to the churches?

> We live in extraordinary times,
> witnessing more manifestations
> of supernatural power than in
> all of history.

For the whole picture, we must go back to the Protestant Reformation during which our basic, biblical, theological paradigm was established. Justification by faith, the absolute authority of the Bible and the priesthood of all believers have been our theological bedrocks ever since. The Holiness Movement at the end of the nineteenth century brought another crucial component to the picture, and the Pentecostal Movement emerged from that, adding the tangible power of the Holy Spirit through gifts and power ministries. It was in 1950 that the great evangelistic harvest began, increasing in volume every decade since. In 1960 the Spirit began speaking strongly to the churches about social ministries and concern for the poor and destitute; today the church is feeding more hungry people than ever before. In 1970 the great prayer movement began, although it had already taken root previously in Korea.

For more than 25 years now, God's people have been "a-praying," as Edwin Orr would say. Possibly previous revivals could not be sustained because there was not enough of the right kind of prayer. David Bryant says, "This prayer movement is a gift from God. Because of our natural aversion to prayer, God must stir up the work of prayer in us. Just as faith is a gift of God, so prayer is a gift of God. Therefore, praying people are a gift from God, and movements of prayer are his gift, too. And if God is giving this gift, he will not fail to answer the prayers that he himself has stirred up in our hearts to begin with. Truly, the prayer movement is a powerfully reassuring sign that national and world revival is at hand."[6]

PROPHETS, APOSTLES AND PRAYER WARRIORS

In 1980 the Holy Spirit began restoring the gift and office of prophet to the whole church. For many, this has been the most difficult step of all to embrace, and some are still resisting it. But at just about the time that traditionalists like me were beginning to understand and accept the ministry of prophets, the Holy Spirit took the next logical step. In 1990 He began to speak to the churches about the restoration of the gifts and office of apostle. This has brought to life the words of Ephesians 4:11, a chief verse on church government which says, "And [Christ] Himself gave some to be apostles, some prophets, some evangelists, and some pastors and teachers." We traditionalists have been used to individuals being recognized in the churches as evangelists, pastors, and teachers, but it has required a paradigm shift for us to admit that apostles and prophets appear in the very same biblical list.

Could it be that the restoration of the office and ministry of apostles is the final element in the preparation of the Body of Christ for the anticipated great outpouring of the Holy Spirit? It does seem we live in extraordinary times. We are in the midst of the greatest harvest of souls that the world has ever known; we have been witnessing more manifestations of supernatural power than in all of history, including the book of Acts; we have more unity of the Body of Christ than we have seen in 1600 years; and a higher percentage of humans are currently exposed to the message of the gospel than ever before. Finally Christians are able to see light at the end of the tunnel of the Great Commission. For the first time ever, it can be fulfilled within the lifetime of our generation!

God is also entrusting His people with equipment for engaging in and winning high-level battles of spiritual warfare that previous generations were not aware of, and perhaps were not ready for, since the biblical government of the Church (as set forth in the fivefold ministry of Ephesians 4:11) had not been reestablished. Such things as strategic-level spiritual warfare, spiritual mapping, identificational repentance and prayer evangelism are now being widely used on all continents. Ten years ago, we did not even have words for these weapons in our Christian vocabulary.

Therefore, the worldwide spiritual climate of the 1990s is undoubtedly more conducive to sustaining the fervor of a revival such as the one in Argentina than has previously been the case. Let me be more specific.

ARGENTINE LEADERS HAVE EARS TO HEAR

My second hypothesis as to why the Argentine revival has been sustained for 15 years is that Argentine pastors, churches and revival leaders have obeyed Jesus' command, "He who has an ear, let him hear what the Spirit says to the churches" (Rev. 2:7).

I have recently read, reread or carefully perused 35 books on revival. Yet I did not find in these books any serious grappling with the fact that almost all the revivals described were relatively short—two or three years, give or take. Charles Finney, for example, thoroughly discusses conditions he feels are necessary to light the revival fire, but he does not address the variables that would separate long-term fires from short-term fires.

Nevertheless, a few significant patterns emerged in the literature on revivals. Three of the most frequent and persistent themes associated with contemporary and historic revival movements have been prayer, repentance and the devil.

There was a great deal of material on prayer in these books, but it revolved mostly around individualistic, pietistic, self-centered prayer. I found almost no discussion of some of the prayer forms being used in the Argentine revival such as aggressive prophetic intercession, prayer invasions of the invisible world, two-way prayer or prophecy, targeting prayer through spiritual mapping, prophetic acts, or even intentional, structured intercession for Christian leaders. The few books that mention these subjects were written very recently.

Repentance is invariably one of the first outward manifestations of the work of the Holy Spirit, and the revival literature strongly reflects this trend. But in these works, repentance is generally assumed to be personal repentance with confession of sins and subsequent steps toward personal holiness. I cannot recall references to corporate or identificational repentance for the healing of the wounds of cities or of people groups or of nations. On the other hand, some of the more notable highlights of the Argentine revival have been public meetings led by Eduardo Lorenzo or Omar Olier or Victor Lorenzo or Marfa Cabrera or Cindy Jacobs or others confessing corporate sin and participating in meaningful, often emotional acts of reconciliation.

SPIRITUAL WARFARE

Accounts of the devil being defeated through revival occurrences are often related in revival literature. But the devil's *modus operandi* is more often characterized in these books by works of the flesh than by

> The new apostolic paradigm, prominent in Argentina, signals the most radical change in the way of "doing church" since the Protestant Reformation.

demonization. The enemy is known to employ the world and the flesh, but, in the revival literature I have seen, the direct activity of the devil through demonization is clearly underemphasized. This stands in stark contrast to the Argentine revival, where overt and structured deliverance ministries are virtually taken for granted as an integral part of dealing with the move of the Holy Spirit.

John Arnott stresses the need for deliverance when he says, "That which is demonic must be dealt with—hopefully the person can be delivered from demonic influence."[7] In contrast to Argentina, Arnott finds that, in Toronto, "manifestations of the flesh and the demonic are actually rare, although they tend to get all the attention."[8] As you will see in the chapter by Pablo Bottari, casting out demons in Argentina is as common today as it was under the ministry of Jesus and the apostles.

In past revivals there are few or no records of Christians engaging the high-ranking agents of Satan, which the Bible refers to as "principalities and powers" (Col. 2:15). The act of breaking curses is given little or no importance in the accounts of more short-lived revivals. In Pensacola, however, perhaps due to the influence of Argentina, strategic-level spiritual warfare and prophetic intercession are part of the lively Tuesday night prayer meetings at the Brownsville Assembly of God. One observer writes, "The spiritual warfare and souls banners are posted at the south end of the building. Prayer warriors stand unified in spiritual battle array with their hands stretched forth in power. Souls are called out from cities, countries and continents to the south. Powers of spiritual wickedness in high places are commanded to release their holds on individuals and communities by the blood and name of Jesus Christ."[9] This prophetic act is then repeated for the west, east and north.

THE APOSTOLIC ORDER

My third hypothesis as to why the revival fire in Argentina has burned far longer than in past revivals relates to the emergence of apostolic ministry and the office of apostle in the 1990s. I will not go into much detail here, because one of the best discussions of this in recent literature is found in the next chapter by Pablo Deiros. The shift from the traditional Christendom paradigm to the new apostolic paradigm, prominent in Argentina, is bringing with it the most radical changes in the way of "doing church" since the Protestant Reformation.

This shift is so new that even those who are at the forefront of the transition are still struggling to understand this enormous move of God, not only in Argentina, but on every continent of the world. In fact, many of those who are now fulfilling an apostolic function in the Church are hesitant to allow the term "apostle" to be applied to themselves, although others have accepted the designation.

The ongoing, mature, apostolic covering of the Argentine revival distinguishes it from many of the more short-lived revivals. One of the closest parallels might be the Wesleyan revival beginning in the 1730s in which John Wesley, Charles Wesley and George Whitefield were recognized apostolic figures who gave direction and government to the movement, which was sustained for decades.

THE ARGENTINE APOSTLES

Four of the authors contributing to this book are acknowledged in Argentina as the key apostolic revival leaders there, although other names might also be included. Omar Cabrera is the precursor. His ministry in the 1970s as itinerant pastor of the 150,000-member Vision of the Future Church, which met in multiple locations around Argentina, was consistently characterized by the outward manifestations of spiritual power now common throughout the nation. But, because these miraculous happenings were so unusual at the time, and because Cabrera used innovative methods such as wearing a clerical collar, his ministry was rejected by the evangelical leaders of the day and relegated by them to the lunatic fringe. No longer! Acts of reconciliation have taken place, and some would now regard Omar Cabrera as the chief apostle of the Argentine revival.

The individual whom God chose to light the revival fire itself was a "nameless, faceless" owner of a nuts and bolts factory, Carlos Annacondia. A layperson with a sixth-grade education and the father of nine children would not be an obvious candidate to become one of the spiritual giants to serve a whole generation. It could not be mere happenstance that Annacondia's first public evangelistic service would be held the very day that the British navy sank the Argentine battleship *General Belgrano* in the Falkland Islands (Malvinas) War in 1982.

For 15 years now, Annacondia has saturated the nation with open-air evangelistic campaigns in which he preaches 30 or 40 nights in a row, while still managing his factory. At every service, between 5,000 and 20,000 will stand (there are no chairs) from 8:00 to midnight to worship God, to receive healing and demonic deliverance, to see curses broken over themselves and their families, to be filled with the Holy Spirit, and to hear a simple message of salvation. When the invitation is given, there is no pleading or closing the eyes or bowing the head or singing "Just As I Am." Sinners typically run toward the altar, sometimes pushing each other out of the way to get there first. Some calculate that up to 2 million have made first-time decisions for Christ at Annacondia's meetings.

Throughout the Argentine revival, rather than allow the fire to die out, God has, from time to time, raised the intensity a notch or two. One of the most notable advances came through Claudio Freidzon, pastor of the King of Kings Church, a Buenos Aires congregation affiliated with the Assemblies of God. Soon after Carlos Annacondia began his meetings, Freidzon, then a professor of theology at River Plate Seminary, along with some interested pastors, met and prayed with Annacondia every Thursday. A short time later, Freidzon attempted an Annacondia-style campaign in the Belgrano district of Buenos Aires, and the King of Kings Church, now with 5,000 members, was planted as a result.

But the most significant change came in 1992. In his moving book, *Holy Spirit, I Hunger for You!*, Freidzon writes, "The year 1992 represented a new period in my ministry. God poured out a salt shaker on my tongue, causing an intense spiritual thirst—a hunger for the Holy Spirit! He not only filled my cup with the Holy Spirit, but he made the Spirit overflow toward others."[10] After reading Benny Hinn's book, *Good Morning, Holy Spirit*, Freidzon visited Hinn's church in Orlando, where Benny Hinn laid on hands and prayed for him. Since then, what has come to be called *la unción*, "the anointing"—characterized by large numbers of people falling out under the power of the Holy Spirit at one time—has become a part of the Argentine revival and is increasingly common in churches across the country.

One of these churches was Central Baptist Church in Buenos Aires, pastored by Pablo Deiros. Central Baptist, 114 years old at this writing, has long been one of the principal features of the ecclesiastical landscape of Buenos Aires and all of Argentina. When Deiros, along with his copastor Carlos Mraida, opened their church to the work of the Holy Spirit through "the anointing," it caused a great stir through all levels of Argentine Christian leadership.

Deiros, with a Ph.D. from Southwestern Theological Seminary, is also a professor at the Baptist Seminary in Buenos Aires and has authored several textbooks used throughout Latin America. Deiros has formed a close friendship with Carlos Annacondia, and even invited the director of Annacondia's deliverance ministry, Pablo Bottari, to serve on the staff of Central Baptist in order to install a local church deliverance ministry. For several years Pablo Deiros has also served with me on the faculty of the Fuller Seminary School of World Mission in Pasadena, California, and I am privileged to coedit this book with the fourth apostle of the Argentine revival.

This apostolic context is a very important reason why the Argentine revival has been sustained until now, and why many are acknowledging this movement as "headwaters of revival" for other parts of the world.

ADDITIONAL FACTORS

In summary, my three principal hypotheses as to why the Argentina revival fire has lasted as long as it has are (1) the timing represents a divine convergence of historical factors; (2) the openness on the part of Argentine leaders to risk joining the new moves of the Holy Spirit; and (3) the presence of an apostolic order to fashion new wineskins.

There are three other factors which should be considered, and which might be instructive for other revival movements.

1. Destruction of the Spiritual Stronghold over Argentina

Throughout all of Latin America, Argentines have cultivated a reputation for being the proudest people on the continent. Granted, they have a beautiful country and much to be proud of, but other Latin Americans have resented displays of Argentine pride. This is no secret to Argentines, some of whom are known to be proud of their pride.

Spiritually speaking, this national pride has been a stronghold which the enemy used to keep the nation in darkness. During the 1970s, evangelical churches in Argentina did not grow well. Argentina was among the Latin American nations with the lowest percentage of evangelicals. Very little of note had happened among the churches of Argentina, with the exception of the short-lived 1954 revival under Tommy Hicks.

One of the best known missionaries to Argentina, Edward Miller, had experienced a strong move of the Holy Spirit in City Bell in 1951. One of the recorded prophecies that he and his group received at that time reflects some of the Argentine pride:

> Oh, Argentina! You who are rejecting My love! Why are you so proud? Because you are rich? Who gave you the riches?...You think you are the highest one; vanity superabounds on your countenance....Humble yourself and I will pardon you. If you do not do this, you will die without mercy for great is your pride.

But God was merciful, and He used the conflict with Britain over the sovereignty of the Falkland (Malvinas) Islands. During the war, the Argentine authorities lied to the public, telling them they were winning the conflict. When Britain emerged victorious, an unprecedented national trauma shook Argentina. Claudio Freidzon says, "It was sorrow and suffering of our nation that prepared hearts for the gospel. The Malvinas war left a tremendous wound in the people's hearts. We lived through days of tension and deep sadness as a consequence of the death of many innocent young boys in that frigid place. *Our pride was shattered by defeat* (emphasis mine). In the spiritual arena, this situation led to the willingness of many people to open up to the Lord."[11]

Satan lost much of the grip he held on Argentina because the national stronghold of pride had been destroyed, and this opened the way to revival. As I mentioned, Carlos Annacondia held his first public meeting and the revival began on the very day that the *General Belgrano* was sunk.

2. A Revival for the Common People

The famous English historian, Arnold Toynbee, has repeatedly made the point that significant religious movements always enter society via the common people, then work their way up the social ladder. This was the case with the beginnings of the Argentine revival. In Carlos Annacondia's meetings, there are many people from the middle and upper classes who are now born again and fully participating in revival manifestations, but in the early days the poor and destitute were those who filled the vacant lots and who were saved. This, combined with the inherent simplicity of a lay evangelist with a sixth-grade education, exemplifies a vital characteristic of the Argentine revival, which has kept it from the dangers of elitism and subsequent stagnation.

The meaning of this social phenomenon is made clear through a cursory examination of the Wilkes Spectrum, first developed and presented in Argentina by Peter Wilkes, pastor of South Hills Community Church in San Jose, California. On this profile ranging from upper-class values on the left and lower-class values on the right, it has been to the credit of the leaders of the Argentine revival that the movement has maintained its position toward the right. Even upper-class revival participants gladly blend into the values of the lower classes on the Wilkes Spectrum.

It is helpful to keep in mind that, while the Wilkes Spectrum distinguishes between social classes, it deals essentially with the *cultural* values ordinarily associated with these groups. There is no claim that one group is superior to the other in any way, including intelligence. Nor should the strictly economic nuances be pushed rigidly if we are going to understand this spectrum. On an international scale, most Americans, especially clergy, would profile toward the "upper class" side of the spectrum, while most Latin Americans would find themselves more toward the "lower class" side. In my opinion, this helps explain why revival would be expected to start south and come north, rather than vice versa.

THE WILKES SPECTRUM
Class Preferences for Christian Values

UPPER CLASS	LOWER CLASS

Personal Inclination

1.	Intellectual	Intuitional
2.	Rational	Emotional
3.	Scientific	Experiential
4.	Deductive reasoning	Inductive reasoning
5.	Time-oriented	Event-oriented
6.	Literacy essential	Literacy optional
7.	You control life	Life controls you

Spiritual Tendencies

1.	Faith is complex	Faith is simple
2.	Conversion gentle	Conversion confrontational
3.	Biblical criticism	Biblical literalism
4.	Systematic theology based on philosophy	Pragmatic theology based on ministry
5.	Relative Ethics	Absolute ethics
6.	Preaching based on study	Preaching based on prayer
7.	Mild demonology	Strong demonology

Trusting Feelings. For example, the American assumption that the more formal schooling one has, the better the person, is not that common in Argentina. American educators feel they need to teach students to *think*, above all. Intellectual reasoning is, to them, more important than facts. Argentines, however, do much of their learning by rote, and as a result, many of them are much more intuitional than cerebral. That means that feelings become very important in reaching conclusions. Argentines do not necessarily buy into the American axiom, "Don't trust your feelings." They trust their feelings quite a bit. This bolsters the faith level of common people, because faith is simple, not complex. Verification of manifestations of the Holy Spirit comes not so much through a rigid application of scientific principles as through personal experience. God is much more likely to do mighty works in this kind of an environment.

Time is also perceived differently. For Americans punctuality is considered a very important value; but, for Argentines, people rank equally high, or even higher as a value. Building and cultivating personal relationships is more important than getting somewhere or starting a meeting on time. Because people are so significant in that culture, theology tends to be pragmatic, not responding so much to the question, *Is it true?* as to the question, *Does it work to bless people?* Debating whether or not God heals today or whether He speaks to us through prophecy does not seem like a worthwhile pursuit to many Argentines. The important things are testimonies like, "God just filled five of my teeth!" or "I was obese and I lost thirty pounds in the revival meeting last night!" or "I fell in the Spirit, and God melted away my resentment toward the man who molested my daughter" or "I began to pray for others and my hands suddenly were full of anointing oil" or "A witch's curse on me was broken, my lust is gone, and now I am reconciled with my wife" or "I had an operation that removed one of my lungs and I now have two lungs again!"

To illustrate my point, I purposely selected a number of actual testimonies that have come out of the Argentine revival, testimonies that are not easy for many toward the left side of the Wilkes Spectrum to believe. The last time I went to Argentina, I heard Omar Cabrera tell of one of his meetings during which God allowed gold dust and tiny chips of precious jewels to rain down on the audience. The material was taken to reputable jewelers for analysis and confirmation; but even with that, many people I know would not believe that it really happened, or that it ever *could* happen.

Is Mild Demonology Enough? Many Christian leaders committed to upper-class values will profess to believe in demons, but quickly add that they are not among those who "see a demon behind every bush." They then typically hesitate to answer the follow-on question, "What do you do when there *is* a demon behind some bush?" This mild demonology may be one reason that some revivals in history have proven to be short-lived. Carlos Annacondia told me that on his first ministry visit to Germany, his hosts told him that he could not minister there like he did in Argentina because demons were not much of a problem in Germany. He began grinning broadly as he went on to tell me that he probably cast out more demons per capita in Germany than he had in Argentina!

The apostle Paul wrote to the Corinthians that "not many wise according to the flesh, not many mighty, not many noble, are called" (1 Cor. 1:26). This was also true in the beginning of the Argentine revival, and continues to be true today.

God loves to work among the common people. This shouldn't surprise us because even Jesus had difficulty getting through to the high-class scribes and Sadducees, but "the common people heard Him gladly" (Mark 12:37).

3. Evangelism Is First and Last

I am convinced that many revivals have not lasted because they were focused on blessing those who were already Christians—renewing their faith in God, increasing their intimacy with Jesus, intensifying their worship experiences, healing their bodies, restoring broken family relationships, providing for financial needs, deepening their hunger for the Word of God, reconciling them with enemies, forgiving their sins, moving them into sanctification, providing the gift of tongues, encouraging them with prophetic words and the like. Evangelizing the lost in the community and out in the world is invariably mentioned, but it is frequently subject to an underlying assumption: namely that we must polish up existing Christians and develop their walk with God first. Then when this is done, we will be properly equipped to move out to evangelize the lost.

There is much underlying truth in that assumption, but the fact of the matter is that many revivals have become stuck in implementing the first part and they have never gotten around to aggressively evangelizing the lost.

The Argentine revival, on the other hand, was kicked off by an evangelist, and a powerful one at that. Because Carlos Annacondia has never deviated a bit from his primary calling to reach the lost, and because Omar Cabrera also maintained this singular focus in the early days of revival, these two key apostles have effectively prevented the Argentine revival from falling victim to the "bless-me syndrome" that has been the downfall of so many others.

Ed Silvoso's best-selling book, *That None Should Perish* (Regal Books), is the strongest argument we have at present for keeping evangelism front and center in movements like the Argentine revival. Silvoso says, "Often our idea of revival is extremely self-serving, and thus, unbiblical. A revival that fails to bring the lost to Jesus is a self-serving revival, centered on man's needs and wants, and not on God's glory."[12]

CONCLUSION

There is a saying, "What is gained by intercession is maintained by intercession." Roy Fish, one of the few authors on revival who does discuss the issue of sustaining revival, says, "If revival is to be sustained, God's people must remain humble before Him; they must continue to be steadfast in prayer; they are to be ever seeking the Lord; and they must live lives characterized by repentance of constantly turning from any wicked way. To a degree, the requirements for securing revival become the requirements for sustaining revival."[13]

Edwin Orr says that one of the requirements for securing revival is for God to get His people "a-praying." I want to close this chapter on this note with a word from Frank Damazio, who says it as well as anyone I have seen. "There has always been a spirit of prayer and intercession associated with spiritual awakening, both in Scripture and in history," says Damazio. "Revival is preceded by prayer, birthed through intercession, and sustained by fervent, persevering prayer. Prayer is the central living element to every spiritual awakening and every moving of the Holy Spirit."[14]

Notes
1. David Bryant, *The Hope at Hand* (Grand Rapids: Baker Books, 1995), p. 130.
2. Wallace Boulton, *The Impact of Toronto* (Crowborough, England: Monarch, 1994), p. 21.
3. David A. Womack, "The Pensacola Revival, Today's Azusa Street," *Enrichment* (Winter 1997) pp. 57-58.
4. John Arnott, *The Father's Blessing* (Orlando: Creation House, 1995), p. 58.
5. Lee Grady, "When God Interrupts Your Agenda: An Interview with the Leaders of Brownsville Assembly of God," *Ministries Today* (November/December 1996), p. 26.
6. Bryant, *The Hope at Hand*, p. 138.
7. Arnott, *The Father's Blessing*, p. 137.
8. Ibid.
9. Renee DeLoriea, *Portal in Pensacola* (Shippensburg: Destiny Image Publishers, 1997), p. 42.
10. Claudio Freidzon, *Holy Spirit, I Hunger for You!* (Orlando: Creation House, 1997), p. 63.
11. Ibid., p. 45.
12. Ed Silvoso, *That None Should Perish* (Ventura: Regal Books, 1994), p. 70.
13. Roy Fish, "How to Keep the Fire Burning," *Revival!* Edited by John Avant, Malcolm McDow and Alvin Reid (Nashville: Broadman & Holman Publishers, 1996), p. 153.
14. Frank Damazio, *Seasons of Revival* (Portland: BT Publishing, 1996), p. 363.

The Roots and the Fruits of the Argentine Revival

By Pablo A. Deiros

Pablo A. Deiros *is pastor, along with Carlos Mraida, of the 114-year-old Central Baptist Church of Buenos Aires. Recognized as one of the foremost Christian scholars in Latin America, Deiros earned his Ph.D. from Southwestern Baptist Theological Seminary in Fort Worth, Texas. He has served for several years as professor of church history at the International Baptist Seminary in Buenos Aires, and he is a member of the faculty of the School of World Mission at Fuller Theological Seminary in Pasadena, California. Deiros has been instrumental in bringing the Argentine renewal into his traditional Baptist church and has served as a bridge to many other traditional evangelicals. With Carlos Mraida, he authored* Latinoamerica en Llamas (Latin America in Flames). *His latest book is* Protestantismo en America Latina (Protestantism in Latin America).

In recent years, people around the world have begun to take notice of the extraordinary work of God which has continued for 15 years in Argentina. Some have acclaimed this movement and its accompanying phenomena, impacting multiple evangelical churches in the country, as true revival. Others who do not expect to see the outward, supernatural activity of God in their churches, claim that these manifestations are serious distortions of the gospel. Then there are those who prefer not to talk about revival per se, but who do agree that we are seeing clear and positive signs of growing spiritual renewal in the churches in Argentina. Many who recognize the phenomena as encouraging new indicators of spiritual growth and development, at the same time assiduously decry attitudes which could be interpreted as triumphalism.

Whatever interpretation we give to the present move of God among the evangelical churches of Argentina, it cannot be denied that over the past 15 years we have experienced a spiritual awakening, numerical church growth, organizational maturity, the emergence of qualified leadership, unity among the pastors, greater evangelistic commitment and a development in discipleship and ministerial formation far more significant than any before in the century and a half of evangelical Christian testimony in this country.

THE SOCIAL AND POLITICAL ROOTS OF REVIVAL

Various historical factors have played a significant role in the development of the evangelical awakening of the last decade. Among them, the long years of military dictatorship in Argentina (1976-1983); the subversive violence of the state; generalized repression; frustration emerging from the War in the Malvinas (Falkland) Islands (1982); the advent of democracy; and a deepening economic crisis. Nevertheless, to many the decisive factor was not political, social or economic, but was, quite simply, an extraordinarily powerful move of the Holy Spirit.

At the top of the list of unique phenomena following in the Spirit's wake are the massive evangelistic campaigns, with a particular emphasis on healing and deliverance, held by several outstanding evangelists. Of these, Carlos A. Annacondia deserves special mention, because of the continuing impact of his ministry throughout these 15 years of revival.

Another revival phenomenon has been the emergence of megachurches, including *Ondas de Amor y Paz* (Waves of Love and Peace) and *Visión de Futuro* (Vision of the Future), among others. Evangelical journalism has also advanced significantly. Today there are several widely-circulated evangelical publications, the pioneer and still the most notable being the newspaper *El Puente* (The Bridge).

INCREASING CHRISTIAN UNITY

Visible Christian unity has accelerated at a rate no one expected. The number of interdenominational consultations, meetings, workshops, conferences, seminars, congresses and other programs serving the whole evangelical spectrum has exploded in recent years. Never before have so many councils of pastors been organized in so many places across the country. About 200 local councils of pastors are now active, characterized by solid spiritual unity and a joint commitment to mission. For the first time in the history of evangelical churches in Argentina, the New Testament model of a single church in each city is taking root. This one-city church is perceived to be made up of many local congregations, linked by close personal relationships and a joint commitment to conquering the entire city for Christ.

Growth of the work in Argentina also has been remarkable. Once a "very happy, small group of people," Argentine evangelicals now constitute almost 10 percent of the total population of the country. In the city of Buenos Aires, recent statistics indicate that, of a total resident population of about 3 million, nearly 80,000 are members of an evangelical church, or almost three percent. There are now about 350 churches in Buenos Aires (Federal District), most of them very young. During the 1960s only two new churches were planted in Buenos Aires. Four churches were planted there in the 1970s, while 10 more were planted in the 1980s. However, in just the first two years of our present decade, 17 new churches emerged in Buenos Aires!

Further evidence of the great move of the Holy Spirit in Argentina includes the proliferation of Christian radio and television programs; the involvement of churches in their communities through social service programs; the development of a distinctly "evangelical culture"; the astronomic rise of evangelical parachurch organizations; the organization of interdenominational cooperative institutions; and the seeming ease of convening large-scale Christian events that bring people together from across the evangelical spectrum.

INWARD FACTORS

Along with these outward signs, some very important, though less visible, inward factors must be considered. For example, theological barriers which seemed insurmountable 20 years ago are coming down. Issues that for decades were the subject of never-ending debates, today are open to calm, cordial discussion and a consensus that these issues may not have been that important after all.

Argentine Christians are rapidly entering what could be termed a "postdenominational" era. Many denominational distinctives that previously seemed non-negotiable, today are met with remarkable flexibility. Churches of many different stripes are open to the influence of traditions different from theirs, and demonstrate a willingness to share their own special insights with others. Similar leveling of the field is also seen with regard to liturgical matters, particularly in the area of worship. Today, it is possible to worship God in almost any evangelical church in Argentina without the need of a hymnbook, since almost all evangelicals know most of the songs that are commonly used in all of the churches.

CHARISMATIC TRENDS

During the 1980s an enormous wave of new spiritual manifestations swept through Argentina. Most of these would be considered Pentecostal or charismatic manifestations, especially in their practices and styles. Thousands of spiritually renewed believers who had never attended a Pentecostal church, nor considered themselves open to that particular doctrinal approach, suddenly found themselves participating in charismatic experiences. Many of these brothers and sisters tried to live out and express these enthusiastic and overflowing new experiences within the context of their own denominational traditions. Many continued to be good Baptists or Methodists or Presbyterians, but they could not deny their sincere practice of the gift of tongues, divine healings, prophecy and other supernatural experiences. Their way of praising the Lord and of expressing their faith was very much like that of the Pentecostals and charismatics, but in foundational doctrine, they continued as faithful members of their denominations.

Some of these believers have found it best to start new congregations or even new denominations characterized by practices formerly found only in Pentecostal churches; yet they decline the label of either Pentecostal or charismatic. Generally, the statements of faith of these new groups differ very little from those of any traditional evangelical denomination. True, their worship services are more lively. But there is also a heightened and renewed commitment to ministry, as well as a more intensive discipleship of believers. They also believe that "signs and wonders" happen in our days just as in New Testament times, and they practice the conscious and outward use of spiritual gifts, including the more spectacular ones.

Many of the leaders of these groups have been trained in traditional, denominational theological institutions, but directly or indirectly they now have been influenced by the charismatic movement. These believers maintain good relationships with Pentecostal and charismatic leaders and have applied some of the effective church growth principles learned from them to their own congregations.

However, in spite of their doctrinal integrity, their denominational loyalty and their appreciation of traditional ecclesiastic structures, many of these new groups are suspect or even blackballed by their denominational executives. Still, few choose to separate themselves from the denomination in which they came to know the Lord and in which they have been discipled in their Christian lives.

THE THIRD WAVE

Around 1983, some leaders began to talk of a "third wave" of the contemporary moves of the Holy Spirit, which had begun to penetrate the historic churches without producing the kind of tensions experienced with the introduction of the charismatic movement back in the 1960s. This movement is referred to by some as the Third Wave because it is considered a successor of both classic Pentecostalism and the later charismatic movement. This new wave comprises evangelicals within traditional denominations who have received and who use the more spectacular gifts of the Holy Spirit, but who reject the label of Pentecostal or charismatic.

C. Peter Wagner, a well-known professor at Fuller Theological Seminary, in Pasadena, California, considers himself to be part of this Third Wave of Christians. He speaks in tongues, but he chooses not to be identified as a Pentecostal or charismatic. He is an ordained minister in the Conservative Congregational Christian Conference. In trying to explain this Third Wave, Wagner says, "I see in the 1980s an openness of traditional evangelicals and other Christians to the supernatural work of the Holy Spirit that Pentecostals or charismatics have experienced, but without becoming Pentecostals nor charismatics."[1]

Towards the middle of the decade, the Third Wave began penetrating the historic Protestant churches in Argentina. Yet the confusion and divisions that had accompanied previous moves of the Holy Spirit were not in evidence, as many non-Pentecostal, evangelical churches gave growing support to the campaigns of Carlos Annacondia, himself very much a Pentecostal evangelist.

Furthermore, we have observed in Argentina, and in many other parts of the world, a growing "pentecostalization" of the Christian experience in general. It might be more accurate to say that in many traditional Christian circles, the doctrine of the Holy Spirit is being taken more and more seriously. The gifts of the Holy Spirit are receiving greater attention, and believers are attempting to live out their faith in a higher supernatural dimension under the lordship of Christ.

AN EXPRESSIVE WORSHIP EXPERIENCE

A principal entry point for the development of the "Third Wave" in the Church is the hunger for a more lively Christian faith and a more expressive worship experience. Obviously, this emotional need cannot be met solely by traditional liturgies and rituals. An uncommitted, formal and cold Christianity is becoming increasingly unattractive. More and more believers prefer "freer" forms of communicating with God, as opposed to the more stylized, ritualistic forms of corporate worship and prayer. This would explain why the majority of those newly attracted to charismatic-style praise are coming from the most formal churches.

If traditional evangelical churches choose not to satisfy these needs, many renewed church members will look elsewhere for satisfaction. By 1983, many Christian leaders within historic Protestantism developed a deep concern over the growing number of believers leaving their churches in order to join a nearby Pentecostal church or an independent charismatic church. The last 15 years in Argentina have seen a great deal of what some have called "circulation of the saints." Thousands of believers have moved from one local church to another, some even changing their denominational affiliation in search of fulfillment of their spiritual needs. For some local congregations, this has caused unprecedented numerical growth, while others seem to be drawing their last breath.

The Third Wave represents a positive response to this trend on the part of many biblical and traditional evangelical churches. As churches become more open to a freer, more "charismatic" worship, they are retaining a greater portion of their members. At the same time, these churches are becoming centers of spiritual attraction for believers in other churches of the same denomination who are unsatisfied with the spiritual coldness and lack of commitment of their more traditional local churches.

MOVING TOWARD THE CENTER

I am not referring here to structural changes in denominations or to differences in their doctrinal statements, but to a way of carrying out worship and applying biblical teaching on the Holy Spirit and His gifts. That is, a Third Wave evangelical church will continue to be

> In Argentina, the differences between Pentecostal churches and traditional evangelical churches are rapidly diminishing.

Baptist or Methodist or Presbyterian or Plymouth Brethren or whatever, but its worship services, its discipleship program, its personal relationships, and its commitment to incarnation and service in the world will distinguish that church from other congregations, while presenting a very attractive and dynamic alternative for believers.

Meanwhile, many Pentecostal churches are moderating some of their more "extreme" practices that the evangelical community has found objectionable in the past. This means the differences between Pentecostal and evangelical churches are rapidly diminishing. In fact, many Pentecostal believers feel very attracted to conservative evangelical Third Wave churches that believe in and practice the gifts of the Spirit, but that are more ordered with a sound ecclesiastical structure and a reliance on better programs for Christian education and preaching. Therefore, the transfer growth taking place in Argentine churches is not all one-way.

Today, almost nobody in Argentina speaks of Pentecostals as if they were a false sect or existing outside the orbits of historic Christianity, as was the case only two decades ago. In general, Argentine evangelicals consider Pentecostals to be an important part of their own religious family, and they appreciate the special contribution that Pentecostals or charismatics can make to the enrichment of those who support a more theologically conservative faith. At the same time, Pentecostal leaders no longer look at their peers in traditional evangelical churches as liberals who may have better theological training, but who ignore the Holy Spirit.

THE THIRD WAVE IN PERSPECTIVE

How can such a recent phenomenon be evaluated objectively? How can we locate the growing Third Wave within the total framework of the historical development of Christianity? C. Peter Wagner raises this same question, and he answers it as follows:

> A growing number of Christian scholars and church leaders believe that God is doing a new thing during these closing years of the twentieth century. The prophecy of Joel, quoted by Peter in his sermon on the day of Pentecost says, "And it shall come to pass in the last days, saith God, I will pour out of my Spirit upon all flesh; and your sons and your daughters shall prophesy, and your young men shall see visions, and your old men shall dream dreams" (Acts 2:17, *KJV*). Whether what is now happening is the fulfillment of this prophecy and the signaling of the last days cannot be known for sure. It is, however, not beyond possibility.
>
> Earlier in our century, the Pentecostals rediscovered God's power and became channels for signs and wonders. Soon after the midpoint of the century, the charismatics became tuned-in and developed Spirit-filled groups within traditional churches. It now may be God's time for those who have not identified with either of these movements to tap into the kind of power described in the New Testament.[2]

It seems to me that, in spite of enormous doctrinal and ecclesiological differences, an invisible string of similar experiences connected with the ministry of the Holy Spirit now binds together the many diverse Christian communities which are experiencing the greatest church growth in Argentina today. Not all churches believe exactly the same things or minister in the same way. But all of them feel themselves spiritually renewed in the context of their own denominational tradition, and all of them are enjoying outstanding numerical growth; not just the transfer growth referred to previously, but largely conversion growth.

THE FUTURE OF THE ARGENTINE RENEWAL

According to projections made in the early 1970s by the World Council of Churches, by the year 2000 more than half of all Christians in the world will (1) not be white, (2) live in the Southern Hemisphere and (3) have a Pentecostal-charismatic flavor. The trends of church growth in Argentina over the last few years would seem to confirm these projections.

> By the year 2000, mega-churches with memberships of over 50,000 will emerge in the nations of the Third World and in the United States.

If current trends hold until the end of the century, it is not beyond reason to predict that by that date Christianity will have a configuration more or less as follows.

Twenty-five percent of the whole of Christianity will be constituted of classic Pentecostals, mostly coming from the Pentecostal movements that thrive in the Third World, especially in Latin America. These Christians will continue to place very little emphasis on liturgy and ritual, and will emphasize the gifts of the Holy Spirit in their regular services. They will likely continue to be the churches with the most rapid growth throughout the world. Some megachurches, with memberships of over 50,000, will emerge in the nations of the Third World and in the United States.

Another twenty-five percent of Christianity will be composed of charismatic Christians belonging to the churches of historic Protestantism and the Roman Catholic Church. These will mainly come from the Western, developed nations in Europe and North America, though they will also have a great influence in Latin America, especially in the large cities. Their worship services will be characterized as somewhat charismatic, and they will typically be believers of the Third Wave type that cannot be labeled as Pentecostals or charismatics. Gradually, their churches will surpass the old liberal or traditional churches in their size and influence. In a sense, these "renewed" churches will become the mainline or historical branch of the churches in the twenty-first century. It is probable that this segment will represent most of Argentine Protestant Christianity.

Non-charismatic Christians who belong to the churches of historic Protestantism and the Roman Catholic Church will make up another twenty-five percent of all Christians. This segment of Christianity will comprise two groups. On one side, there will be the "liberal" churches that will continue to decline in number of members. On the other side, there will be the conservative, non-charismatic, evangelical churches that will continue to grow, but slowly. Liberals will have less power within denominational structures, but they will continue to control the world ecumenical movement. The most conservative evangelicals will continue to oppose the charismatic or renewal movement, and more and more they will take a defensive posture, seeking refuge in their fundamentalist shell.

Finally, the last twenty-five percent will be constituted of nominal Christians from all churches and denominations, those who will not practice their faith and who will remain Christians only in a cultural sense. Most of them will fall in a progressive apostasy. These cultural or nominal Christians will constitute the majority of the members of the Western churches (mostly whites from the Northern Hemisphere). They will consider the church to be irrelevant for the modern human being, and, as apostates, they will have their names on the list of church members, but they will not attend worship services nor participate in the Church's mission. Others will totally abandon the Church.

PENTECOSTAL GRASSROOTS CHURCHES

Quite probably the future of Christianity will be most strongly influenced by the Pentecostal and grassroots churches of the underdeveloped Third World, in dynamic interaction with the vigorous charismatic elements of the traditional evangelical churches. Recent growth of the Church in Africa and Latin America indicates that the fate of Christianity in the twenty-first century may be in the hands of Pentecostal national churches that are emerging in the Third World and of a reborn Roman Catholicism, inspired by the charismatic renewal.

It is difficult to affirm or deny that these forecasts of the composition of worldwide Christianity in the twenty-first century paint an accurate picture of what will happen in Argentina in the coming years. However, indications are that the spiritual renewal in Argentina will, in all probability, continue to deepen until well into the next century and will expand to all the Christian world. Maybe this is the place to recall the exhortation of James, the brother and servant of the Lord: "Be patient, then, brothers, until the Lord's coming. See how the farmer waits for the land to yield its valuable crop and how patient he is for the autumn and spring rains. You too, be patient and stand firm, because the Lord's coming is near" (Jas. 5:7,8, *NIV*).

"THE ANOINTING"

One of the most interesting phenomena taking place in evangelical Protestantism in Argentina is what, since 1992, has been called "the anointing." Basically, this is the experience of the fullness of the Holy Spirit, in ways that are more or less in accord with standard evangelical teaching on the subject. Among the many manifestations associated with this phenomenon are the falling out under the supposed influence of the Spirit, outbursts of crying and raucous laughter, tremblings in different parts of the body, sensations of heat or cold or tingling and a peaceful ecstasy that is described in terms of "spiritual drunkenness."

The occurrence of such experiences is not something new. The history of Christianity records hundreds of similar cases throughout the centuries. In general, such experiences have been associated with times of spiritual renewal and revival. John White, an outstanding Christian psychiatrist and former associate professor of psychiatry at the University of Manitoba, Canada, has documented and described some of the current forms of this unusual behavior.[3]

From a different point of view, David Pytches, formerly the Anglican bishop of the dioceses of Chile, Bolivia, and Peru, considers these same phenomena to be legitimate manifestations of the work of the Holy Spirit for spiritual renewal among believers and revival among unbelievers.[4]

BENNY HINN'S INFLUENCE

However, the anointing did not actually originate in Argentina, but it is traced to the influence exerted by two best-selling books, *Good Morning, Holy Spirit* and *The Anointing*, both written by charismatic American pastor Benny Hinn. These have been listed among the most widely distributed religious books in the United States in the 1990s and have enjoyed tremendous circulation in Argentina and in the rest of Latin America.[5]

Hinn is an evangelist who has served as pastor at the Orlando Christian Center in Orlando, Florida, an independent charismatic congregation of about 7,000 members. His preaching and ministerial style, as well as the operation of his church, are typically charismatic. However, Hinn has drawn international attention with his regular practice of praying for the fullness of the Holy Spirit, and seeing the manifestations that accompany that experience. He has been severely criticized for this and also for alleged doctrinal errors. Those who have most strongly criticized him, both inside and outside of the United States, include both charismatic leaders and fundamentalist evangelicals. Hinn's TV ministry (more than 15 million viewers per week) and the contents of his books (more than 1.7 million English-language copies in print) have come under the scrutiny of many.[6]

CLAUDIO FREIDZON

Hinn's influence in Argentina has spread, not only through his books, but also through the ministry of an Argentine pastor of the Assemblies of God, Claudio Freidzon. In 1992, Freidzon, pastor of the King of Kings Church in Buenos Aires, went to visit Hinn in Orlando. According to Freidzon, it was there he received "the anointing" that he later began to minister to his congregation. In just a few months, his church grew remarkably, as pastors and members from evangelical churches in Argentina and neighboring countries attended the worship services at King of Kings in order to receive the fullness of the Spirit. What is interesting about this is that most of the pastors for whom Freidzon prayed belong to historic and traditional denominations. Nevertheless, the phenomenon of falling out in the Spirit, spiritual drunkenness and other manifestations characteristic of the anointing of the Holy Spirit began to be repeated in the home churches of these same pastors!

In the last months of 1992 and the first half of 1993, the number of local evangelical churches that were being spiritually renewed by the anointing increased dramatically. Meanwhile, Freidzon was attracting more and more people to huge soccer stadiums in evangelistic healing rallies, accompanied by prayer for the anointing. This phenomenon could not be ignored by traditional evangelical denominations, and the issue became a hot topic of discussion. Few churches have actually become divided on this issue itself, although in some cases it has caused deeper, existing problems to surface. Opinions on the anointing have been, and still are, divided.

One way or another, however, the atmosphere of spiritual revival, of religious enthusiasm and of willingness to commit fully to serving the Lord in any way is quite evident in those congregations that are open to these kinds of spiritual experiences. The phenomenon of the anointing is now appearing in other Latin American countries and may soon become characteristic of a large portion of Latin American Protestant churches before the end of this century.

It is interesting to note that this phenomenon, of a distinctly Pentecostal-charismatic nature, is experienced differently within the framework of each denominational tradition and is adjusted to the theological perspective of each one, yet retains many common characteristics across the board. Major adjustments are not being made in institutional forms to accommodate the anointing. Rather, the anointing seems to operate as a secondary element, only one component of a more comprehensive process of spiritual renewal.

THE PRAISE MOVEMENT

Argentina has also been shaken by an authentic praise movement. The explosive growth of Christian music throughout Latin America is just one expression of this. A revolution is also taking place in churches, bringing changes in liturgies and new forms of corporate worship. Traditional evangelical hymns, sung from a hymnbook, are being replaced by a new range of contemporary songs.

The new music is more joyful and lively than many of us in Argentina are accustomed to. Derived largely from contemporary folk and rock music, the new music is played on instruments found in modern bands, such as guitars, electric basses, drums and other percussion instruments, keyboards, and wind or metal instruments—trumpet, saxophone, clarinet—commonly used in the performance of jazz. Congregational singing is generally accompanied by the clapping of hands, the raising of arms and dancing.

The use of an overhead projector to display song lyrics takes hymnals out of the hands of worshipers and permits a more active participation of the whole body in the event of praise. Emotion is increased, with the songs following each other in a continuum spanning a much longer period of time than in traditional, hymn-singing churches.

The lyrics of these songs are not so much didactic or moral, as they are emotional and experiential. They are often built directly on biblical texts with a praise-oriented content and put to music with a distinct rhythm. The time for praise generally comes at the beginning of the service and takes up a considerable portion of the service. It is a festive, joyful and noisy celebration of the presence of the Lord in the midst of His people. This time of spiritual rejoicing is ordinarily followed by a time of worship, in which, through softer, slower, more prayer-oriented songs, the congregation approaches the throne of God recognizing Him for who He is.

MARCOS WITT

This new distinction between a time of praise and a time of worship owes a great deal to the teachings and ministry of Marcos Witt, Latin America's best-known worship leader. Few individuals have had a greater influence on this generation of Latin American churches. Witt, the son of American missionaries, was born and raised in Mexico. It is from Mexico that he practices his ministry of producing Christian music and promoting new forms of worship. His visit to Argentina at the beginning of 1993 was most impressive. Since then, Witt has been doing worship workshops in our country almost every year. On March 28, 1997, during a visit to Buenos Aires, he led in worship a multitude of more than 45,000 people, filling the Velez Sardsfield Stadium to capacity.

The most interesting thing about the new worship is the liturgical leveling taking place in Argentina. Churches belonging to diverse denominations, even those far removed from Pentecostalism or the charismatic movement, are adopting a charismatic style in their praise and worship. Witt himself has pointed out, "Praise, worship and music should be factors that unite, rather than set us apart."[7] And it seems this is happening.

Liturgical movements such as those promoted by Witt; the increase in Christian music production throughout South and Central America, especially Guatemala; and a greater freedom, variety, creativity, spontaneity and contextualization in praise in Latin American churches— all these signal a time of great revival. Undeniably, this innovation of worship has clear Pentecostal-charismatic overtones. Could it be that this rapid spread of contemporary worship substantiates the thesis that I have expressed throughout this chapter, namely that the profile of evangelical Protestantism in Argentina and around the world in the twenty-first century will be of a largely Pentecostal-charismatic nature?

IS THERE A REVIVAL IN ARGENTINA?

Is there a revival in Argentina? In recent years I have heard this question many, many times. The answers I have heard have been quite diverse, often meeting with skepticism. However, I do not believe that I have ever heard anybody raising questions about the question itself. It seems, then, that this a valid question for us to reflect upon.

A good part of the problem lies not so much on spiritual discernment and an understanding of historical facts, as on how we label them. I do not think that anyone would offer the thesis that God is doing *nothing* to redeem people in Argentina. Such a conclusion in the face of the facts would be absurd. Surely, God is moving to make the presence of His kingdom real in this country. The question is how we are to understand or qualify what He is doing.

This issue of labeling is important. We run the risk of losing the content by concentrating on the label of the container. Besides, it seems evident that not all who speak or write the word "revival" are referring to the same thing. For some, the term points to events similar to spiritual awakenings, such as the Great Awakening in the American colonies in the first half of the eighteenth century. Others consider processes of spiritual renewal over a longer period of time, such as the emergence of Pentecostalism and the charismatic movement, to be revival.

There are those who argue that a revival is a program of massive and intensive evangelization. Still others will speak of revival every time the spiritual condition of a portion of the people of God deepens. There are also those who identify certain external manifestations of the faith, especially signs, wonders, miracles or the exercise of the gifts of the Holy Spirit, as indicators of an authentic revival. There are even those who feel that a process of institutional renewal or restructuring or the updating (*aggiornamento*) of certain old forms constitutes a kind of awakening.

WHAT IS A REVIVAL?

In my opinion, a spiritual revival is neither restructuring, nor renewal, nor updating (*aggiornamento*), nor restoration, nor revitalization, nor reformation, although all of these may come about as a result of revival. The essence of spiritual revival is a combination of dynamic ingredients which moves the Church to return to its theological roots in the Scriptures, accompanied by a missionary commitment in obedience to the lordship of Christ and under the power of the Holy Spirit. The Church was constituted by Jesus Christ to fulfill a mission. Consequently, spiritual revival has to do basically with the recovery of this reason for being (*raison d'etre*) of the Church.

This is not simply a return to an ideal past. As Wilbert R. Shenk, professor at Fuller Theological Seminary, indicates, "The founding of the church was linked to its purpose in relation to the world in which the church was located. The church exists for the *missio Dei* on behalf of the world. Authentic renewal will be manifested in intensified witness in the world to the reign of God. This must be the clue that guides the (re)institutionalization of the church at a particular moment in history."[8]

> Authentic spiritual revival always coincides with evidence of the powerful action of God, through His renewed and obedient people, for evangelization.

It is precisely because the Church has been charged by Christ with a mission in the world, that its vitality—that is to say, its degree of spiritual revival—must be evaluated in terms of its missiological commitment. Every time the Church surrenders itself in obedience to the lordship of Christ and is filled with the Holy Spirit, committing itself to the mission of God in the world, the supernatural manifestation of God's grace that we call "revival" occurs.

An authentic spiritual revival is the result of a deep outpouring of the Holy Spirit in the lives of those who have been regenerated by Him according to their faith in Christ as Lord. This operation of the Spirit in the lives of believers results in the outreach of the Church to the world to proclaim the gospel of the Kingdom. Filled with the Holy Spirit, believers, both individually and as a confessing community, proclaim the good news of Christ to every human being and to the circumstances in which they are immersed. At the same time, the Spirit confirms "the message of his grace, by enabling them [the believers involved in the missionary action] to do miraculous signs and wonders" (Acts 14:3, *NIV*). An authentic spiritual revival always coincides with evidence of the powerful action of God, through His people who have become spiritually renewed and obedient, for evangelization.

A PARADIGM SHIFT

Let's raise the question once again: Is there a spiritual revival going on in Argentina today? Perhaps a better way of framing the question would be: Is there a revival going on in the world today? The present phenomenon of the globalization of the Church not only forces us to evaluate local phenomena adequately within their own space-time frame, but also within a global context. From this perspective, it is helpful to observe that, in spiritual and missiological terms, something unusual is indeed happening throughout the entire world today. Argentina is not excluded from this extensive movement of God.

Though I will not go into great detail here enumerating all that is happening in the worldwide Church today, I would like to draw attention to a fact which, from a historical perspective, seems to be very significant to our consideration of what is happening in Argentina. We may be able to find an interpretative key, not only to understand what revival is, but also to understand on a global level the direction of the extraordinary spiritual changes that are taking place. By doing this, we can better discern the powerful hand of God working through His people throughout the world, and specifically in Argentina.

The singular element I am referring to is the deep *paradigm shift* we are experiencing in the last years of the present millennium and into the beginning of the next one. This shift has generated enthusiasm and expectation in some, fear and uncertainty in others, and rejection and resistance in the rest.

A look at the history of the Church will help us to better understand what is happening today in the world. Loren Mead, in his book *The Once and Future Church*, suggests a very interesting interpretative framework, which may help us understand the "birth pains" of the present time. According to him, the Western church has known only two dominant paradigms in its almost 2,000 years of life. And we now are living in the critical *kairos* of the transition between the second and a third paradigm.

THE APOSTOLIC PARADIGM

The first Church model, which Mead names the Apostolic Paradigm, encompasses the first three centuries of Christian testimony. Because Mead's paradigms are based on shifts in what the Church understands to be its mission in the world, it can be said that the first primary and fundamental mission of the apostolic Church was testimony, the proclamation of the gospel of the Kingdom.

The primitive Church saw itself as a faithful people surrounded by a hostile environment, in which each member was called to be a witness to the love of God according to His manifestation in Christ. The mission was immediate and urgent. The field was the world, and all believers were participants. All of them were endowed with the charismata and the power of the Spirit to carry out the task, and all of them understood that, in the name of Jesus, they had authority to proclaim the gospel of the Kingdom, heal the sick and cast out demons. Each disciple of Jesus was a carrier of the message of the gospel, announcing everywhere that Jesus had died, resurrected and reigned as Lord. They taught that Jesus, the Christ, could rescue those who were lost and transform them into new men and women who, once redeemed, were to live according to the values of the kingdom of God, separating themselves from the values of a decadent world.

THE CHRISTENDOM PARADIGM

With the "conversion" of the Roman Emperor Constantine at the beginning of the fourth century, came a new paradigm for the Church: the Christendom Paradigm. In the year 313, with the Edict of Milan, Constantine put an end to the oppression of Christians within the Roman Empire and granted them the condition of being an officially tolerated religion. Overnight, the Church went from being a persecuted minority—the congregation of the "called-out" (ekklesia)—to being the congregation of the "called-in," accommodating itself to the ruling system.

In this way, the Church, the world, and the Roman Empire turned out to be one and the same. The Roman Empire extended throughout much of the known world, and to be a citizen of the empire was to be a Christian. It was no longer necessary for Christians to go to the world, because they were now part of it. The mission was not outside the Church, but inside, and the fulfillment of the mission was not the responsibility of all Christians, but of some called by God to that purpose. To be a witness to the Kingdom did not presuppose a willingness to die for Christ (i.e., to be a martyr) but, at most, to take the mission of the Church to the new territories conquered by the empire. The purpose of that mission was to convert the barbarous pagans to the Christian religion and the Christian civilization.

The constantinization of the Church and the establishment of the Christendom Paradigm radically changed the understanding the Church had of its identity and the definition of its mission. From the hands of all confessing believers, the mission was abdicated to the hands of the established religious leaders. A clergy was constituted, whose primary occupation was the management of the religious mysteries and rites. All other believers constituted a laity, whose principal role was to support the clergy and receive the benefits of its religious mediation.

The clergy came to be the symbol of the sacred. The dispensers of the ministry of the Word to the spiritually ignorant people, the clergy had exclusive access to the gifts of the Holy Spirit. They were the only ones capable of exerting apostolic authority, of receiving prophetic word, of evangelizing, of caring for the herd, of teaching the faith as it had to be taught. The clergy was responsible for discerning the truth and what was from God and what was not; for dispensing the grace through the sacraments; and for forgiving the sins of the penitent. They also were a very important factor in maintaining social control, serving as agents who generated cultural consensus. They were in charge of presiding over the public ceremonies of worship and the rites of baptism, confirmation, matrimony and death.

The more consecrated "laity" provided for the support of the Church and the clerical class. They helped maintain the institution, serving on an infinite number of committees and internal organizations. The laity also contributed finances and facilities, so as to provide the clergy with all that was necessary to fulfill "their ministry."[9]

INWARD LOOKING INSTEAD OF OUTWARD LOOKING

Far from being focused on the fulfillment of the commission to proclaim the kingdom of God, the churches of the Christendom Paradigm have for centuries been more concerned about strengthening their power structures, defining their dogmas and practices, establishing their denominational identities and persecuting and harassing those who claimed a different experience and a different understanding of their faith. Churches have spent a great deal of energy developing programs of activities oriented inward to the religious community and getting entangled in the processes of institutionalization. Above all, they have dedicated their energies and resources to the maintenance of what has been accomplished in all these aspects.

It is precisely in this last point where the present crisis of traditional Christianity can be located. These churches are decadent, having built their organizational structures around the purpose of maintaining what they already have, instead of focusing on the fulfillment of their mission in the world.

This Christendom Paradigm has been in force, with a few notable exceptions, during almost the whole of Christianity (Catholic, Protestant and Orthodox) up to approximately our own days. Why do I say "up to approximately our own days"? Because I believe that in recent years a paradigmatic change of great significance is taking place on a global scale. By this, I do not mean that the Christendom Paradigm has been relegated to the past or that it is easy to describe the new paradigm. On the contrary, I think we are in a period of transition, precisely because of the difficulty we have in seeing clearly what is happening. I insist that our question of the revival in Argentina is an expression of this confusion. Nevertheless, I will try to summarize my understanding of the direction in which I see the Church moving in the world, and particularly in Argentina.

THE NEW APOSTOLIC PARADIGM

I am convinced that we are moving toward a new paradigm which would deserve to be called a "New Apostolic Paradigm." Some have called this phenomenon the New Apostolic Reformation.[10] No matter what name we give it, it is evident we are talking about not only a new way of living as Christians, but also a new way of being the Church of Jesus Christ in the world.

For the purpose of understanding this, let us briefly change our historical approach. Traditionally, we have read history from the past to the present. In an apocalyptic time like the one in which we are living, and with a magnified *eschaton*, history must not be read from the past to the present but from the future to the present.

To be sure, there is a great eschatological expectation in our days. Many skeptics and historians consider this to be nothing but a recurring phenomenon that accompanies any transition from one century to another. Naturally this phenomenon would be intensified by a change of millennium. One way or another, and beyond any particular eschatological theory, clearly there is a great expectation regarding the *telos* and a very diffused consensus that we are nearing the "end times," and that the return of the Lord is close at hand.

Assuming we *are* living in the end times, let us look at history from the future to the present. From this perspective, the Christendom Paradigm, which is deeply internalized in all the traditional expressions of Christianity, after so many centuries is in crisis. This is, I suppose, not because of human initiative but because of the redeeming intervention of God in preparation for the glorious return of Christ. The Lord comes to look for His Bride, for His Church, but He will not return to meet the "harem" that has been formed during the centuries in which the Christendom Paradigm ruled.

DEMOCRATIZING THE CHARISMATA

The prophecies associated with end times describe a people of God more similar to the apostolic church than to the churches of present, traditional Christianity. Today the exercise of the charismata is becoming more democratic and is being returned to the believers, from where it was previously usurped by the clergy. The new zeal in the testimony of Christians is accompanied by signs and wonders, healings, miracles, demonic deliverance and spiritual power encounters. This might be a sign of the already announced outpouring of the Holy Spirit over all flesh (not only those who confess His name for salvation) so that all human beings can have the opportunity of coming to confess Jesus Christ as Lord in their own languages.[11]

Some will no doubt take issue with this eschatological interpretation. But it seems to me to be beyond question that the Christendom Paradigm is in a terminal condition, and that it deserves a decent burial. Several elements characteristic of this paradigm are notably declining, including denominationalism and its historical products. One would have to be blind not to see the constant numerical decline of denominational Christianity across the planet, but especially in the North Atlantic world which was its cradle. And there are no clear signs of recovery despite the enormous efforts being made for survival, especially in mainline Protestant churches.

At the same time, the process of theological and liturgical homogenization seems evident. A generation ago, each denomination had more than enough reasons for taking pride in its own distinctive theological and liturgical traditions. However, it is becoming more and more difficult today to make such distinctions.

In the face of the decline of the Christendom Paradigm, a new way of doing Christianity is dawning. Because of its incipient character, we could speak about an "experimental Church," or a Church that knows it is more a pilgrim than ever before, marching toward the future in search of a new identity. That is to say, it will be a Church that wants to continually hear what the Spirit is saying to the churches, so as to become involved with His mission immediately, through a process of incarnation and service.

EXPERIMENTAL MODELS

This experimental Church is emerging around the world, and at a tremendous speed. This includes Argentina. Churches of the new paradigm no longer want to conform to the Christendom model. They meet in gymnasiums, schools, cinemas, parking lots and especially in homes. Those who have studied this phenomenon describe it and analyze it in different ways, but all of them affirm that these will be the churches that will survive the transition and will come to characterize twenty-first-century Christianity.

One interesting observation is that one can worship God in any of these new congregations without feeling a radical change in tradition or form from one to the other. What is this due to? As I pointed out previously, paradigms have to do primarily with the mission of the Church. The present paradigm shift in Christianity is not so much a change in doctrine as it is a change in our understanding of the nature of the Church and its mission. In the Christendom Paradigm, the mission, understood as proclamation of the Kingdom, was transferred to faraway lands and to pagan peoples, but it did not include reaching the lost of one's own culture.

Today, however, many churches which have previously subscribed to the Christendom Paradigm now recognize the need to be evangelized themselves and to evangelize the lost of their own cultures. An ever-increasing number of Christians recognize that the true mission of proclaiming the Kingdom begins in the local church and extends to the whole world, and that this is the task of every believer filled with the Holy Spirit. For many today, the conclusion that the Church is in mission seven days a week and 24 hours a day is a discovery of Copernican proportions.

THE OLD NEW PARADIGM

However new this understanding of the mission of the Church might be to some, it is not new in the history of Christian testimony. This dynamic understanding of the mission of the Church is similar to that of the Apostolic Paradigm. Thus, the accurate designation of what we are seeing today is the New Apostolic Paradigm. It is not strange, therefore, that the charismata are exercised once again, and that spiritual ministries of common people are being reestablished. Signs, won-

> The New Apostolic Paradigm will be the last of its kind to emerge before the glorious return of Christ.

ders and miracles are not institutionalized, but liberated. The growing numbers of believers active in ministry are now widely affirmed by a Church that boldly proclaims the gospel of Christ in obedience to the command of God, who does not want anyone to perish, but desires that everyone come to repentance.

Under the New Apostolic Paradigm, churches understand that the missionary commitment requires a new priority of context over structure. The local church is no longer turned in on itself, but it is addressing the world and its needs. It is not so concerned with doctrine as it is about spreading the message of redemption. Very little emphasis is placed on cultivating prestige for the local church, but their energies have been redirected toward making the presence of the Kingdom a reality amidst human circumstances. The same church is not as interested in its political power as in its spiritual power. The agenda of activities now takes a back seat to obeying the will of God and committing to Him and His mission.

For certain, in assuming this attitude, a church becomes vulnerable and is exposed to a great number of dangers. Nevertheless, it is ready to assume the risks because it understands that this is how it must operate to fulfill the mission given by Jesus in John 20:21.

In the New Apostolic Paradigm, the needs of people determine the priorities of the Church's testimony and action. As Wilbert Shenk writes, "In the apostolic model of witness, the 'other' is invited to set the terms of interaction—whether it be an appeal for healing, exorcism or the solution to a perplexing issue. The presence of the witness is essential in making such an exchange possible at all; but whether it takes place depends on the attitude and initiative of the other."[12]

A NEW WINESKIN

Is there revival in Argentina today? Unfortunately, we have not reached a consensus in the Christian community as to what the term means. I do want to affirm, however, some clear impressions that I have:

1. We are undergoing a deep period of transition in all the Christian world.
2. This transition is of a paradigmatic character; that is to say, it signals a radical change in our values and our understanding of the world and our reality.
3. The Christendom Paradigm, which has ruled for almost 17 centuries, is in danger of impending dissolution.
4. A new paradigm is emerging which can be called the New Apostolic Paradigm.
5. The dominant characteristic of this paradigm shift is a change in attitude, from one of institutional maintenance to one of incarnational mission and service in the power of the Holy Spirit. This new church paradigm is reminiscent of the apostolic profile outlined in the New Testament.
6. It is my personal conviction that this new paradigm will be the last of its kind to emerge before the glorious return of Christ.

An authentic spiritual revival cannot be separated from the mission of the Church. They are essentially linked. Both emerge from the same biblical and theological foundation. The covenant of God with Abraham called for Abraham to be a blessing to all nations (see Gen. 12:2,3). This covenant was renewed and reaffirmed by the Messiah, Jesus. The Church, that is His body in the world, exists for the same evangelistic purpose of God to bless the nations. That is why every time the Church gives itself away and assumes a deep detachment from worldly demands; when it surrenders itself to the lordship of Christ and is filled with the Holy Spirit; when the Church obeys the will of God and submits to the inspired record of His revelation; when it goes out into the world to fulfill God's mission, *then* there is an authentic spiritual revival.

The remaining question is whether it is possible or necessary for the whole Church to move away from the Christendom Paradigm to the New Apostolic Paradigm. Is it possible to affect a worldwide change from an attitude of maintenance to one of mission? Can we do that without losing forever everything we have till now venerated as secure and effective? These questions cannot be answered in other than a radical way—a way as radical as the way of Jesus' cross. It has to be as radical as the wheat seed that dies to its structure and form to give way to something new, just as the old wineskin is put aside to allow the new wine to be poured into a new wineskin.

Ralph W. Neighbour, coming out of a tradition within the Christendom Paradigm, suggests that we must "give it up and start something new." With some confessed pessimism as to the viability of traditional churches, Neighbour says, "I began to ask myself the question, 'Can new wine be put into old wineskins?' The answer is 'no.' Attempts at renewal don't work for one reason: Our Lord told us over 2,000 years ago it could not be done. Every time we try to ignore His clear teaching, we fail. In retrospect, I could have saved myself 24 years of dreaming the impossible if I had taken His admonition literally."[13]

THE OUTPOURING IN ARGENTINA

Looking at the work of God in Argentina, I believe the Lord is doing remarkable things never before seen nor experienced in our country. The powerful outpouring of the Holy Spirit and its remarkable manifestations during these 15 years have no precedent in the history of the Church in Argentina.

The evidences of His supernatural operation are abundant and growing. Only those who are inattentive, who are overly preoccupied with the negative, who are unaware of their own prejudices and presuppositions, who have turned into themselves or who are chained to institutional commitments, cannot see that there is a special grace of God operating through the people who confess His name in Argentina.

If what is happening in Argentina today is truly from God, I do not want to waste my time debating it or analyzing it, but rather living it in all its intensity. My prayer today is the same that I made on November 22, 1992, in the morning service of my local church in Buenos Aires, when I received the powerful anointing of the Holy Spirit: "Lord, if this is Yours, I want it all...."

Notes

1. Peter Wagner, "A Third Wave?" *Pastoral Renewal*, No. 8 (July-August 1983), pp. 1-5. See also C. Peter Wagner, *Spiritual Power and Church Growth* (Altamonte Springs: Strang Communications, 1986), pp. 13, 14, and his book, *The Third Wave of the Holy Spirit* (Ann Arbor: Servant Publications, 1988).
2. Peter Wagner, "Signs & Wonders Today" (Wheaton, Ill.: *Christian Life* magazine, 1983), p. 78.
3. See John White, *When the Spirit Comes with Power* (Downers Grove, Ill.: InterVarsity, 1988), pp. 7-10.
4. See David Pytches, *Come, Holy Spirit* (London: Hodder and Stoughton, 1985).
5. Benny Hinn, *Good Morning, Holy Spirit* (Nashville: Thomas Nelson Publishers, 1990); and *Idem, The Anointing* (Nashville: Thomas Nelson Publishers, 1990).
6. See Stephen Strang, "Benny Hinn Speaks Out and Explains Changes in His Teachings and Ministry," *Charisma* (August 1993), pp. 22-29; Stephen F. Cannon, "Good Morning, Holy Spirit? Benny Hinn and Revelation Knowledge," *The Quarterly Journal*, No. 11 (July-September 1991), pp. 1, 10-15; G. Richard Fisher, "Benny Hinn's Anointing: Heaven Sent or Borrowed?" *The Quarterly Journal*, No. 12 (July-September 1992), pp. 1, 10-16; Perucci Ferraiuolo, "Christian Leaders Admonish Hinn," *Christianity Today* (August 16, 1993), pp. 8-39.
7. Marcos Witt, "Somos siervos, no artistas," *El Puente* (June 1993), p. 24.
8. Wilbert R. Shenk, "Envisioning the Church of the Future: Mission and Renewal," paper presented to the Faculty of the School of World Mission, Fuller Theological Seminary, Pasadena, California, March 4, 1997, (photocopy), p. 10.
9. The word "laity" is the typical designation used to refer to Christian believers who are not a part of the clergy in the Christendom Paradigm. The present standing in the use of this term is further evidence that the constitutive elements of this paradigm are still operating in contemporary Christianity.
10. C. Peter Wagner has thus named a new course he teaches at the extension of the School of World Mission of Fuller Theological Seminary in Colorado Springs, Colorado. His first book on the subject, *The New Apostolic Churches*, is scheduled for publication by Regal Books to coincide with the release of this book.
11. The prophecy in Joel 2 was partially fulfilled on the day of Pentecost, according the interpretation of Peter (Acts 2).
12. Shenk, "Envisioning the Church of the Future," p. 11.
13. Ralph W. Neighbour, *Where Do We Go from Here?* (Touch Publication, 1990), p. 92.

three

POWER EVANGELISM, ARGENTINE STYLE

BY CARLOS ANNACONDIA

Carlos Annacondia *has been the key figure in the Argentine revival for 15 years. His massive evangelistic campaigns, featuring healing ministries and overt confrontation with the demonic, have drawn worldwide attention. Annacondia lives with his wife, Maria, and their nine children in Quilmes, a city near Buenos Aires, where he operates a nuts and bolts factory. As few others have, Annacondia has transformed the life and ministry of the Church in an entire nation. In recent years, he has responded to invitations to minister in many other countries. His impact on the Church in Japan has been notable.*

Over the last 15 years, our massive, open-air evangelistic campaigns have attracted widespread attention for the important role they have played in the Argentine revival. The attendance figures have reached record proportions, and the surprising events that take place in these meetings are unprecedented in the history of evangelical Christianity in our country. Our campaigns are centered around powerful proclamation of the gospel of Christ, accompanied by the operation of miracles, signs, wonders, healings and especially deliverances from the demonic. The remarkable manifestations of the power of God working for the well-being of those who come to seek Him has been astonishing and very humbling.

I am particularly grateful to God for the growing level of unity among evangelical pastors in Argentina. As we continue to see an increase in the number of churches all across the denominational spectrum the country, one of the ripple effects of our campaigns in the cities of Argentina has been the establishment of pastors' associations in each city. Nearly all of the almost 200 pastoral councils now functioning in Argentina can trace their origins back to a committee organized on the occasion of an evangelistic campaign during which I had the privilege of proclaiming the gospel in that city.

FROM BUSINESSMAN TO EVANGELIST

My name is Carlos Annacondia. I was born in the city of Quilmes, province of Buenos Aires, on March 12, 1944. I am a typical Argentine from the coastal region of my country; that is, I am a descendant of European immigrants. My mother, Maria Alonso, is Spanish, while my father, Vicente Annacondia, was of Italian descent. I grew up, together with my brothers, Angel and Jose Maria, in a happy family in Quilmes. We were not wealthy, but later I was able to make ends meet through a family business. Since 1977, I have been the head of Bulonera Quilmes S.C.A., a business that is still operating and helps me to support my large family. I married Maria Lujan Rebagliatti in 1970, and we have been blessed with nine children.

By the time I was 35, I was a well-known and respected businessman in my native city. I had more than 20 employees and earned a good income. But I soon realized that my life consisted of nothing but the quest to make more money. I thought that if only I could have a weekend house, I would then find the peace I did not have in my heart. When I finally got that house, however, I immediately began looking for a larger and more comfortable one. I still did not have peace. I purchased an apartment in the resort city of Mar del Plata, where I hoped to enjoy my vacations and find the peace I was seeking, but it was to no avail. The same was true of the luxurious cars I bought. I became increasingly concerned about the state of my life, and especially about the future of my children. I had heard people speak of Jesus Christ and the gospel. But I always thought that Jesus was for others, and not for me.

Nevertheless, I continued to be worried about my children. I wanted the best for them, and I did not want them to fall into the sins which were consuming so many youngsters in our city. My life was permeated with fear: fear of death, fear of losing everything I had achieved, and fear that something evil might happen to my family. It was in these circumstances that the Lord Jesus came to meet me.

I accepted Christ as my Lord and Savior on the occasion of an evangelistic campaign held on May 19, 1979 in the city of San Justo in the province of Buenos Aires. The preacher was Manuel A. Ruiz, a pastor from Panama. I stood at the back of the meeting room. I had come to this place, moved by simple curiosity. I wanted to know if God was as powerful as people said. I do not know if I really heard the sermon, because there was a lot of noise around me, and the sound system was not working very well. Nevertheless, I experienced an unmistakable encounter with God, an encounter that impacted me beyond measure. The Holy Spirit touched me in a marvelous way that night. He spoke to my heart and said, "You are very worried about your family, about your children and about earthly things. If you give me your heart and all your life, you will not have to worry anymore for your children or for your home, because I will take charge of guarding your home, your family and your life."

I had never mentioned my personal worries to anybody, not even to my wife. I then understood that God was real, that He existed, that He knew who I was and that He loved me in a personal way. I understood that I was a sinner in need of Him, that I had lived apart from God, in spite of professing the Roman Catholic religion. Indeed, I was, for all intents and purposes, an atheist—a "Christian atheist" who did not seek God personally, even though I professed to believe in Him. But God came upon me and overcame me that night.

BORN AGAIN!

At that very moment, in the back of the meeting room, I began to cry. I was unable to stop. My wife was by my side, and she also began to cry. When the preacher gave the invitation, I raised my hand as an expression of my faith in Christ, and from that very moment, God began to radically transform my life. I was born again as a new creature. I quit smoking and drinking alcoholic beverages. I stopped having doubts and filling myself with fears. I began a new life in the love of Jesus Christ. Ten days after my conversion, I was baptized in the

Holy Spirit. Filled with Him, I was ready to serve the Lord.

As soon as I had been converted, I asked the Lord about the ministry He wanted to assign me so that I might serve Him. I thought it likely that God would want me to make more money so that I could support the ministries of those who preached for a living. But I then began to wonder if He wanted me to preach. I asked the Lord to reveal His will to me, so that I would not make a mistake and head in a direction God did not intend for me to take. Suddenly, deep in my heart, I felt a powerful desire to be an evangelist. At the time, however, I did not have the faith necessary to bring that desire to fruition. I thought that if it were to happen, it would be sometime in the distant future.

THE FIRST EVANGELISTIC CAMPAIGN

The following year, a few of us were making plans for a campaign to which we were planning to invite preachers from abroad. We were having a very difficult time, however, in raising the funds necessary to bring in speakers. One of our intercessors began praying fervently about the financial problem. She soon found herself praying that God would raise up the evangelist we needed from amongst ourselves. Much to our surprise, the Holy Spirit clearly indicated to her that I was to be the evangelist! At that point, the intercessor became very confused, because I had been a Christian for only a year and a half. By the end of the meeting, however, as we continued to pray, she prophesied that I would not only preach in Argentina, but throughout all the Americas.

This is how I was invited to preach in my first evangelistic campaign. That was in 1981, and the meetings were held in a very poor slum area in the city of Bernal. I did my best, and I was astonished to see how God was moving. This was the beginning of my ministry as an evangelist.

"LORD, WHAT SHALL I DO?"

God's call to evangelistic ministry began the very moment I surrendered my life to Christ. I am thankful that, from the beginning, I had the support and the counsel of my pastor, Jorge Gomelski. When I was a babe in Christ, God placed him in my life to disciple me and to teach me in His ways.

I had made a covenant with the Lord. I promised to serve Him and, in exchange, I asked Him to give me what the world had promised but was never able to provide: peace, happiness, security and quietness. All this God gave me from the moment I committed my life to Jesus Christ. Thus, from the beginning of my Christian life, I was ready to serve my Lord with all my strength.

I asked God to bless me with a ministry that would glorify Him. He did so, and He prospered me in such a remarkable way in spiritual things, that some have come to regard me as a successful evangelist. However, I want to make something very clear. If I do have strong gifts from God, it is by His grace alone. When God gave me this ministry, He asked me, "Are you ready to pay the price?" The price for my ministry was not some sacrifice that I had to make in order to earn gifts from God. No, the price was to carry on my shoulders the burden and responsibility of that ministry, which meant being away from home, not being with my children as much as I would like, facing criticism and opposition, investing large sums of money out of my own pocket and so forth.

However, I know that I have stored up treasures in heaven, where moth and rust do not corrupt. But it is not always easy. Sometimes, my knees bend, and I cry out, "God, I cannot stand any longer!" Then He reminds me, "Were you not ready to pay the price?" Ministry is a gift of grace to the man or the woman ready to serve God. But the price is non-negotiable. That is why success in ministry comes with certain requirements. The first one is to walk in the perfect will of God. And for that, a radical life conversion is necessary. The second requirement is that one must completely withdraw from evil in order to serve God. And this involves total consecration.

BEGINNING WITH THE POOR

My ministry began among the very poor, in very humble neighborhoods, where I would visit hospitals to pray for the sick. I struggled mightily at the beginning, because I was unsure whether the Lord wanted me to give up my business and all my worldly possessions. I seemed to hear the voice of God telling me, "Your heart is still set on your things."

So I said, "Lord, use me! Use me!"

And God answered, "Go to the slums, and give Me your business."

I was not ready to do either one of those things, so I spent a full year crying and struggling, until I finally told my wife, "All right, I will give everything up. I cannot stand this situation any longer." I gave my car away, then I went to consult with my pastor. He said, "If you are ready to abandon everything for God, do not throw it out like you did your car. Keep it; then when God demands it, give it to Him." This was good news. I felt as if a burden weighing 5,000 kilograms had been lifted from my shoulders. I followed Pastor Gomelski's advice, and from that moment on, I felt that my whole life was finally consecrated to the Lord. I could now go to the slums to preach the gospel to the poor, as God had told me to do.

During my search for the ministry that God had set for me, the Lord spoke to me through Ezekiel 37, the passage on the valley of the dry bones. I was sending to preach, He said to me, "so that those who are dead in their trespasses and sins can live; and even for My Church itself to be renewed in the Holy Spirit." On another occasion, I received a prophecy through a friend, indicating that I would start a revival in Argentina, and that, from the south of the continent, revival would spread to the entire world.

One day in 1981, my eldest son, Carlos Alberto, began to prophesy in tongues. It seemed that he was speaking in German, because I heard him say, "*Argentinien, Argentinien.*" I asked my wife to interpret, and she did, saying, "Soon, soon, soon. Great revival in Argentina! 'Argentina will be mine,' says the Lord."

MESSAGE OF SALVATION

The ministry now known as "Message of Salvation" was launched in 1980 when Pastor Jorge Gomelski and I purchased time on Radio Real from Uruguay. The area covered in Argentina by this station was fairly large, and the available time was very convenient. Pastor Gomelski presented the message, while I only prayed. Later, the pastor asked me to serve as the master of ceremonies and also to provide the closing words.

The radio producer had asked me to write a few words his announcer could use to introduce the program. I remember writing, "Listen to a message of salvation through the voice of pastor Jorge Gomelski." But when the announcer introduced the program, he instead said, "Listen to message of salvation...." And the name stuck. God used a non-believer to give us a wonderful name for our ministry.

Very soon, Pastor Gomelski began receiving invitations to preach in different churches. When he could not accept an invitation, he sent me. This is how the Lord began to burden our hearts with the need to carry out evangelistic campaigns—first in very humble neighborhoods, in the open air or in rented rooms. I never had an opportunity to attend seminary or a Bible institute. Neither did I study homiletics or preaching. So I tried to imitate the best preachers I knew, especially the man of God who led me to Christ, the Panamanian pastor Manuel Arlindo Ruiz. Some say that I still preach like him, even with his Central American accent. That may be true, as I learned all I know about preaching from watching him.

PREACHING IN THE FULLNESS OF THE GREAT COMMISSION

Soon after I began to preach, I felt that I should put into practice a new understanding of the Great Commission that the Lord had given me. Beyond basic evangelism, the Great Commission has four aspects. The first of these, *salvation*, is implicit in Jesus' words, "Go into all the world and preach the gospel to every creature" (Mark 16:15). The second aspect of the Great Commission is *deliverance*, expressed in the phrase "in My name they will cast out demons" (Mark 16:17). The third has to do with manifestations of the *anointing of the Holy Spirit*. Jesus said, "They will speak with new tongues" (Mark 16:17). This is a source of power that all believers need. And, finally, the fourth aspect of the Great Commission is *healing*. The Lord told His disciples, "They will lay hands on the sick, and they will recover" (Mark 16:18).

So I set myself to obey the Lord's command. Besides proclaiming the gospel of salvation in Christ, I began to put a strong emphasis on healing the sick and on casting out demons. I learned to rebuke, strongly and directly, the high-ranking principalities of darkness; to address Satan and his demons with full authority in the name of Jesus; to bind them publicly; and to cast them out of the lives of the captives in my audience.

This understanding of the Lord's command and the practices of proclaiming, healing and casting out demons continue to be foundational to my ministry. The ministry of deliverance is a notable characteristic of my campaigns. That is why I dedicate a good portion of my public presentation, night after night, to warfare prayer. I find myself investing an incredible amount of energy to this strategic-level spiritual warfare. I am certain of the power of the Lord to deliver those who are held in slavery because of what I find in the Bible and what I have learned through experience.

THE GREAT EVANGELISTIC CAMPAIGNS

My early evangelistic campaigns were marked by miraculous increases in attendance and decisions of faith for Christ. The following is the sequence of campaigns I carried out in the first years of my evangelistic ministry.

Year	Place*	Decisions
1981	Don Bosco (Beccar)	110
1982	Villa Domínico	100
1982	Florencio Varela (Alpargatas)	70
1982	Florencio Varela (Barrio San Eduardo)	279
1983	Quilmes (Kolynos)	700
1983	Don Bosco (Beccar)	1,000
1983	Ezpeleta	350
1983	Bernal (IAPI)	750
1983	Francisco Solano	700
1983	Quilmes Oeste	800
1983	Wilde	1,500
1983	Bosques	600
1983	Tres Arroyos	100
1984	Berisso	2,000
1984	Ranelagh	1,600
1984	City Bell	1,700
1984	La Plata, Ensenada and Tolosa	50,000
1984	Monte Grande	8,500
1984	Lomas de Zamora	1,800
1984	Mar del Plata	83,000
1985	San Justo	60,200
1985	San Martín	57,000
1985	Moreno	16,000

* All these places are located in the province of Buenos Aires.

Since 1984, God has allowed me to minister the gospel of Christ to great multitudes. By that time, my ministry, Message of Salvation, was well-organized with an excellent staff. A basic infrastructure was in place with the ability to gather several thousands of people in open-air meetings. We owned huge tents, lighting equipment, platform, chairs, sound equipment, vehicles of all sizes for the trans-

> Behind the platform we have a 150-foot tent where we minister deliverance. Some call it our "spiritual intensive care unit."

portation of materials, etc. This allowed us to bring together a large number of churches in a given area and to extend each evangelistic campaign for a longer period of time. In some cities, we would hold two full months of continuous preaching every single night, even under heavy rains or in intense cold. After more than 12 years of ministry, I continue to serve the Lord with the same enthusiasm, rejoicing over the harvest of abundant fruit, and desiring to harvest the fruit that remains.

For each campaign, we create the climate of a popular fiesta which makes the event very attractive to the people living in the area. Powerful lights surround the large vacant lot where the crowd will gather. We construct a huge, well-decorated platform, and behind it we place a 150-foot tent with yellow and white stripes. This is where we minister deliverance, and some call it our "spiritual intensive care unit." Another tent is dedicated to praying for the sick, and yet another holds a bookstore.

Around the outside of the lot, we place several stands to sell food and refreshments. The joyful music, the singing and the traffic jam caused by a steady stream of vehicles and people approaching the site, work together to build great expectancy among the enormous crowd. The informality of the meeting and the freedom to move, since most of the people are standing, help the hours to pass without anyone feeling too tired.

REBUKING SPIRITS OF DARKNESS

A time of lively praise and worship to the Lord is followed by the necessary announcements. I then go on the platform to present the message of
the gospel of salvation. Before preaching, I always pray loudly, rebuking
and binding all spirits of unbelief, doubt or rejection, so that the people
can not only understand the message, but so that they will also receive
it into their hearts. I firmly believe what the Bible says, that Satan, the
god of this age, "has blinded the minds of unbelievers, so that they cannot see the light of the gospel of the glory of Christ" (2 Cor. 4:4, *NIV*).
That is why this prayer of direct rebuke is absolutely fundamental.

Afterwards, I preach in a simple, clear manner, appealing not only
to the understanding of the people, but also to their emotions. My
messages are brief, testimonial and always based on a portion of the
Bible, generally a story taken from the Gospels. Because I have not
studied homiletics, my presentation is more narrative than argumen-
tative or didactic.

After the message is presented, I invite unbelievers to put their faith
in Christ as the only Lord of their lives. The Holy Spirit touches their
hearts, and it is moving to see thousands of persons of all ages come
down the aisle, literally running to the altar with their hands up and
confessing their sins. I pray for them and, many times, demonized persons begin to manifest there. In fact, these manifestations happen from
the beginning of the meeting, often as people approach the place of
our gathering.

There is not a fixed order for the campaign program. However, after
counselors take the information about the persons who have expressed
their faith in Christ and after some songs, I pray for the sick. I believe
that most health problems are provoked by evil spirits. That is why I
rebuke each spirit of sickness, one by one, according to the words of
knowledge that I receive from the Holy Spirit. I ask the persons to put
their hands where their ailment is whenever possible. Many fall to the
ground, touched by the Holy Spirit, and they are miraculously healed.

CASTING OUT DEMONS

Later, with the authority I have received from God through the blood
of Christ, and in the name of Jesus, I turn directly against Satan and

his demons who have been keeping the lives of these dear people under bondage of darkness. I outwardly rebuke all spirits of witchcraft, sorcery, mental control, *macumba*, *umbanda*, spiritualism, and other pagan religions. I come against the emotional and physical bindings over the lives of the individuals there. This is a moment of great inner tension for me and a visible tension in the audience. I let the Spirit guide me to declare freedom in Christ to those points of the lives of those present bound by the chains of Satan.

Demonic manifestations at this point can become terrible. Persons fall with convulsions, jerking, yellings, cries, guttural noises and spasms. Trained workers (in our jargon we call them *"camilleros,"* or "stretcher bearers") discern those who are manifesting because of demons (in contrast to those resting peaceably in the Spirit) and usher them out to the yellow-and-white-striped deliverance tent, where other teams of brothers and sisters, thoroughly trained by my staff, begin to minister deliverance to them. Some of the resulting scenes are horrible, demonstrating clearly how devastating and destructive the work of the devil is in the lives of those who have been oppressed by him.

TESTIMONIES OF HEALING

After a time of songs of praise, we then invite those who have received healing to come to the platform to give testimony to the glory of God. Of course, we take all precautions possible to insure that these testimonies represent authentic and verifiable healings. The staff thoroughly interviews each person coming to give testimony, and many are turned away when there is doubt.

After four or five hours of meeting, we come to the end of the event, when I and some members of my team pray for the anointing of the Holy Spirit for each person who wants it. Many fall to the ground, touched by the Spirit, where they are strengthened, healed, restored and comforted in their faith. On many occasions, I then go out to have dinner and relax a little afterwards, getting home at about two or three in the morning!

In general, this is the way I minister whenever I have the opportunity to proclaim the gospel of the Kingdom. For me, there is no difference if I am speaking before a crowd of 20,000 persons in the open air, or if I am ministering to 200 persons gathered in a church. It makes no difference to me if it is a campaign of 30 consecutive days or three days on a weekend. Actually, no matter where I am, God allows me to serve Him, and I see His hand moving in power and authority, almost always with the same awesome results.

CAMPAIGNS WORLDWIDE

God has allowed me to preach to more than a million people, not only in Argentina, but in almost all the world. The year 1985 was a very special year for me. After great campaigns in the cities of San Justo, San Martin and Moreno, others followed in Beccar, Haedo, Rosario and La Boca. Each of these attracted huge attendance and consisted of more than a month of daily preaching. Later, the Lord allowed me to minister in many other places outside the province of Buenos Aires and internationally. I have proclaimed the good news on several occasions in the United States and at campaigns in Spain, Germany, Russia, Peru, El Salvador, Finland, Puerto Rico, Bolivia, Japan, Uruguay and many other countries.

Each campaign is different. Often the attendance increases as the campaign goes on. For example, in 1996, in San Martin we had about 3,000 people per night the first three days of the campaign. On the fourth day, we counted 3,451, not including small children. But from the fifth day on, the attendance jumped to more than 4,500 people. In comparison with other campaigns, this one had poor attendance, largely due to the fact that we were preaching in a location with relatively low visibility.

Our campaigns come to town with very little professional publicity. In fact, most people come because somebody brings them. As the days pass, the word gets out that God is working miracles and extraordinary things are happening. This attracts more and more people as the campaign goes on. It is necessary to build a strong organization in order to handle such tremendous crowds of people. Besides the permanent team that accompanies me in my campaigns, a local committee is appointed for the campaign, and they take responsibility for all the local arrangements. This committee coordinates the huge number of volunteers necessary to pull off an event of this magnitude. Ushers, counselors, people in charge of the offerings, *camilleros* (stretcher bearers), counselors for deliverance, security personnel and many others gladly serve the Lord night after night.

AN EYEWITNESS TESTIMONY

How do our meetings look to those who observe from the outside? Here is the way an American pastor describes his first visit to a Message of Salvation campaign. I think this will provide helpful insight into the ministry that I have been performing over the last 15 years to the glory of our Lord.

I went with a group of Presbyterians by bus to the campaign. As the bus approached the campaign site, we saw dozens of strings of bare lightbulbs hanging around the grounds, giving a small-town, carnival-type atmosphere. The site itself was a large, open space, mostly dirt, bordering a well-traveled street. When we arrived, everything was in full swing. The platform was about six-feet high and on it were musicians and singers and a master of ceremonies excitedly inciting the crowd to join in. The huge speakers on either side of the platform would pierce the ears of anyone standing too close.

Annacondia came on stage and gave a reasonably normal gospel message. He gave the invitation for salvation and hundreds of people flocked forward, filling the area which had been blocked off all around the platform by a human chain of uniformly attired men and women, members of local churches. After a prayer for salvation, Annacondia went into what I can only describe as a tirade against the demonic hosts which were present in the area. All over the audience, people went into demonic manifestation. Some fell to the ground and started writhing or slithering, some started flailing and screaming, some started shaking or in some way reacted to Annacondia's diatribe against the demonic host present at the campaign.

Several men were near the platform. These were the spotters. They would see someone go into a manifestation of some type and send the carriers to bring the person out of the crowd to take them to the intensive care tent behind the platform. It was a huge tent capable of seating some 5,000 people if it rained at the campaign site. So two men would run into the crowd and pick up the person who was in manifestation, if they could, and they would carry this person back to the tent. It was an incredible sight. Some people looked confused, but not as much as we who were visiting the campaign for the first time that night. Most of the crowd took the situation pretty much in stride. The lower class of Argentina, and that is what the majority of the attendees of the campaign were, are well aware of things which happen in the spirit realm. They are generally aware and may have some experience with demons, witches, warlocks, shamans and religious sects which have rites which release power for good or evil.

INSIDE THE DELIVERANCE TENT

After watching this scene for 15 minutes, we went into the tent where they were doing deliverance. Inside, people were spread around in groups of three throughout the entire tent. Two would be ministering deliverance to the one person who had been brought in. That person may have been in their right state of mind because the deliverance had already occurred and they were sitting calmly on their chair being counseled. Possibly, the person was on the ground writhing and screaming and the two ministers, laypeople from local churches, generally, were either holding the person, speaking to them, screaming at them or in some way trying to evict the demonic intruder. Some of the people were unconscious, or still in some other stage of the demonic manifestation. Probably 60 people were in the tent receiving some kind of ministry to free them from demonic bondage.

Later, Annacondia prayed for the sick and made the rounds through the tent, sort of like the attending physician. He gave instructions now and again to the ministers in the tent and sometimes stepped in and dealt with a demon....After the time in the deliverance tent, Annacondia went outside and started praying for the believers right in front of the platform. He had them all line up in a straight line. There were hundreds of them. He had some workers get behind the line of people. He then asked them to extend their hands and he blew on them. About 90% fell down backwards into the waiting arms of his workers. This activity continued until well after midnight.

I attended many other Annacondia campaigns while in Argentina, and the pattern was almost identical in every situation. I have also seen Carlos minister to Christians in conference settings. Even in this setting, there have been spectacular healings follow his ministry.[1]

WHAT IS THE SECRET?

God has allowed me to preach to tens of thousands of persons of all languages, races and colors. Hundreds of thousands in these meetings have chosen to put their faith in Christ as Savior. How has this been possible? What is the secret? The secret of this ministry, and of any ministry that is carried out in His name, consists of believing that God has already given us the power to do it. The Lord says in His Word that He has *already* given power to His people for them to accomplish the mission. This He did through His Son, Jesus Christ.

The Bible affirms that "when Jesus had called the Twelve together, he gave them power and authority to drive out all demons and to cure diseases, and he sent them out to preach the kingdom of God and to heal the sick" (Luke 9:1,2, *NIV*). What did those disciples do? "They set out and went from village to village, preaching the gospel and healing people everywhere" (v. 6).

Later, Jesus commissioned another 72 of His disciples, and said to them, "Go! I am sending you out like lambs among wolves....When you enter a town and are welcomed...heal the sick who are there and tell them, 'The kingdom of God is near you'" (Luke 10:3,8-9, *NIV*). And what did these disciples do? The Bible says they "returned with joy and said, 'Lord, even the demons submit to us in your name'" (v. 17). Filled with satisfaction, Jesus said to them, "I have given you authority to trample on snakes and scorpions and to overcome all the power of the enemy; nothing will harm you" (v. 19).

Note that the three times that Jesus sent His followers out to preach the kingdom of God—the 12 according to Luke 9:1, the 72 according to Luke 10:19, and all believers, according to Mark 16.17—Jesus gave them the authority and the power to do the things that He did.

Moreover, Jesus promised His followers that they would do not only the things that He did, but even "greater works than these" (John 14:12).

A MATTER OF FAITH

If this is the Lord's command, and if we believe that we have the power and authority in His name to carry it out, then what must we do for this to be fulfilled in our lives and ministries? What we need is faith. Faith

> I have the power of God. I can count on it. He gave it to me. I must put it into practice.

in the Word of God. Time after time I repeat to myself, "I have the power of God. I can count on it. He gave it to me. I must put it into practice." Only faith can release the power of God in your life and ministry.

Remember, this promise is not just for a few anointed, inspired or privileged individuals. That kind of thinking is falling prey to Satan's deceit. The promise is for anyone who believes in Him (see John 14:12). And Jesus further promises, "I will do whatever you ask in my name, so that the Son may bring glory to the Father. You may ask me for anything in my name, and I will do it" (v. 13,14, *NIV*).

So I see this as essentially a matter of faith. The Word indicates that "the righteous will live by faith" (Rom. 1:17, *NIV*). The Word also specifies that "without faith it is impossible to please God" (Heb. 11:6, *NIV*). Now, this faith, the faith necessary to operate under the supernatural power of God and with authority in His name, is not a rational conviction, nor does it require a certain religious knowledge. These things are hidden from the wise and learned and have been revealed to little children (see Matt. 11:25). These things are for those who, with a simple heart, begin to put into practice the command of the Lord of going and preaching, trusting Him that the promised supernatural signs will follow.

The order of God is for preaching to come first. Then signs will confirm the truth of the gospel of Christ with miracles and wonders, just as Jesus affirmed. It is not enough just to talk about the gospel, but it is necessary to also put the gospel into practice with all of its visible and outward consequences and effects (see Matt. 7:24).

This is so, "for the kingdom of God is not in word but in power" (1 Cor. 4:20). And this power has to be made evident through the manifestations of the supernatural operation of the Holy Spirit. How can you obtain this power of God? Jesus' promise is quite clear as He answers this question. "You shall receive power when the Holy Spirit has come upon you; and you shall be witnesses to Me...to the end of the earth" (Acts 1:8). This was how the first Christians received power and authority and, as a consequence, they filled the known world with the gospel.

This is also how the apostle Paul was able to experience such a fruitful ministry. According to Paul, his Christian testimony was "not with wise and persuasive words, but with a demonstration of the Spirit's power" (1 Cor. 2:4, *NIV*). This was the case, so that the faith of his hearers would "not rest on men's wisdom, but on God's power" (v. 5). It is evident that the apostle Paul only preached under the power of the Holy Spirit. He writes, "I will not venture to speak of anything except what Christ has accomplished through me in leading the Gentiles to obey God by what I have said and done—by the power of signs and miracles, through the power of the Spirit" (Rom. 15:18,19, *NIV*). This explains how it was possible for a weak and limited individual such as Paul to affirm without exaggeration, "from Jerusalem all the way around to Illyricum, I have fully proclaimed the gospel of Christ" (v. 19).

MINISTERING BY GOD'S GRACE

So, then, it is necessary for each of us to minister according to the grace that we have received from God, according to the power that He has given us. The apostle Peter exhorts us, saying, "If anyone speaks, he should do it as one speaking the very words of God. If anyone serves, he should do it with the strength God provides, so that in all things God may be praised through Jesus Christ" (1 Pet. 4:11, *NIV*). Our faith, then, must be accompanied by visible works of power. Otherwise, it will be a dead faith, because "faith, by itself, if it is not accompanied by action, is dead" (Jas. 2:17, *NIV*).

Do you want God to use you? Is it your desire to receive revelation from the Lord? Believe like a child and He promises to do it. This brings joy to His heart (see Luke 10:21). It is only when we fully trust Him, that "his incomparably great power for us who believe" is made effective in our lives and ministries, "like the working of his mighty strength" (Eph. 1:19, *NIV*).

Note
1. Michael D. Richardson, "Revival in Argentina" (Paper, Fuller Theological Seminary, 1997), pp. 10-12.

four

DEALING WITH DEMONS IN REVIVAL EVANGELISM

BY PABLO BOTTARI

Pablo Bottari, a barber in Buenos Aires, developed an extraordinary gift of deliverance while being mentored by Carlos Annacondia. For 12 years he served as the director of Annacondia's deliverance ministry, supervising the activities in the deliverance tent at the campaigns. Bottari has personally participated in casting demons out of more than 60,000 individuals. He now serves on the pastoral staff of Central Baptist Church in Buenos Aires, where he has developed what is arguably the most sophisticated local church deliverance ministry today. He is in increasing demand internationally, especially for teaching pastors about deliverance in the local church.

During the first days of January 1985, I found myself in the midst of a multitude of people who were praising God with songs, clapping their hands and shouting, "Hallelujah!" and "Amen!" The meeting place was surrounded by numerous lights and was the center of a lot of bustle and activity. My Plymouth Brethren background had not prepared me for this kind of a situation. But there I was, along with my wife, Margarita, and our two children, Gabriel and Elizabeth. We were astonished at the hubbub, but we had come to the meeting with a definite purpose in mind. We wanted to see how these people dealt with individuals who had serious spiritual problems. A special case which was facing us personally had us deeply concerned.

A DEMONIZED WOMAN IN OUR CHURCH

A rather elderly woman in our church was suffering from a very serious spiritual problem. We readily admitted that solving this problem was far beyond our reach or experience. In a meeting of the elders of our church, I suggested we might consult someone with experience in the ministry of demonic deliverance. I was assigned the task of dealing with this thorny issue.

So it was that my family and I journeyed to the city of San Justo, where evangelist Carlos Annacondia was leading one of his evangelistic campaigns. We had been invited by one of the pastors of our church to see for ourselves how this unusual ministry was carried out. We went on a Friday night. Of course, we questioned many things we were seeing, among them, people falling to the ground when they were prayed for, speaking in tongues, enthusiastic shouts of praise, public rebuking of demons, dramatic manifestations of those who were demonized, the festive character of the gathering, the food stands and the general informality of it all. Many of the things I was seeing and hearing for the first time, I could not understand. But, somehow, I felt that the presence of the Lord at the meeting was strong and very real.

"LISTEN TO ME, SATAN!"

One of the most difficult things for me to digest was when the evangelist, after reading the Word and preaching a simple message, confronted the very devil himself, shouting, "And now, listen to me, Satan! I come against you in the powerful name of Jesus Christ of Nazareth! I rebuke you, I bind you and I order you to get out of this place! Out! In the name of Jesus! Loose the lives you have in bondage! Now!" And he continued like this for several minutes in a loud voice. His rebukes over the loudspeakers were deafening. I actually felt my hairs standing on end, and my skin became like goose flesh. But I also felt the powerful presence of God in that place in a very special way.

There was a ring of authority in the voice of the evangelist that I had never heard from anyone before.

Suddenly, it dawned on me that my family and I were there, in a Pentecostal meeting, with our hands raised as if we were ready to receive something. As good Plymouth Brethren, we felt quite strange in the midst of that boisterous multitude. But, we had come with the sincere desire to take something from God back home with us. Carlos Annacondia had finished his preaching, and more than a thousand people rushed forward to accept Christ as their Savior.

GOD OPENED MY EYES TO SEE

I sensed there was something special from God in the heart of that evangelist who, though short of stature, had a loud, harsh voice and was full of an incredible amount of physical energy. I was impressed with the spiritual authority and power which Carlos Annacondia seemed to be taking for granted. During the meeting, he had preached, he had invited sinners to come to Christ and he had prayed for deliverance and healing. The manifestations had been spectacular. Persons who manifested under demonic power were taken to a yellow-and-white striped tent. I saw convulsions, spasms, yelling, crying, fainting, vomiting and occasional violence. Each of the demonized persons was given individual attention. Meanwhile, others took the microphone and gave testimony of healings they had received during the ministry time.

What really got my attention were the testimonies of persons who affirmed that their teeth had been healed with new bridges or crowns or perfect fillings. Here was a phenomenon I had never heard of in my entire life. We could not fully believe what we were seeing and hearing! But there we were, with our arms raised, ready to receive from God some blessing through His servant. At that moment, Carlos began to pray.

Margarita, my wife, fell to the ground, touched by the power of the Holy Spirit. My children were frightened. But Margarita lay there with her hands raised to heaven. Her face was full of peace. I comforted my children, telling them, to my own surprise, that everything was OK because it was God who "had touched" her. In a few minutes she stood up. Then I asked her what had happened to her. She told me that she could listen to everything, but she was in another dimension—a place where she had felt God's presence so deeply that she did not want to come back. At that moment, a biblical word came to my mind: "Test everything. Hold on to the good." To myself and to God, I exclaimed, "Lord, I accept your challenge!"

That very night, I searched for and found the coordinator of the meeting and told him what had happened to my wife. I told him that I had questions about all I had seen and heard, and that I had a deep desire to know more about these things. This brother introduced me to the vice president of the campaign, who advised me to get a letter of presentation from the pastors of my church where I served as a deacon and musician. They said that the letter would be necessary for them to give me a credential that would allow me to visit all the components of the campaign. I did this, and over the next several weeks I attended the campaign with the purpose of "testing everything."

THE CALL

Of all the aspects of the campaign, the one that had the greatest impact on me was the deliverance ministry. Pehaps this was because of my denominational background. I had a Baptist background, but I was discipled among the Plymouth Brethren, deeply absorbing the principles of traditional evangelical fundamentalism. There, in the deliverance tent, I met a pastor of my own denomination, Floro Olivera. I asked him what he was doing there and what he thought about all that was happening. He answered by saying that both the evangelist and the organizers of the campaign (most of them of a Pentecostal conviction) were his brothers in Christ and that, even though he did not agree with all that was being done, nevertheless many of the souls that had been saved at Annacondia's campaigns became faithful members of his church. He then added, "I do not know if you are going to agree with what I'm going to tell you. But I believe that we are the Pharisees of this century. We are full of wisdom, but without the anointing of the Holy Spirit. That is why God is putting us to shame by using a simple, straightforward man, a man without much human schooling, but filled with the Holy Spirit."

His words were just what I needed. That very night, when the meeting was over, we met with some brethren in the deliverance tent. Those who had been ministering there were exhausted after many hours of physical, emotional and spiritual struggle. (They did not have the knowledge and experience in casting out demons that we have today, so the ministry in those days was very tiresome and extremely prolonged.) The members of the deliverance team asked for somebody to pray for them. Floro Olivera began to pray, laying hands on each one.

At that moment, a young girl about 20 years old appeared. When Pastor Olivera laid hands on her, the girl began to tremble. I thought, *This girl must be manifesting with a demon.* Suddenly, she began to speak in tongues, something that at that time I was not familiar with. Floro began to interpret. Addressing us, he said, "The Spirit of God is speaking. Kneel down and humble yourselves before the Most High." I thought that maybe he was speaking to others in the group. But Mario Tucci, a deacon of my church who was with me, said, "He is speaking to *us*. What shall we do?" I answered him, "If the Lord wants me to kneel down, I kneel down. But I will kneel down before Him alone, and not before any other human being."

We knelt down, as the girl continued to speak in tongues, with Floro interpreting. The words referred to the text of 2 Chronicles 7:14, "If My people who are called by My name will humble themselves, and pray and seek My face, and turn from their wicked ways, then will I hear from heaven, and will forgive their sin and heal their land." I still didn't understand. When the girl finished reciting the biblical text, she exclaimed, "Holy, holy, holy!" Immediately she began to sing with a sweet, harmonious and melodious voice.

When she stopped singing, we stood up, and she began to speak in tongues once again. Floro interpreted: "The Spirit of God is speaking. Kneel down and humble yourselves before the Most High." We prostrated ourselves flat on the ground. I felt a great brokenness and understood that the Lord was calling me to His service. At that very moment, the Lord made me know that He would always be with me in every situation, and that He would give me the strength to resist the enemy and to be faithful to Him. Floro continued to interpret, saying, "Fire from heaven! Great awakening and subsequent persecution." The girl ended exclaiming, "Holy, holy, holy!" But this time, she did not sing.

THE AUTHORITY

We stood up, having prostrated ourselves before the Lord. The pastor then said to me, "I feel the Lord is ordering me to lay hands on you for you to receive the anointing, so that from now on you, too, can lay hands on and pray, even for pastors." And he prayed for us.

In the days that followed, unimaginable things began to happen to me. I prayed for people, and they fell to the ground under the power

I was seeing the power of God in full operation.

of the Spirit. I laid hands on the sick, and they were healed. On occasion evil spirits would manifest themselves. Little by little I came to understand that, in all these things, I was seeing the power of God in full operation.

When the campaign in San Justo was over, pastor Olivera invited me to his church to sing, something that I liked to do as a service to the Lord. He also asked me to give a testimony of what God was doing in my life. The church was celebrating its anniversary, and there were several pastors visiting the congregation. Among them was brother Ed Silvoso from Harvest Evangelism. When I finished singing, Ed approached me and publicly told me that the Lord was showing him that they should anoint me and pray for me, because God was going to give me a renowned public ministry. I had no idea what he was talking about, but I did tell the Lord, "Well, Lord, if you want it, I will not put barriers in the way." I knelt down. They prayed for me and laid hands on me, dedicating me to a ministry, though none of us had the slightest idea of exactly what God had in mind.

I was very much impressed with what had happened during the campaign in San Justo, especially by the girl that had spoken in tongues, something totally alien to my personal experience at that time. I knew that God had anointed my life with His Spirit, but I did not speak in tongues. I am a musician, and since I was a little boy I have enjoyed singing. Praise and worship were the focal point of my ministry as a deacon in the local church. So I prayed and told the Lord, "You know what I want: I want to worship you in spirit and in truth." The Lord responded to me, "Tongues for you, not yet. But I give you authority." From that very moment, I knew that, of all the gifts the Lord had given me, the gift of deliverance was the tool with which I would serve Him for much of the rest of my life. It was then that the Lord called me to the deliverance ministry, and He gave me full authority in the name of Jesus to carry out the ministry with power and effectiveness.

THE NEED

Never before has the occult thrived and proliferated in Argentina as it has in recent years. Deeply entrenched in some rituals of the Roman Catholic Church, the occult has multiplied through sects and new religious movements, especially among the spiritualist Afro-Brazilian cults and Afro-Caribbean cults and within most of the indigenous religions of Latin America.

For far too long, we in the traditional evangelical churches have stayed on the sidelines, acting as mere spectators to this powerful satanic advance. The majority of church members who are suffering from curses or demonization due to their involvement with the occult have no other remedy but to go back to the same occult practitioners in search of a solution. Often as a result they are defeated by the enemy, their final condition being worse than the first. It is paradoxical that millions of human beings have to go back to the very *cause* of their problems to find a *solution*. But this continues to happen because the Church seems powerless to help them.

The longer we choose to be spectators and not participants in this war, the more we play into Satan's hands. The only way to put an end to the Umbanda, Quimbanda, Macumba, spiritualism, Satanism, voodoo, sorcery, witchcraft, quackery, Santeria, magic, divination and other expressions of the occult, is with the power of the gospel of Christ. We Christians have the true and effective answer to put an end to spiritual oppression. This is what God wants us to do. "Is this not the fast that I have chosen: To loose the bonds of wickedness, to undo the heavy burdens, to let the oppressed go free, and that you break every yoke?" (Isa. 58:6).

The secret things of the invisible world are not the property of warlocks, sorcerers, seers, mediums, magi and parapsychologists. These things belong to God, and they can be ours through His revelation. The Bible states, "The secret things belong to the Lord our God, but

those things which are revealed belong to us and to our children forever, that we may do all the words of this law" (Deut. 29:29). Those
who do not recognize and do not follow the revealed truths in the
Word are more likely to practice the occult and live their lives in cap-
tivity to Satan.

This is why the Church must take the ministry of deliverance very
seriously. When demons are driven out, the love and power of God is
on public display. I have seen thousands of lives, tormented by the
enemy, change radically when they received ministry in the name of
Jesus. Delivered and restored by the Lord, they then found in Him the
answer to their spiritual needs. God has equipped us as a Church to
fulfill this task. In Christ, He has provided us with all that is necessary
for us "to preach good news to the poor...to bind up the brokenheart-
ed, to proclaim freedom for the captives and release from darkness for
the prisoners" (Isa. 61:1, *NIV*).

THE MINISTRY

After the campaign in San Justo, where God had touched my life so
deeply, I anxiously waited for the next Message of Salvation evangelistic campaign in the city of San Martin. When the meetings began, I
realized that those who were ministering in the deliverance tent were
the same ones who had ministered in San Justo. One of them asked me
to cut his hair. (I am, among other things, a barber.) Then the brother
who was in charge of the campaign asked me if I would cut his hair.
So, the next day, I took my hair-cutting tools with me. I was busy cut-
ting hair, when Maria, the wife of evangelist Carlos Annacondia,
passed by with a few of her nine children. The coordinator asked if I
would cut the children's hair. This is how I first met Carlos
Annacondia's family and, later, Carlos himself. I began to build a personal relationship with him (and I also cut his hair).

The more I got to know Carlos Annacondia, the more I realized I
was in the presence of a simple, humble person, a true man of God. He
taught me many things related to the ministry of deliverance. Little by
little, I assumed some of the responsibilities in the deliverance tent,
ministering to some of the persons who were brought there every
night. This experience brought me to a deeper understanding of the
need for this ministry, especially when persons who professed to be

believers were manifesting with demons. This led me to investigate with urgency this sphere of Christian service.

During a later campaign in Paso del Rey, near the city of Moreno, I went looking for more from God. I felt that I myself needed a fresh touch from the Lord. I wanted Him to anoint me powerfully with His Holy Spirit. Everybody around me talked about the importance of receiving new tongues through a divine touch. I had asked the Lord in prayer that, according to His will, He would bless me by giving me a language in which I could praise Him with greater freedom. By the middle of the campaign, my wish was satisfied.

"You Will Pray with Me in Public!"

One day, at a campaign in Haedo, I was talking with Annacondia and with Baptist pastor Eduardo Lorenzo. We were discussing the diverse reactions of the Argentine churches to this ministry. As we were talking about some recent criticism and opposition, Carlos said he felt that, in the future, God might limit the freedom with which we were ministering, but that now He was giving His church a special opportunity to awaken and to take the authority that had been provided in the name of Christ and to move into this ministry of power. When he had said this, he pointed to me and said, "Tomorrow you're going pray with me in public, with the laying on of hands."

All of my body began to tremble. I said that I could not do that, because I was a mere nobody. But Carlos insisted. So I asked, "Is this what you feel from God?" "Absolutely!" he answered. So I began to pray together with him. Carlos would pray toward a certain sector of the audience, and I would pray toward another. We did this for several nights. Then other pastors took my place, and I began praying specifically for children. Gradually, I was becoming a part of the Message of Salvation team, specializing in the ministry of deliverance.

My First Campaigns with Carlos

During the campaign in Rosario, I would close my barber shop in Buenos Aires on Friday and travel three and a half hours to spend the weekend in Rosario. Annacondia began to hand over certain difficult cases to me. To my surprise, these people were released and healed by God's grace.

I remember the case of a young man, a bus driver, who came to see me and told me that when Carlos prayed, he could not remain in the place where the campaign was held. He had to leave because something within him forced him to go. I assured him that the Lord was stronger than the spirits who were controlling him, and that if he wanted to be free, Jesus could deliver him. Then we began to pray. I realized there was hate in his life, caused by painful circumstances from his childhood.

He was known locally as the "Piranha Kid," because when he fought, he fought to the death. He would become blinded by rage, even biting his opponent savagely. He was totally driven by the hate which controlled him. As he was responding to the Lord and renouncing this hate and all that had caused it, he perspired copiously. His struggle against the demons that oppressed him was terrible. Finally, through confession, through renouncing, through the power of the Word and through prayer offered with authority in the name of Jesus, the young man was finally set free. It was a precious victory. I have ministered to thousands of persons, but I remember this young man in a special way because it was among my first experiences of this kind. The "Piranha Kid" has since written to me three times, telling me he is serving the Lord in the evangelical church were he attends, that his marriage is in order and that he continues to be free from all satanic oppression.

God was confirming me in this ministry. It was during this campaign in Rosario that I was officially incorporated as a member of the Message of Salvation team. What a privilege it has been for me to serve the Lord together with Carlos Annacondia, and also with the precious group of men he has gathered around him, all consecrated to the cause of the kingdom of God.

THE "QUEEN OF MARIJUANA"

Among the precious fruits that remained from a 1985 campaign in La Boca is Liliana, known then as the "Queen of Marijuana." I found this young woman sitting in the middle of the huge site where we held our campaign. She told me that she wanted to die. Because of a motorcycle accident, she had become hemiplegic, paralyzed on one side. Each time a demon was rebuked, she manifested strongly. During the campaign, God partially healed her of her physical ailment and totally healed the wounds in her heart. The devil lost his stronghold. Liliana was transformed into a vessel very sensitive to the Holy Spirit, and now she is a great blessing to the kingdom of God, serving the Lord in an evangelical church.

Late one night, after the La Boca meeting, Carlos Annacondia was celebrating his birthday with some members of the team when a group of young hoodlums approached and threatened us. As Carlos began to deal with one of them, another one ran toward Carlos with a knife in hand. Just before the young man reached Annacondia, I shouted to the demon, "I bind you, in the name of Jesus!" Instantly, the young man fell to the ground, subdued by the power of God and yielding to the word of authority. That night, besides celebrating Carlos's birthday, we ended up rejoicing over the deliverance of those kids.

TAKING CHARGE OF THE DELIVERANCE TENT

At the beginning of 1986, during a campaign in Cordoba, Annacondia asked me to take charge of the deliverance tent. My legs trembled as I did not feel at all capable of taking such a heavy responsibility, but I

> I must not judge the persons
> I minister to, as if I were
> better than they. I am
> what I am solely by the
> grace of God.

knew I could count on the Lord's help. Annacondia's confidence in me was also very important, because I had great respect and admiration for him. I understand now that he was increasing my ministerial responsibilities for three reasons. First, he saw in me a genuine interest for souls, since I cannot bear to see persons bound by the devil. Second, there was the depth of my biblical knowledge, which I obtained through the Baptist and Plymouth Brethren churches in which I was spiritually formed. Third, I insisted on getting down to the root causes that gave license to the devil to bind the lives of the people.

For those who suffer from demonization, it is necessary to provide adequate pastoral care. To that end, much love and compassion are necessary. I must put myself in the shoes of the other and understand as much as possible the affliction they are suffering. I am convinced that I must not stand as a judge over the persons I minister to, as if I were better than they. I am what I am solely because of the grace of God. Both the person I am praying for and I, too, need the mercy and grace of Christ.

THINGS THAT ONE LEARNS

In the early campaigns, we experienced some great victories, but at the same time we made some serious mistakes. For example, we tried to minister by shouting as loud as possible at the demons. The only thing that seemed to accomplish was that they manifested even more violently. We bombarded the person by repeating unending lists of all the possible demons we could imagine, trying to cover all our bases. This required enormous amounts of physical and emotional energy, both on the part of the deliverer and the deliveree. Little by little, we learned how to do deliverance more efficiently and with greater success.

The campaign in Cordoba not only produced many beautiful experiences, but it also helped me to understand better the meaning of some important biblical texts, which, up to that moment, had only been theory for me. I began to see how many of the theories actually worked out in practice. I learned on the job, gaining valuable experience as the one leading the ministry in the deliverance tent. I was called upon to deal with very complex and difficult cases. As I faced situations that seemed far beyond my ability, I could only humble myself before the Lord and ask Him, "Lord, how should I do this?" Faithfully the Lord would give me the clues I needed to minister to the individual each time.

Today, after almost 12 years of continuous, systematic deliverance ministry, with more than 500,000 persons having come through the deliverance tent (and more than 20,000 that I have dealt with personally) my attitude remains the same. I humble myself before God, I depend totally on the Holy Spirit, and I believe that I have authority to cast out demons in the name of Jesus.

GETTING TO THE ROOTS

Let me explain something important about deliverance. From the outset, I knew that I had to rebuke the demons and order them, in the name of Jesus, to come out of the individuals. But I soon found that, in many lives, this was not enough. The only thing I would accomplish in some of those cases would be to cause the persons to suffer more from increasingly violent demonic manifestations, which could last up to several hours. I found that if I took the approach of dealing with the persons with more of a pastoral attitude, showing them that I loved them and talking to them about their lives, I could then come to know the root causes that had given place to the invasion of the devil. With more experience, I could readily discern certain common denominators in cases which had similar roots, and quickly uncover specific elements characteristic of a particular situation.

At the campaign in Cordoba, for example, I came to understand how sexual bindings were produced. A young lady came to the tent who had been separated from her husband for some time. She had been under psychological treatment. When Annacondia rebuked the demons, this woman entered the tent with terribly violent demonic manifestations. We rebuked the demons, but nothing happened. When she came back another day, I asked her, "What do you see or feel?" She answered, "I cannot get my psychologist out of my mind." Guided by a word from the Lord, I asked her if she had had sexual intercourse with her psychologist. When she answered affirmatively, the Lord brought to my mind the text of Mark 10:8, "the two shall become one flesh." Illicit sexual relationships unite persons in one flesh (see 1 Cor. 6:16), so that the spirits that dominate one person can dominate the sexual partner as well.

Likewise, I discovered that persons, generally moved by felt needs, make pacts with the devil in a conscious or unconscious way, opening the way for spiritual bindings. To be able to diagnose and deliver these cases properly, it is not enough to know what the covenant with the enemy consisted of, but it is also necessary to know what the causes were that led the person to make the covenant in the first place.

"Lobison" Becomes a Wolf

One evening, a young man known as the "Lobison" came to the meeting in Cordoba. He was given this name because he would manifest like a wolf (wolf in Spanish is *lobo*); that is, he howled and foamed at the mouth. To avoid doing military service (which in Argentina was mandatory at that time), he had made a covenant with Difunta Correa (Correa the Deceased), a goddess with a large following in the western provinces of Argentina. The shrine of Difunta Correa, located in the province of San Juan, is a center for popular idolatry and the occult (see Deut. 32:17 and 1 Cor. 10:19-20). This young man had remained spiritually bound by the covenant he had made with Difunta Correa.

One day, as he was riding his motorcycle over a hill, the motorcycle broke down. He saw a nearby *ranchito* (a small hut made of adobe), and approached it. There he met an old woman who invited him to have *mate*, an Argentine tea. The young man asked her if he could leave his broken motorcycle there, but the old woman told him, "The bike is running." When he tried starting it, the engine ran fine. On the following day, he drove by the place where the old woman had been, but the hut was no longer there!

The young man did not do military service. In his official papers, the reason given was: "Exempted for being a *lobison*." In Argentina, Paraguay and Uruguay, people call *lobison* the man, generally the seventh male son, to whom popular tradition attributes the capacity to transform himself into a wild beast during nights of a full moon. This is exactly what had been happening to this young man. When there was a full moon, he would go out in full demonic manifestation as a wolf and commit much violence. It was at one of those times that he showed up at the Annacondia meeting. After hearing his story, I broke the covenant he had made with Difunta Correa and ministered deliverance. He was delivered, but I could tell that there were other fears and deeper bindings which had caused him to make the covenant in the first place. Because the campaign was coming to an end, I was never able to get to the bottom of his problems. I just cite this case to indicate that even those of us who are very experienced in deliverance ministry also come to points of frustration when we wish we could have done more.

Through the 12 years of supervising Carlos Annacondia's deliverance ministry, one of the most important things I have learned has been that the Church of Christ is fully equipped by God to face the enemy. The first Christians received from Jesus power and authority to cast out demons. We serve the same Lord and we can count on the same resources. The ministry of deliverance is not an exclusive ministry, but a task that the Lord entrusts to all believers, no matter how humble and simple they are. Anyone who has the power of Jesus in his or her life can cast out demons. The fundamental requirement is obedience and submission to His authority. If we are ready to do what He wants, He will accompany us in a faithful and powerful way and give us the authority we need to break down the gates of Hades in His name.

DELIVERANCE AND REVIVAL

Among my more recent roles has been to serve as minister of pastoral counseling on the staff of Central Baptist Church in Buenos Aires under pastors Pablo Deiros and Carlos Mraida. At the end of 1994, a group of 70 pastors from Germany, Switzerland and Austria came to visit us. They had traveled to Argentina specifically to learn what they could about the ministry of deliverance. As I taught them the principles that have to do with submitting our lives to the lordship of Christ, they came to understand that, if they were to minister deliverance, they must totally surrender every part of their lives to Christ as the only Lord. The Holy Spirit began to minister powerfully to them as individuals. These pastors confessed openly those areas in their lives in which they had not experienced victory, and in which they themselves needed deliverance. During an awesome time of extraordinary deliverance and healing, old bindings fell to the ground, unresolved covenants were broken, heavy yokes were shattered, oppressions that for years had limited their Christian service came to an end and, most of all, these men and women of God were filled with a new and powerful anointing of the Holy Spirit for their own ministries.

This opened our eyes to the need of many church leaders to experience deliverance from their own bindings, yokes, oppressions and inner wounds, if they are going to serve the Lord with effectiveness, fruit, satisfaction and victory. This revelation placed an enormous burden on my heart. Under the covering of my pastors, I organized a seminar for pastors and leaders called "Pastoral Clinics," the purpose of which is to combine teaching with personal ministry to the servants of God. The results have been astonishing and long-lasting.

DELIVERANCE IN THE LOCAL CHURCH

I have since held many Pastoral Clinics, both in Argentina and abroad. This has allowed me to broaden my ministry, not only ministering deliverance, but also teaching others how to do it and helping them to live free and strong that they may better serve the Lord. With this, I believe that the Lord has completed my ministerial calling, fulfilling a prophecy that my wife and I had previously received. The Lord had said, "Speak to My church. Teach My church. I will send you far away, where you cannot imagine." I never even imagined that I would ever be able to teach anything, much less go outside of my country to do it. However, at 58 years of age, I made the decision to obey the command of the Lord, and do what He was asking me to do.

I expressed this feeling to Carlos Annacondia, with whom I had been working as a full-time member of the Message of Salvation team. We prayed together, and we agreed that I should follow my call to serve the Church and its leadership. We soon saw the hand of the Lord in this decision, as opportunities to minister to hundreds and hundreds of pastors and leaders from all over the world began to multiply. It is my conviction that the kingdom of God will not function properly in our cities and in our nations until effective deliverance ministries are part and parcel of each local church.

I believe that God is preparing to ignite the final great revival before the glorious return of Christ. This revival will not come from outside the Church, but through the Church. That is why it is imperative for the Church to be "Sound and Free to Serve," which is the motto of our ministry. But this will not be possible if the leadership is not a leadership that lives in holiness, health and freedom. Only when this happens will we have the power and authority to confront the hosts of wickedness in the final battle, and defeat them in the name of Jesus.

five

VISION OF THE FUTURE

BY OMAR CABRERA

Omar Cabrera *is widely recognized as the dean of the Argentine revival. Cabrera had been ministering with signs and wonders and demonic deliverance for years before Carlos Annacondia burst upon the scene. Because most Argentine church leaders did not have a paradigm to understand ministry accompanied by supernatural power in the late 1960s and through the 1970s, they rejected Cabrera as a charlatan. Today, Cabrera is pastor, along with his wife, Marfa, of the Vision of the Future Church, a centrifugal church with 145,000 members. The disagreements of the past have been forgotten, and no church leader is more widely respected in Argentina than Omar Cabrera.*

God, in his grace, called me to His service when I was scarcely 12 years old. From the beginning, I was interested in the supernatural operations of the power of God. I first experienced an awesome manifestation of divine power with the healing of my brother. At the tender age of 21, he had been declared beyond help by doctors. After thorough testing and examination, his physicians informed him that that he had only three months to live, due to a tumor at the base of his skull. But my brother received wonderful healing from God! Sadly, he would eventually depart to the presence of the Lord...45 years later!

After this experience, I grew up with a dynamic faith, trying to learn the Word of God by heart. I had a deep inner conviction that, in due time, I would be able to preach the message of the gospel of our Lord Jesus Christ, and that I would reach multitudes with His Word. Thus, since I was a youngster, I have felt the call of the Lord on my life to be part of His army of servants, dedicated to the proclamation of the gospel of the Kingdom.

For this reason, when I was 17 years old, I enrolled in a Bible school for the purpose of receiving preparation to better serve the Lord. Upon graduation, I went out to preach in the interior part of the province of Buenos Aires, trying to plant churches among peasants of low income in rural areas. Little by little, I began seeing and experiencing the supernatural manifestation of the power of God in my ministry. I felt a great fire burning in my heart, and I attempted to make continual spiritual progress in all areas of my life. I was very young, but the Lord was working deeply, building in me a tenacious character and stern willpower, surrendered to Him in obedience. I was certain that, in His plans, there was a great ministry awaiting me in my country.

ARGENTINA IN CAPTIVITY

Argentina has long been among the most difficult places on earth to preach the gospel. For centuries, Argentine Christianity was wrapped in the dominant religious tradition of Roman Catholicism. The people, captive to popular Catholic and pagan idolatry, hopelessly wallowed in unbelief.

Instead, the people embrace anything that has to do with magic and the occult. Millions here have turned to such esoteric practices to meet their spiritual and physical needs. Although medicine in my country is fairly advanced, generation after generation has looked to the power of witch doctors and sorcerers to cure their ills, perhaps due to the people's lack of economic resources.

My spiritual eyes have always been open to the reality of a spiritual and supernatural world. For me, this invisible world was more real than the physical world and the tangible forms therein which accompany our everyday existence. I thought that the truth of the power of the gospel was something vitally real. And although our evangelical churches did not teach that we could reach and touch our generation with the operation of the supernatural power of God, I knew there was a power that could be manifested in my life in the same way it was manifested in the life and ministry of our Lord Jesus Christ. I was convinced that this power had continued operating in the primitive Church, not only through the ministry of the disciples, but also through new members who came to be a part of this spiritual body. Up to then, however, I had not experienced the operation of this miraculous power flowing through my own life and ministry.

After I married my wife, Marfa, and after I had finished some advanced theological studies in the United States, my family and I came back to Argentina with the purpose of testing, through practical ministry, whether God could and would manifest Himself through us. We were certain He would, even overriding our own lack of faith.

It was toward the end of the 1960s that we started a very challenging work. I preached for 540 nights in a row, with people gathering night after night to listen to the word of God and to witness the miracles that the Lord began working in our midst.

A NEW VISION FOR ARGENTINA

A year and a half later, after some needed rest, study and reflection, I returned to Argentina with a new vision. The Holy Spirit had given me clear instructions as to what I had to do. He had commanded me to introduce the message of Christ into the minds and the hearts of those who, for years, had heard about the power of God but had never experienced it personally.

Early in the 1970s, a very influential and popular youth movement swept Argentina. Fostered by leftist ideologies, this subversive movement proclaimed revolution as the only solution for the social problems of the country. Guerrilla units were organized, in rural areas at first and then urban. Thus, the country entered a dreadful period of chaos and became engulfed in an atmosphere of generalized violence. This irrational leftist subversion led to the irrationality of military repression. The resulting terror, death and atrocities were horrifying.

It was within this context of fear and insecurity that Marfa and I were placed by God to serve Him. In 1972, we started a new work, especially and uniquely oriented to those who were immersed in the ritualistic and sacramental religion of the state, Roman Catholicism. The Lord commissioned me in a particular way to focus my evangelistic ministry on winning nominal Roman Catholics to the faith in Jesus

Christ. To our surprise, thousands and thousands answered the call of the gospel. Up to 20,000 people gathered at one time during the first week of our meetings.

PREACHING WITH PERSECUTION

As I have said, Argentina—like many other places in the world a quarter of a century ago—was almost completely closed to the preaching of the message of Christ. Regretfully, the people were tied to one religious tradition, the Roman Catholic Church. That meant that, due to the fusion of church and state in Argentina, every time we attempted to carry out an evangelistic campaign, we faced terrible opposition from the system, often resulting in severe persecution. Many times police and security authorities came with dogs and tear gas, to disperse the people who had gathered to participate in our meetings. More than once my team and I were arrested and thrown in jail.

During those years, I was hauled into court four times and accused of everything. I was accused of practicing medicine without a license. I was accused of fraud for promising false healings. In other cases, I was taken to jail for not obeying the authorities. I frequently made use of Peter and John's argument before the council of the Sanhedrin: "Judge for yourselves whether it is right in God's sight to obey you rather than God" (Acts 4:19, *NIV*). On one occasion I was taken to court for practicing hypnotism in public, because people fell to the ground under the power of God.

GETTING THE GOSPEL TO THE PEOPLE

As a teacher in Bible schools for many years, I had studied all the known methods of evangelization. Nevertheless, and in spite of our enormous efforts, the local church had never obtained commensurate results. Since we made few efforts to preach outside our own church building, we had no vision of preaching before multitudes. By remaining within the four walls of our church, we saw many people in the streets passing by without enjoying salvation. But we felt powerless to make them enter into our services in order to listen to the gospel. During this time, many great international preachers had visited Argentina, but even with great publicity, very few would answer to the invitation of accepting Jesus into their hearts. In general, it seemed as if the Church of Jesus Christ were sleeping soundly, with scarcely any concern for the unsaved.

In 1954, pastor Tommy Hicks had stirred the city of Buenos Aires with his powerful message, accompanied by signs, wonders and miracles. During the weeks of Tommy Hicks's visit, one of the most glorious events in the history of Argentina took place. More than 200,000 persons attended a single evangelical rally! Argentine evangelicals had never seen such a thing! I was there and had the privilege of witnessing the marvelous operation of the power of God.

People of all governmental, social, political and educational strata were touched when they saw the power of God in action. Persons from every part of the country came to listen to the message of eternal life and power. But, as it happens, the Church was not ready for such a great harvest. We were not prepared to preserve such an abundance of fruit. The afterglow of this spiritual revival, which moved the entire country, dwindled little by little, although a few pastors would continue to attempt more aggressive evangelistic ministry outside their churches.

PREACHING AND SPIRITUAL WARFARE

I am convinced that the Holy Spirit does visit people and entire cities, with great miracles and healings accompanying the proclamation of the message of salvation. During my ministry in the 1970s, it was as though a veil were drawn back before my eyes. I began to see that the mission of the Church was not only preaching the gospel, but that there was also a spiritual battle which must be fought and won if multitudes are to respond to the gospel.

At that time, virtually no Christian leaders were talking about spiritual warfare or about taking our cities for Christ. However, through personal experience, I was finding that intercessory prayer was of vital importance to our ministry, clearing the way for us to act with the faith that God desired. Not only were our prayers answered, but I found that I could operate in the spiritual world where the power and the work of the Holy Spirit can be personally experienced. It is only from there that the Word of God, the incorruptible seed, can effectively be sown in the hearts of those in need.

Reflecting in detail on the meaning of warfare prayer—and direct confrontation with principalities and powers—would require more space than I have been allotted here. Nevertheless, in my personal experience, spiritual warfare is fundamental. We can pray for hours on

> Evangelizing without actively engaging the enemy in spiritual battle is like trying to row a boat with only one oar.

end, but if we do not come out of the prayer closet to engage the enemy on his own turf, proclaiming the gospel of Christ, the effort will not be what God wants it to be. Evangelizing without actively engaging the enemy in battle is like trying to row a boat with only one oar.

ENGAGING THE POWERS OVER A CITY

In my own case, I came to understand that, after a time of fasting and prayer, I could effectively engage the spiritual hosts of evil keeping peoples and cities in spiritual darkness. My proof was that areas formerly marked by apathy and indifference would suddenly open up and that the powers of unbelief were impotent to keep the people from answering God's call. I was continually astonished and filled with wonder as I saw the multitudes drawn by the Holy Spirit to receive the word and to accept Christ Jesus into their hearts. From one place to the next, people were deeply moved by the presence of God. The method was the same, and the outcome was the same.

Thus, little by little, I learned how the enemy's territory could be penetrated to establish the Kingdom with God's power. Many places which had been completely closed and indifferent to the gospel immediately opened like fertile soil. The preaching of the gospel shattered the power of religious tradition, indifference was broken, and even those who were proud of their intellectual capacity realized that they needed God.

I found that receiving revelation from God as to the identity of the forces of darkness operating over a given city was always helpful. Many who were involved in magic and the occult were drawn to attend our meetings and receive the message of salvation. Centers where Satan was worshiped were annihilated by God's divine presence falling on the city. Furthermore, many of those who were leaders of these occult movements ended up committing suicide or disappearing entirely.

POWER EVANGELISM

While preaching to the masses, I tried never to proselytize. People somehow know when somebody is trying to give them a message of proselytization. Nor would I use mass psychology. I would not take a negative approach, speaking wrongly or looking for points of controversy with the official religion, Roman Catholicism. On the contrary, I tried to avoid anything that might cause friction with or separation from those who received my Christian testimony. My purpose was not to convince people that they should abandon the Roman Catholic Church, but rather that they should enter into the kingdom of God through their faith in Jesus Christ.

Whenever possible, I have tried to avoid the impression I am asking anyone to change their religion. I have always done my best to avoid confrontations and unnecessary controversies. At the same time, I never compromised the fundamental message of the Word of God, and I clearly explained the meaning of idolatry and sin according to the Scriptures.

As a result, many who came with great burdens, problems, difficulties and illnesses, both emotional or physical, found answers through a personal encounter with the Lord. The power of God freely manifested through miracles, signs and wonders. The operation of Christ's redeeming love was marvelous to behold. I taught that Christ was powerful enough to make everything new in the lives of those who trusted in Him for salvation and who surrendered to His lordship. Convinced that the gospel "is the power of God for the salvation of everyone who believes" (Rom. 1:16, *NIV*), I preached the message "not with wise and persuasive words, but with a demonstration of the Spirit's power" (1 Cor. 2:4, *NIV*). I ministered the Word, fully expecting to see repentance for salvation and miracles of healing and deliverance in the lives of the people.

At times during my ministry, there was such a wave of divine visitation, that multitudes started coming to Christ by the thousands. I have held meetings with 3,000, 10,000, 20,000, up to 48,000 people attending a single gathering. The manifestation of the power of God on the cities to which I had the opportunity of ministering was so great in some cases, that people would arrive eight or 10 hours before the beginning of the meeting in order to find a place. In the mornings, new converts could come to take courses on the development of their faith, on prayer and on how to lead a Christian life. I could see that the transformations taking place in the lives of persons were genuine and the conversions were real. People experienced a true encounter with the Lord. Many began to enjoy the benefits of Calvary through a new life in Christ.

FROM AN EVANGELISTIC MINISTRY TO CHURCH

At the beginning of my evangelistic ministry, I thought that its purpose was to enrich the existing Body of Christ. My goal was to serve as an itinerant evangelist and to contribute to the development and growth of the local churches. But, regretfully, some of the methods I used did not conform to the expectations of existing evangelical leaders. Not all evangelicals understood my specific calling to attract to Christ the masses of nominal Roman Catholics. The Lord had promised to give me a special love for His lost sheep of the Roman Catholic Church. But other evangelicals were jealous, upset, concerned and frustrated because, according to them, I was breaking all the rules and sacrificing the fundamental truths of the faith, which I never did. That is why, most of the time, my wife and I had to fight alone, together with the small group of faithful workers who accompanied us. They had all come to be saved under my ministry, and they had become my disciples. Many of them had even left their jobs and professions in order to dedicate themselves full-time to the extension of the kingdom of God through my evangelistic ministry.

Plowing new furrows is not an easy job. One must have God's wisdom to present the message in a way that people understand it. Today, missiologists call this "contextualization." Understanding the message is a fundamental step if the message is to be accepted and treasured in the heart. As Jesus pointed out, each time we sow the gospel, it might happen that some seed will fall along the pathway (see Matt. 13:4).

According to the Lord's own interpretation, these are the ones who listen to the word of the kingdom and do not understand. Then, "the evil one comes and snatches away what was sown in his heart" (Matt. 13:19, *NIV*). Then there are those who belong to the good soil and produce abundant fruit; these have heard the gospel and understand it (see Matt. 13:23).

When I first began my ministry, I had no idea exactly how far it would reach. In each town or city that opened up to the gospel, the people wanted to continue hearing the word. Nevertheless, due in part to opposition and persecution, we were forced to try a new method of evangelization. After preaching in a city for anywhere from 10 to 45 days, I would fix a date to return each month for only two or three days. We did this to confirm the new believers and help them to grow in their Christian life. Before we began to do this, we were losing much of the fruit. However, through our periodic visits, new groups of believers were formed which met regularly and, in many cases, experienced growing attendance. Later, these groups of believers formed the nucleus of new churches planted in cities and towns throughout the country.

VISION OF THE FUTURE:
A SCATTERED CHURCH

This is how we came to preach the gospel to more than 4 million persons in Argentina. In 1985, I was preaching monthly, face-to-face, to 145,000 persons. That was our total monthly attendance at these meetings for several years. I want to make it clear that I was not the pastor of one local church with 145,000 members. My church, Vision of the Future, was a scattered church to which I would preach from city to city in the role of an itinerant senior pastor. Still, 145,000 persons congregated with each other on a regular basis to learn, to pray, to study the holy Scriptures and to attempt to live a life in obedience to Christ.

That is how our strictly evangelistic ministry gradually became a church scattered over numerous congregations throughout the territory of Argentina. In fact, this unusual outgrowth of our campaign ministry became a new model for how to plant and organize a church. We developed what has been called by church growth experts a *centrifugal* church, one in which the pastor goes to the people instead of the other way around.

As we think back to the days of the evangelistic campaigns, we can hardly imagine how we survived the physical wear and tear that ministry demanded of us. We lived in a car, where we slept, ate, prayed, planned, etc. Those years required great sacrifices from my wife, my children and from me. But it was worth it. The evangelistic ministry has now become a great church scattered all over the country: Vision of the Future.

RESULTS AND NEW CHALLENGES

We calculate that, of all those we have reached with the gospel through the years, some 64 percent have proved to be fruit that remains. Today we have about 92,800 people attending the different meeting places of our centrifugal church throughout Argentina. At this writing we have organized Vision of the Future congregations in 187 towns and cities in Argentina, and, in some of these locations, there are up to five different preaching places.

By the grace of God, the mass media has opened to us. Formerly, we had no access to the media because of control exerted by the government and the restrictions they imposed on evangelicals. In some cases, the authorities acted under the pressure of the official church, which enjoyed exclusive access to radio and television media. However, God has now given us the radio waves, and we are on the air in the evenings, seven days a week. We also have had occasional opportunities to preach on television, although we are limited due to the high costs of production and television time. Funds are scarce, and for the majority of evangelicals, buying significant time on radio or television is impossible.

Radio is the most viable medium for us at present, so we have attempted to begin radio ministries in as many cities as possible. This serves the purpose of softening and preparing the soil for the sowing of the gospel, especially if the program can be aired for at least two years. Thanks to the radio ministry, we have often gone to a new place with an evangelistic campaign to find that there were already from 500 to 3,000 persons ready to receive the Word. For an itinerant ministry like ours, this is strategically important.

In 1985 we began to raise up discipleship cells in homes. We called them "family nuclei." This solidified the work greatly, because in the cells, people could learn biblical doctrines more deeply and, at the same time, enjoy opportunities for Christian fellowship and minister to one another. We calculate that about 40 percent of those who have given their lives to the Lord through our ministry made their first decision in

> Spiritual warriors cannot stand alone. If the Holy Spirit does not move in our towns and cities, we will have "much ado about nothing."

these home meetings. We continue to develop this work. Our goal is that each church member be directly or indirectly connected to a cell. Thus, we can immediately address the needs of our members, and we can recognize those brothers and sisters who, because of trials or struggles, have a weak faith and who need special pastoral care.

WHAT IS THE SECRET?

We attribute the lasting results of our ministry largely to our successful engagement in strategic spiritual warfare. But spiritual warriors cannot stand alone. It is necessary to maintain a constant dependence on the work and the power of the Holy Spirit. Note that these are complementary: spiritual warfare and Spirit dependence.

If we concentrate on spiritual warfare, but the Holy Spirit does not descend and move in towns and cities, we will have "much ado about nothing." If we do not act with evangelistic zeal, preaching the gospel where it needs to be heard, the result will be completely fruitless. There must be a perfect blending of spiritual warfare and the total operation of the Holy Spirit.

NO PLACE IS TOO HARD

We must never allow our hearts to be penetrated by the idea that the spiritual soil of a place is too hard or too difficult to till. Perhaps we may not see great manifestations of power immediately. But whenever we have taken enough time for prayer and fasting, engaged the forces of darkness, and then gone out to proclaim the message of the Word of God, presenting Christ Jesus as the only Lord and Savior, the results have been extraordinary.

I thank God that in the 1980s, He raised up other powerful evangelistic ministries in Argentina. Thousands of pastors have dared to go outside their temples, battering down the gates of hell with fervent faith and preaching. Today, we can say with complete conviction, that in Argentina the strongman over the nation has been bound, and that we are living in a time of genuine freedom in the spiritual world for Christ to be made known to the multitudes. The soil has been fertilized by the Holy Spirit, and Argentine people are more ready than ever before to receive the gospel of the Kingdom.

At this moment, we are experiencing a great spiritual unity movement among evangelical pastors, who are now praying together more than ever before. But Argentina as a nation is undergoing one of the greatest crises in its history. The people have lost much of their trust in the government and in the economy. The country has fallen behind the rest of the world in educational matters, in health care, in justice and in human rights. In recent years, the nation has been rocked by scandals and corruption.

Meanwhile, the Church of God has also suffered deeply because of scandals coming to light within the evangelical community. It is as if God were exposing the corruption of the world at all levels and in all places, even inside the Church. This has shaken the Church to its foundation. In this context, it is not easy to overcome the spirit of rebuke and judgment. A scandal always affects many, weakening faith and credibility. This makes it difficult for us to present the message. On the other hand, it is also true that we are learning to confront this national misery with the love and unity that Christ brings.

IS THIS REVIVAL?

Many feel that we cannot use the word revival to accurately describe what is happening in Argentina. I do believe we can affirm with certainty that we are living in a time of consolidation. For years the Church has been fishing and we have gathered all kinds of fish. But now it is time to clean them, to process them and to put them in a container. There are many who, at a given moment, once expressed their faith in Christ, but who have fallen back on old traditions and returned to their heathen and occult practices. It is necessary to reach them again and bring them back to Christ's sheepfold, to heal their wounds and help them grow and mature in their faith.

Some people say there is no revival in Argentina because the Christian Church has not significantly altered corrupt social structures, nor has it cured the evils that the country is enduring. We can affirm that there have been radical changes in those who have received the miracle of the new birth. But it is difficult to say the same about those who exert authority, such as the president of the nation, governors, ministers and people in high governmental positions. In the same way, we have been largely unsuccessful in reaching businesspersons, controllers of the mass media, educators and community leaders with the gospel.

I do believe, however, that there is a significant change of attitude toward the gospel in many of these power circles, especially in the interior of our country. Someone who has suffered as much opposition and persecution for the sake of the gospel as I have, can clearly see the marked difference in attitude. In my judgment, this attitude is considerably more positive and favorable than it was only a few years ago.

THE FRUIT HAS COME

Indeed, in the past 10 years, we in Argentina have seen much enduring fruit of the gospel of the Kingdom. The people are much more open to hearing and receiving the message of salvation. Many now dare to break with the religious traditions of the past, with an ever-increasing number desiring to be integrated as members of an evangelical church. Not long ago, the social prejudices and political resistance made this almost impossible.

My impression is that the Lord is more enthusiastic than many resident evangelical Christians about what the Holy Spirit is doing in Argentina. True, we have failed in many things, perhaps because the heavenly blessings were so great and unexpected that we were not ready for them. Churches that have long been praying for this spiritual revival are now faced with the problem of not having enough workers to move and keep up with what the Lord is doing.

The most important thing is that we take advantage of this special moment in which we are living. There is no doubt that, today in

Argentina, we are presented with unprecedented opportunities for the proclamation of the gospel of the Kingdom. The worst that can happen to us now is that we allow Satan to cheat us and seduce us to disobey the Lord, falling into moral sins or into sins of pride and spiritual arrogance. In fact, we need to be on guard against falling into a pernicious self-sufficiency, produced by pride or vanity, that displaces Christ from the center of our lives.

VISION OF THE FUTURE

What can Argentine Christians expect from God? We must believe that what God has begun among us, He will bring to completion at the day of Jesus Christ.

But if this is merely a time of consolidation in the Argentine Church, how do we achieve effective and ongoing revival? And how do we reap all that the Lord has given us up to now? For starters, it is necessary that we live in constant dependence on God, and that we never neglect that precious daily time in the presence of the Lord. In order to live and remain in a revival, we must constantly drink the living water, both through the Word of God and through the anointing of the Holy Spirit.

Also, we must not be overly anxious in our desire to see immediate, radical changes in the lives of our converts. We cannot expect these new Christians to develop overnight a deep, mature life in Christ. Babies are not born with mustaches! We must be patient and allow the stream of the Holy Spirit to move at its own speed. No matter how good our new discipleship methods and our healthy doctrine might be, nothing can produce more wonderful results than those produced by the Holy Spirit in a human being. Only His light can make darkness flee and His truth destroy the devil's lies in the minds and hearts of persons.

HOLINESS IS ESSENTIAL

If our fruits are to remain, there must be true holiness in our lives. Our hearts must be constantly purified by Christ's blood. Sometimes, sins and faults are committed, whether because of negligence, weaknesses or direct demonic attacks. When this happens, it is necessary to be ministered to by other members of the Body of Christ, so as to remain in a state of grace. If we are to be used by the Lord in His kingdom, we must allow the Lord's grace to flow on us and in us, so that we do not fall into the error of wanting a kingdom for ourselves. All that we have and all that we are, we have received through the Lord's grace.

Each of us must then be under the care of a spiritual body of honest servants of God to whom we surrender. We must be ready to receive help and spiritual counseling from them. We must join with them in prayer to maintain the unity of the Body and to be edified in love. We must be perfectly aware that we have been called as simple collaborators of Jesus Christ, who is the One who truly builds His Church and makes it grow.

At the same time, the message we preach must be well-balanced, because there is a heaven and a hell, blessings and curses. There is a broad road that leads to destruction, and a narrow road that leads to eternal life. The worst we can do in such times of opportunity as these, is to give an uncertain message. These are times that demand spiritual warfare and conquest. And, as the apostle Paul points out, "if the trumpet does not sound a clear call, who will get ready for battle?" (1 Cor. 14:8, *NIV*).

THE HAND OF GOD

I can testify that God has moved in our ministry during these 25 years, with great manifestations of His saving and healing power. The Holy Spirit has worked creative miracles, raising the dead and encouraging us with direct words from the Lord and with visitations of heavenly beings. We have seen the hand of God intervene in times of danger, when we have suffered life-threatening accidents and illnesses or when we have faced opposition and persecution. Nevertheless, I believe we have not yet begun to see the fullness of all that God has prepared for those who love Him.

There is a wave of divine power on the way, one that is greater than anything we have known and experienced in Argentina up to now. I believe this because the Church here has grown spiritually, acquiring a more personal and direct dependence on the power of the Holy Spirit. I also see that God is raising up many young people who will win their own generation for Christ.

From the depths of my heart, I want to express my infinite gratitude to the Lord for having allowed me to be a direct participant in this new spiritual revival in the land that I love so much.

The Holy Spirit, the Anointing and Revival Power

By Claudio Freidzon

Claudio Freidzon pastors, along with his wife, Betty, the 5,000-member King of Kings Church in Buenos Aires. Prior to that he served as a professor of theology at the Assemblies of God River Plate Seminary. For years he was mentored personally by Carlos Annacondia, then he received a special touch of the Holy Spirit under Benny Hinn's ministry in 1992. He brought this "anointing" back to Argentina, where he is now recognized as one of the foremost leaders of the revival. His book, Holy Spirit, I Hunger for You! *has been translated into many languages. Claudio spends much of his time traveling and ministering in other nations.*

We are living in glorious times. God is pouring out His Holy Spirit, and the first flames of the revival have begun to burn with unrestrained strength. The prayers of the saints and the many tears that have been poured out in secret through the years are finally bearing fruit. The Church is being restored so that God's original plan will be accomplished. Jesus Christ said, "I will build My Church" (Matt. 16:18). And He is doing it!

This restoration begins in our hearts. Before we touch the world,

God must touch our lives. The first phase of any great revival has to do with the personal relationship of God with His people. Revival begins with the vertical axis of the cross, with our communion with the Lord. Only then is revival projected powerfully in a horizontal sense, allowing us to reach the nations for Christ.

ANOINTED WITH A PURPOSE

The following item is from an article published in the foreign missions journal of the Assemblies of God, *Mountain Movers*, titled "Revival in Argentina: A New Surge of Spiritual Power":

> In December 1992, Claudio Freidzon rented a 12,000-seat auditorium—Brazil's largest—for a service. When the building was filled and police closed the doors, 25,000 people were still waiting in line, closing off two major avenues. They waited three hours for a second service.
>
> Among those waiting two blocks from the auditorium was a very wealthy, unsaved woman. She was unhappy and suicidal. The power of God touched her, and she fell to the ground. Believers gathered around her and led her to Jesus. A week later she testified to the changes God had made in her life.
>
> While the revival began in Claudio's church, it has spread to hundreds of pastors and churches. Several churches hold multiple Sunday services to accommodate the increased attendance.[1]

The article from which this passage is taken was written by Donald Exley, area director of the Southern Cone and Brazil for the Assemblies of God in Latin America, and missionary Brad Walz. These respected men of God were reporting the glorious events we began to experience in that year in Argentina—and some of the visible results of this divine visitation.

I am glad to report that the Holy Spirit is still moving, and I believe that this move of God has a definite purpose. As the prophet Elijah said to King Ahab, "Go, eat and drink, for there is the sound of a heavy rain" (1 Kings 18:41, *NIV*), so are spiritually-tuned Christians today "hearing" that a great revival is approaching. Everywhere I go, I perceive extraordinary zeal and clamor for revival. The Church is raising its eyes, looking into God's face, and the torches have begun to burn in holiness and love for the unsaved.

God has granted me the privilege of carrying out a world revival ministry. In only four years, more than 1.5 million persons have participated in our revival and evangelization campaigns! My wife and I have had the opportunity to minister in Argentina, Germany, the United States, Spain, Uruguay, Costa Rica, Burkina Faso, Australia, Hungary and many other countries. And we have seen God working in the Church, and through the Church, reaching the unsaved. My book, *Holy Spirit, I Hunger for You!*, published by Creation House, has now been translated into eight languages. From many parts of the world, I receive wonderful testimonies of how God is working. This is happening because people all over hunger for God! As the Scripture says, "'Behold, the days are coming,' says the Lord God, 'that I will send a famine on the land, not a famine of bread, nor a thirst for water, but of hearing the words of the Lord'" (Amos 8:11). These are the days in which we are living.

THE LAME WILL WALK

I was recently invited to conduct a campaign in the city of Guayaquil, Ecuador. More than a 160,000 people from all parts of the country attended over the three days. The Modelo football stadium in Guayaquil was filled to capacity under the motto, "Holy Spirit, Glorify Christ." And His name was truly glorified! Thousands of persons, among them a large number of young drug addicts, accepted Jesus Christ as their Lord and Savior. The healing testimonies had tremendous impact. At one point, I was taken by surprise when a section of the stadium, far removed from the platform, erupted in loud and sustained shouts of joy. I later found out that a crippled man there had left his wheelchair and was running along the field! Glory be to God!

A woman, who for years had also been confined to a wheelchair, unable to walk at all, was filmed at the beginning of the meeting in her pitiful state. She had come to the stadium specifically expecting a miracle from God. After praying for the sick, we saw this lady again and, sure enough, she was walking! God moved in a glorious way.

Another woman, very well known in the city, had been unable to walk for several years due to a childhood illness. She was instantly healed by the power of God. We saw her walking, running and jumping in happiness for the miracle that God had worked in her body. Many others testified of having been healed by God, some even before they arrived at the stadium!

"And these signs will follow those who believe...," our Lord said (Mark 16:17). As a result of the Holy Spirit healing bodies, liberating hearts and restoring families, we gathered an abundant harvest of souls in Ecuador. There was a huge party among the angels in heaven! I give Guayaquil as an example, but it is not an isolated experience. God wishes to show His power and salvation everywhere. He wants to anoint each believer with His Holy Spirit for ministries of power, and He is doing it in our day!

GOD ALWAYS HAS MORE FOR US!

There is a story in the Bible that might help us better understand the times in which we live and the purposes of God for His people today:

> One day Elisha went to Shunem. And a well-to-do woman was there, who urged him to stay for a meal. So whenever he came by, he stopped there to eat. She said to her husband, "I know that this man who often comes our way is a holy man of God. Let's make a small room on the roof and put in it a bed and a table, a chair and a lamp for him. Then he can stay there whenever he comes to us."
>
> One day when Elisha came, he went up to his room and lay down there. He said to his servant Gehazi, "Call the Shunammite." So he called her, and she stood before him. Elisha said to him, "Tell her, 'You have gone to all this trouble for us. Now, what can be done for you? Can we speak on your behalf to the king or the commander of the army?'"
>
> She replied, "I have a home among my own people."
>
> "What can be done for her?" Elisha asked.
>
> Gehazi said, "Well, she has no son and her husband is old."
>
> Then Elisha said, "Call her." So he called her, and she stood in the doorway. "About this time next year," Elisha said, "you will hold a son in your arms" (2 Kings 4:8-16, NIV).

This story from the Old Testament is very suggestive. The Scripture tells us that this servant of God visited Shunem from time to time, and he was invited to eat in the home of a very important lady of Shunem. For sure, these sporadic visits of the prophet opened the spiritual eyes of the woman. She was very sensitive to spiritual things. And one day she told her husband, "I know that this man who often comes our way is a holy man of God" (v. 9)

FIVE-HOUR MEETINGS?

In Argentina, and in many other parts of the world, we are experiencing a glorious visitation of God. The presence of the Lord comes upon our meetings in a powerful manner. We see miracles and supernatural manifestations. Meetings will last for four or five hours, and still nobody wants to leave because God is there. We have allowed the Holy Spirit to take control of our worship services. Praise and worship times are now fresh and spontaneous. Leaving behind their religious routines and spiritual lukewarmness, many have given testimony of the joyful return of their first love, when all that mattered was the presence of the Lord.

> If we allow Him, the Holy Spirit will take us deeply into the heart of God, instilling in us a new zeal for sharing the good news.

Have we recognized our privileged position? Do we really understand who visits us and what His purposes really are? Are we opening our spiritual eyes to see the powerful presence of the Lord? The Shunammite woman understood who was visiting her. And equally important was the fact that she understood the need, that the visit would not be a one-time experience, but that it would be ongoing. In these times of renewal, many, not understanding the depth of God's river, seem to be content with very little. They enjoy a few restoring moments from the work of the Spirit. They have a spiritual party and rejoice before God. Now and then, they experience an extraordinary manifestation of the Spirit. And I think this is beautiful! But, let me tell you something: There is still more! There is still more that God has for you!

If we allow Him to, if we break our hearts before Him, the Holy Spirit will take us deeply into the heart of God. He will make us feel pain for the unsaved, for those multitudes who march blindly to hell because nobody is preaching to them. When we experience God's goodness, the Holy Spirit will instill in us a new zeal for sharing the good news. This is a natural consequence of having tasted His mercy. However, it is very difficult for us to cry for the unsaved if we have not first cried for our own sins.

THE FOCUS: UNSAVED SOULS

A while ago, I heard a 19-year-old girl share her experience with God:

> The Lord showed me His heart. He showed me the souls being lost in hell, and that many of us are the ones whom He has chosen to rescue them. The Lord showed me what a privilege we have of knowing Him personally, a privilege that they do not have. We are here to influence those persons and to touch their hearts. The devil lies to us, but we have God's power. We were chosen before the foundation of the world, to take salvation to others. And we do not understand! When God showed me these unsaved people, I cried. I could hear their moaning, and I could not bear it. *This is horrible!* I thought. *There are so many people with whom I can share the gospel and I am here, alone.* But God told me, "Rise up, and I will also raise others." If we wait on God only to receive blessing for us, we will soon be so "mature" that we become like burned-out candles. It is the time to move with the heart of God, and the heart of God is to reach lost souls. This is the only thing we can ultimately take to heaven with us. We will not take a car, a house, a position or a degree. In heaven, the only valuable thing we bring in our hands are the souls who have been saved.

Can a sincere Christian set aside these words? The Lord Jesus made clear the purpose of the anointing in His own life when He said, "The

Spirit of the Lord is on me, because he has anointed me to preach good news to the poor. He has sent me to proclaim freedom for the prisoners and recovery of sight for the blind, to release the oppressed, to proclaim the year of the Lord's favor" (Luke 4:18,19, *NIV*).

We are marching towards a great revival! I believe it with all my heart. We must imitate the attitude of the Shunammite woman, who was not satisfied with just an occasional visit. She wanted to provide a permanent dwelling for God's messenger—a place where he could be comfortable, so comfortable that he would want to live there forever! With that in mind, she made her decisions, she worked, she invested. There was a price to pay. But her desire to be in the presence of the one who represented God was crowned with fruit. She not only enjoyed the presence of the prophet in her home, but God also satisfied her most intimate need, her most cherished desire. He granted her a son.

Is this not our need today? We need spiritual children! God's eternal purpose is having a family of many children who reflect Jesus Christ. As the apostle Paul indicates, "For those God foreknew he also predestined to be conformed to the likeness of his Son, that he might be the firstborn among many brothers" (Rom. 8:29, *NIV*). If we prepare our hearts in holiness, the anointing that remains will be outwardly manifested and the fruit will be spiritual children. You, like this woman, need children. You must desire them as a barren woman would. You must claim like Rachel, "Give me children, or I'll die!" (Gen. 30:1, *NIV*).

FILLING THE EARTH WITH GOD'S GLORY

Recently, a group of young people from our church participated together in a wonderful time of prayer. The Lord opened their eyes, so they could see as He sees. He made their hearts sensitive, so they could feel as He feels. I set aside time during the next worship service for them to share what God had given them. One young girl testified, "God pours this anointing on the Church so that the whole earth can be filled with the knowledge of His glory. He calls us to preach and to serve Him. He asks us to give up our selfishness, those things that are important to us. He wants us to be concerned about those things important to God, those things that are in God's heart. We are not our own masters. We are Christ's servants. We are on the earth to do His will, to obey Him and to serve Him. Christ is coming soon. In the wink of an eye, He will take us to His presence, and He says, 'I want you to bring hundreds with you.'"

Another sister told the congregation, "When I prayed, when I sought God, I realized I was worrying about my own things, about my own goals. I did not realize that, around me, there were people who needed me to share the gospel with them. I now see those around me as opportunities that God is giving me and I must not waste them."

The apostle Paul carried a heavy burden of love in his heart toward his Jewish brothers. "I speak the truth in Christ—I am not lying, my conscience confirms it in the Holy Spirit—I have great sorrow and unceasing anguish in my heart," wrote Paul. "For I could wish that I myself were cursed and cut off from Christ for the sake of my brothers, those of my own race" (Rom. 9:1-3, *NIV*). That pain led him to claim, "Brothers, my heart's desire and prayer to God for the Israelites is that they may be saved" (Rom. 10:1, *NIV*).

E.M. Bounds, that great man of prayer, expressed it this way: "The highest state of grace is shown through compassion towards the poor sinners. This kind of compassion belongs to the grace and not only sees men's bodies but also their immortal souls, stained by sin, miserable for not knowing God and in imminent danger of getting lost forever....The gathering of the harvests of the earth in heaven barns depends on the prayers of God's people."[2] God will add anointing to your life if you understand His heart and purpose.

THE ANOINTING AND THE JAR OF CLAY

The anointing and its accompanying divine authority are revealed in hearts that are 100 percent consecrated. The great evangelist John Wesley said, "What is it that hinders the work? I consider that the first and principal cause is ourselves. If we were holy of heart and life, entirely consecrated to God, would we not all preachers burn and spread this fire all along the country?"[3]

The prophet Isaiah, before hearing God's voice calling him to the need of the people, was confronted with his own sin. He saw the Lord in glory, and he did not adopt a superficial attitude of low commitment, but one of deep humiliation and confession. This same thing is taking place in our congregation, and it fills me with hope, because I know that we are reaching the very core of the gospel. There is a sweet fragrance of the Spirit, which, like valuable perfume, only flows through broken vessels. The Lord Jesus said, "If anyone thirsts, let him come to Me and drink. He who believes in Me, as the Scripture has said, out of his heart will flow rivers of living water" (John 7:37,38).

In my ministry, I attempt, through the preaching of the Word of God and then by prayer and praise, to take the congregation into the presence of God, to be face-to-face with Him. When this happens, and we are directly confronted with the holiness of God, there is visible brokenness. We are all shaken by His presence! No one can maintain the status quo before God! When the jars break, the anointing flows, and the anointing of God changes our lives.

Back in 1992, I was working harder than ever before. Every morning I did an evangelistic radio program. That done, I would go to the church to direct my staff and keep appointments with parishioners. At night, I either taught classes or preached in public meetings. I was going strong 14 hours a day, seven days a week. For many years, I limited my annual vacation to five days, always from a Monday to a Friday, because I did not allow myself to be absent from church even for a weekend. I was fully devoted to taking care of a good, growing church. Nevertheless, I knew intuitively that I lacked something, but I did not know what it was.

HEARING THE HOLY SPIRIT

I received my answer through the visit of a beloved brother, pastor Werner Kniessel. Brother Werner is the pastor of the largest church in Switzerland, located in the city of Zurich. He had been a missionary to Argentina for many years and was the head of the seminary where I had studied. In order to pay my student fees, I had worked as Werner's secretary in the afternoons after class, and we had become very well acquainted. His wise advice greatly blessed me back in those days of my training.

After several years, we met again to share a good dinner in a restaurant, and to enjoy the excellent Argentine beef (which Werner missed so much). We had a lively conversation. That night, he had spoken in our church service. At dinner I began telling him how hard I was working in the church, and how many other important activities I was involved in. To be honest, I expected him to congratulate me. I thought he might say, "Oh, Claudio, how good it is to see all that the Lord has given to you!" But, instead, he only asked me a question—a question that shook my life. He said, "Claudio, how much of what you do in a day do you dedicate to hearing the Holy Spirit?"

I almost choked on the piece of steak in my mouth! Werner continued, "You have grown a lot and the church is beautiful, but there is something you are not doing well. The Holy Spirit wants to talk to you, and you have no time to listen." At that moment, I understood what Moses felt when Jethro, his father-in-law, told him, "What you are doing is not good" (Exod. 18:17, *NIV*). After hearing this from Werner, I felt an urgent need to stop much of what I was doing and to think things over. I began to understand what I was missing.

I had always exercised my prayer life regularly. And I attempted to prepare spiritually for each of the tasks on my schedule. But there was a level of communion with the Holy Spirit I had not explored. I had been a professor of theology for years, and I even taught a course on the Holy Spirit—His names, His attributes, etc. I knew quite a bit about the Holy Spirit. But suddenly the Holy Spirit had stopped being the content of a seminary course, and He stood before me as a person who wanted to talk to me and have a relationship with me.

A renewed thirst for God was born in my heart. "As the deer pants for the water brooks, so pants my soul for You, O God. My soul thirsts for God, for the living God" (Ps. 42:1,2). My heart became a sponge which would eagerly absorb the smallest drop of the Holy Spirit that came near to me. I asked different servants of God who were filled with the Holy Spirit for their prayers. I met as often as I could to pray with them. My prayer life was renewed. My highest priority was to seek God's face. An intimate and fresh communion was born in me. For a time, I did not sleep at all during the night so that I could have communion with Him. My whole life and ministry changed.

The Bible shows us that every man who experienced contact with the glory of God was broken and transformed. In Peniel (which means "God's face") Jacob received a new name: Israel. Before that, however, he had wrestled with God and had become lame. Consider Job, a righteous man, but one who justified himself before God. When God revealed Himself to him, Job exclaimed, "My ears had heard of you but now my eyes have seen you. Therefore I despise myself and repent in dust and ashes" (Job 42:5,6, *NIV*). Remember Habakkuk, the complaining prophet? What happened to his complaints when God talked to him in a vision? "I heard and my heart pounded, my lips quivered at the sound; decay crept into my bones, and my legs trembled" (Hab. 3:16, *NIV*).

We have already mentioned Isaiah, who discovered he was a prophet of unclean lips. And what can we say of Jeremiah, this patient servant of God, called to be ignored by everyone and persecuted? When he lamented his condition before God, the Lord admonished him, "If you repent, I will restore you that you may serve me; if you utter worthy, not worthless words, you will be my spokesman. Let this people turn to you, but you must not turn to them" (Jer. 15:19, *NIV*). Jeremiah might have complained in response, "But, Lord, I'm your servant. I have preached in your name for years. I suffer for you. Why must I repent?" But God was showing him areas in his life that required conversion. This was a call for Jeremiah to examine himself and his ministry.

For years, I experienced a great dryness in my ministry. There was no fruit. Our small church in the Parque Chas neighborhood was like a desert. My colleagues in the ministry seemed to move forward, but I was seeing no such advance. Those were times of brokenness. I was dying to myself, learning to depend on God alone, and growing in faith. Those were times of seeking God's face. After seven years of traveling through that desert, guided by a vision from God, in 1986 we planted a prosperous church in the neighborhood of Belgrano, in the city of Buenos Aires. This church, King of Kings, now has over 5,000 members.

There is no anointing without a broken heart. God will use all the circumstances in our lives to achieve this end. The apostle Paul expressed it thus:

> But we have this treasure in jars of clay to show that this all-surpassing power is from God and not from us. We are hard pressed on every side, but not crushed; perplexed, but not in despair; persecuted, but not abandoned; struck down, but not destroyed. We always carry around in our body the death of Jesus, so that the life of Jesus may also be revealed in our

body. For we who are alive are always being given over to death for Jesus' sake, so that his life may be revealed in our mortal body. So then, death is at work in us, but life is at work in you....For our light and momentary troubles are achieving for us an eternal glory that far outweighs them all (2 Cor. 4:7-12,17, *NIV*).

THE ANOINTING THAT REMAINS

Many Christians do not reach for God's fullness and, unwittingly, they live a double life. I refer to those who enjoy God's presence in the worship service, feeling His glory, but in their private lives and with their families, they live in another spiritual realm. What is happening? The phenomenon is similar to the one described by the prophet Haggai when he says, "Now this is what the Lord Almighty says: 'Give careful thought to your ways. You have planted much, but have harvested little. You eat, but never have enough. You drink, but never have your fill. You put on clothes, but are not warm. You earn wages, only to put them in a purse with holes in it'" (Hag. 1:5,6, *NIV*).

In the church these people have joy, holiness and warm fellowship. But in their homes, all that is lost. There, they live with loneliness, sadness, spiritual emptiness, arguments and shouting. From an atmosphere of glory, they return home to a different spiritual atmosphere. Could it be that we lose the anointing on the way home from church? Is that God's will? This is certainly worthy of further meditation.

The Shunammite woman made changes in order to be able to receive the man of God in a permanent way. We, too, must make changes to our lives in order to remain under the anointing. The Word of God sheds light on this issue. We find precious symbolism in the law on leprosy regarding houses (see Lev. 14:34-57). This was a sanitary law given by God to the Israelites to help them fight this terrible disease. Undoubtedly, the extent of what the Word teaches in these verses is still greater for us. Leprosy in the Scriptures is a symbol of sin, as are blindness and paralysis in other passages.

The parallelism is impressive. Sin, as leprosy, can begin with something very small, but soon it will spread and affect the whole life until the life is quenched out. Furthermore, sin, like leprosy, is highly contagious. This is why you must be very careful to avoid all contamination. Finally, leprosy makes the affected zone insensitive, so that the leper does not feel pain as he does in the rest of the body. In the same way, when you give room to sin in your life, you can sear your conscience and thus become insensitive to the voice of God.

No Room for Sin

You might be saying, "Pastor Claudio, why are you speaking about this to me?" My answer is: "Because I love you and I want to be very open with you." The presence of God will not manifest in your home if you give room to sin in your life. If you open the door to some kind of spiritual pollution, this will deprive you of your precious communion with the Holy Spirit.

> What are the symptoms of spiritual contamination in our homes today? Sadness, depression, lack of peace, permanent uneasiness and feelings of anguish.

God revealed to the Israelites specific symptoms they were to watch for in order to prevent leprosy. "He who owns the house comes and tells the priest, saying, 'It seems to me that there is some plague in the house'....And he shall examine the plague; and indeed if the plague is on the walls of the house with ingrained streaks, greenish or reddish, which appear to be deep in the wall, then the priest shall go out of the house, to the door of the house and shut up the house seven days" (Lev. 14:35,37,38). There were certain symptoms that needed to be dealt with.

What are the symptoms of spiritual contamination in our homes today? They are sadness, depression, lack of peace, permanent uneasiness and feelings of anguish. When spiritual contamination is there, we find that we cannot maintain our prayer lives or study of the Word. Our minds think impure thoughts and we find ourselves arguing or fighting. We must pay attention to these symptoms! If they affect our lives when we are at home, then we must go quickly to our High Priest for Him to examine us and cleanse us.

You cannot change your relatives (who may oppose the things of God), but you can make correct decisions in order to be a light at home. That is your responsibility. The apostle Paul was in jail in the inner cell in the prison of Philippi. But nobody could put his spirit in prison. He was filled with the joy of the Lord and he made God's heart glad with his spiritual songs. You can do it, too! But you must take care of your spiritual life when you are at home.

SPIRITUAL HOUSECLEANING

It is interesting to know that the people of Israel, on many occasions, as God had anticipated, took possession of houses that had been built by the Canaanites. In some cases, these pagan peoples had hidden small idols inside the walls of the houses, as part of their worship of demonic spirits. When the Israelites discovered these idols, they took them out of their houses. Perhaps, in your house, you might have some hidden idols which you have not yet discovered. Television is only one means by which the evil one brings worldly idols into our homes. What do you talk about? What do you watch? What do you comment on in your family circle? Is there any room in your home for the Holy Spirit?

Jesus, our High Priest, is the only one who can determine when there is leprosy in your home and when there is not. That is why you should ask yourself certain questions. Am I fulfilling my role of priest in my home? Am I praying and guarding the spiritual health of my children, my wife, my husband? Am I embittered against somebody? Have I been wounded by someone in my family? Is television a blessing or a curse in our home? Am I wise and cautious in its use? Am I obsessed by worldly news, materialism, comfort, frivolity? In short, am I a good Christian at home?

These are the answers God demands in this time of visitation of the Holy Spirit. Donald Exley and Brad Walz, in their article in *Mountain Movers*, refers to this. "The revival [in Argentina] has brought a renewed hunger for God evidenced by the tears of repentance shed by pastors and lay people alike. An emphasis on personal holiness has caused many people to change their lifestyle. Less time is spent watching television. Pastors talk about the hours spent in prayer and a new joy in ministry."[4]

We must make concrete and firm decisions. To eradicate the leprosy, the Israelites were required to tear out the contaminated stones, have all the inside walls of the house scraped and dump the scraped-off material outside of town (see Lev. 14:40,41). Contamination has to be pulled out. In the same way, we must repent and decide conclusively to do things differently.

Remember, these are practical decisions that can change the spiritual atmosphere of your home, beginning with your own life. Leviticus 14 tells us that in the purification rites a little bird was offered in atonement and sacrifice, while another one was set free. The symbolism is quite clear: God is generous and merciful to forgive, and He gives you freedom to enjoy a new time of glory in your home.

THE YEAR OF THE LORD'S FAVOR

Let me give you some encouraging words. Very often we hear the demands of the Word of God, but we do not take into account the wonderful grace that enables us to fulfill them. Holiness and the victorious Christian life can be attained only by God's grace. If you have failed before Him, if you have concluded that His demands are too high, if you feel frustrated just thinking about it, you need a revelation of the divine grace.

Consider the biblical story found in 2 Samuel 9:1-13 that helps us to better understand the meaning of God's grace. King David asked those subject to him, "Is there anyone still left of the house of Saul to whom I can show kindness for Jonathan's sake?" (v. 1, *NIV*). The answer arrived through a servant of Saul's household, called Ziba. "There is still a son of Jonathan," he said, "he is crippled in both feet" (v. 3). This son of Jonathan, called Mephibosheth, lived in an isolated place in Lo Debar. The situation of this man was desperate. As Saul's descendant, he had lost everything: his good name, his fortune, his family. He could even fear for his life, since in those times it was customary for a new king to execute all the lineage of the king who was removed from office. We can imagine Mephibosheth hidden in a solitary place, bearing both his pitiful sickness and his hopelessness. But somebody remembered him.

The king had asked, "Is there anyone still left of the house of Saul to whom I can show kindness for Jonathan's sake?" David made no requirements. He said "anyone." Ziba in his report, made it clear that Mephibosheth was "crippled in both feet." It was as if he had said, "There is still one left, but I do not know if you will like him. Perhaps it would not be elegant to have a cripple in the royal court." But David, typifying the King of kings, had made a covenant of mercy. He took interest in that man beyond his painful condition. "Where is he?" he inquired (v. 4).

In these latter days, from His glorious throne, God is looking for men and women who want to receive the benefits of His grace. He made a covenant of mercy on the cross of Calvary, and He is not about to break it. He has decided to love us beyond everything. As David extended his invitation to Mephibosheth, the Father wants to seat us at His table as His beloved children. How wonderful it is to think that we are eating from the same table as Elijah, Elisha, Moses, Paul and Peter! At the wedding of the Lamb, we will see these great servants of God face-to-face, sitting at the same table as we. The angels in heaven, seeing our weaknesses, could tell the heavenly Father, "Lord, these will make your throne ugly." But God, who calls the things that *are not* as if they *were*, looks at us with different eyes. He looks at us through the eyes of faith and mercy.

Among the first words David said to Mephibosheth were, "Don't be afraid" (v. 7). Mephibosheth considered himself "a dead dog" (v. 8). Many believers today think they are prevented from living a victorious Christian life. They feel frustrated, depressed, drowning in feelings of self-condemnation. Satan lies to them, saying they will never deserve God's favor. And the truth is we will never *deserve* it. But God still wants to give it to us, because He loves us! That is why, in His Word, He extends His invitation to us. "Let us therefore come boldly to the throne of grace, that we may obtain mercy and find grace to help in time of need" (Heb. 4:16).

I want to encourage you to put the Word of God into practice. I wish to exhort you to make the correct decisions in order to receive the anointing of God, and allow it to remain over your life. This is the year of the Lord's favor! It is God's time for great revival. If you allow God to touch your heart and to cleanse you, you will be one of the vessels that God will use as a conduit for His divine revival power in your home, in your church and in your community.

Notes

1. Donald Exley and Brad Walz, "Revival in Argentina: A New Surge of Spiritual Power," *Mountain Movers* (October 1993), p. 7.
2. Source unknown.
3. Source unknown.
4. Exley and Walz, "Revival in Argentina: A New Surge of Spiritual Power," p. 7.

seven

CONFRONTING THE POWERS IN ADROGUE

BY EDUARDO LORENZO

Eduardo Lorenzo *is pastor of the First Baptist Church of Adrogue,*
a suburb of Buenos Aires. He is a warrior and a pioneer, introducing
the concepts of spiritual warfare on all levels to the Body of Christ
in Argentina. He has gained great credibility by making practical
application of these principles in local church ministry. Lorenzo is also
the Argentine director of Ed Silvoso's ministry, Harvest Evangelism.

The Word of God is sharp and penetrating, dividing even soul and
spirit (see Heb. 4:12). I find the Word to be a constant stimulus for
reflecting upon and adjusting the plans, the strategies and lifestyle of
the church I shepherd. Together, the Word and the Holy Spirit make
an explosive combination that puts the power of God into action in
ways far beyond our expectations. Our congregation in Argentina discovered several years ago that if God decides to do something we do
not understand, the best thing to do is simply to obey!

The Lord has reasons for doing what He does. Sometimes He shares
them with us. Sometimes He doesn't. Much of the time we find ourselves in the position of Israel leaving Egypt—simply following the
"cloud" in obedience (see Exod. 13:21).

After Jesus had preached to the 5,000, He told His disciples to give
them something to eat. The disciples began to count the money they

could collect. Then they came back to report to Jesus, "Lord, we managed to collect two hundred denarii, but that is not enough; we cannot feed them with so little." In fact, they were pointing out to Jesus that His proposal was absurd. "What you're saying is impossible. We are ready to obey you, Lord, but be logical! Don't ask us irrational and impossible things." But we know the rest of the story. The 5,000 were all fed with five loaves and two fish (see Mark 6:36-44). What God does may seem absurd to our understanding, but even so, the best thing for us to do is to obey.

THE CHURCH IN THE CITY OF ADROGUE

The story of our congregation in the city of Adrogue (pronounced Ah-drow-*gay*), a suburb of Buenos Aires, is a story about learning this very lesson: Obey God, even when doing what God is telling you to do may seem absurd!

When I arrived in Adrogue with my family in 1974 to assume the pastorate of the Baptist congregation, the church had already known 52 years of Christian presence and testimony in the city. Theirs was a beautiful building in the downtown area, with a capacity of about 200 people. The membership of the church was about 60 persons, only five percent of whom lived in the city itself.

From the beginning, God let me know His marching orders for this small church: "I want the city of Adrogue." This order was repeated several times and under diverse circumstances, leaving me no doubt that God wanted the city of Adrogue for His kingdom. However, during the first years of my ministry there, all my efforts to get the residents of the city into our meetings amounted to nothing. In the eyes of most people, the ministry of the church was a success. The church was growing a little each year. Neighbors were astonished by the numbers of people who began attending. Still, every new believer we baptized came from a neighboring city, not from Adrogue.

I began to immerse myself more and more in the life of the city. I had many opportunities to give a Christian testimony. For nine years I served as president of the parents' association of the most important elementary school in town. I then held the same position in the National High School for four years. As the congregation grew, my prestige also grew. Our social involvement also grew, but still the people of Adrogue remained indifferent to the gospel. And God continued to say, "I want the city of Adrogue!"

To make room for the growth in attendance, we bought some property very close to our place of worship and built a huge gymnasium there. This was a big step of faith for us, because we had to do it all with resources from the congregation. We might have looked for help from the outside, but God clearly and expressly prevented us from doing so. At the time, I did not fully understand God's reasons for this. So I applied the principle that it is better to obey Him than to insist on understanding Him. We have since learned that Mammon, the god of riches and the goddess of opulence, dominated the city. The Lord used an action of faith precisely to confront those powers. The provision of God and the generosity of believers have been keys to attaining victory over the enemy.

THE HOUSE OF OUR GROWTH

When the construction of the gymnasium was completed, we called it "the house of our growth." All that we had done, we had done with much effort and much joy, but it left us with a strange feeling. In the old church building, there was standing room only, giving us the false impression that everything was working well, simply because the place was packed. A congregation that once appeared to be thriving, now in a new home that could accommodate 1,500 persons, suddenly seemed small. We looked like a huddle of "wet chickens." Nevertheless, we celebrated the Lord and dreamed His dreams.

It was then that Satan began to bombard us. Our dealings with the spiritual world, up till then, had been superficial and occasional. It seemed to us a simple and easy thing to order demons to come out of persons. When we did this, the evil spirits came out. So we did not feel the need to develop a stronger ministry of deliverance.

The truth was that the principalities and powers of darkness did not want us in Adrogue. Time and again, evangelical churches had been planted in the city, but all of them had failed. And now it seemed it was our turn to fold. Strong demonic manifestations began to interrupt virtually all our meetings. This happened to such a degree that many decided to leave the congregation, leaving the remaining church members in a state of confusion and fear. A small group helped me minister to the most difficult cases. We invested hours and hours fighting against demonic forces we did not understand. We prayed! We cried out for the Lord's assistance! Little by little we began to see the light. Thank you, Holy Spirit, the One who guides us to all truth! Through our experiences, we learned about the nature of the demonic realm, and what we could do to drive out the demons attacking us.

POWERS IN THE INVISIBLE WORLD

We learned that in the invisible world there are spiritual powers who manifest themselves and who can affect the plans of the church. As the struggle continued, our vision became clearer. Then God revealed to us something surprising. He revealed to us the identity of a spiritual principality over the entire southern zone of Greater Buenos Aires. This principality was located in our city of Adrogue! He was the one who had succeeded in creating in our city an environment of indifference to the gospel, and this indifference had prevented the people from attending our meetings. When we took authority over this principality in the name of Jesus, two things happened. First, our growth accelerated. Second, 40 percent of all the people we baptized from that time were neighbors from the city of Adrogue itself. The church had now been in the city for 67 years, and for the first time in its history, the church was harvesting spiritual fruit from among the people of Adrogue!

With a total population of 480,000 people, Adrogue serves as the county seat of the Almirante Brown county, a political region that comprises various other cities. Our place of worship is located in the heart of the downtown area. This allows us to directly influence about 150 city blocks with approximately 35,000 people. This community houses the middle and upper classes of the entire region. Our neighbors are people of means, with a higher-than-average level of cultural and academic achievement. Adrogue is the very image of a rich and proud city.

This sector of a society always comes under the greatest influence of the demonic realm. The reason is quite evident. The upper classes constitute the top of the social pyramid, the one that usually determines the standards by which the rest of society will live. Other social strata are either busy climbing the social ladder (i.e., the middle class) or simply surviving (i.e., the lower class). In any city, the area where most political and economic power is concentrated will probably lack a strong and effective testimony of the gospel. Churches that are located in such places frequently struggle to maintain a healthy congregation and an evangelizing presence. To disciple a nation, it is necessary to spiritually conquer that part of its cities.

Since discovering and implementing these principles of spiritual warfare, the life and ministry of our church has changed in a radical

> God is not calling our churches to be filled to capacity. The desire of His heart is for us to fill our cities with the gospel of Christ.

way. The past few years have been characterized by (1) a deeper understanding of the Word of God; (2) a closer relationship with the Holy Spirit; (3) an awareness of the daily, living presence of Jesus in the midst of His people and (4) decisive encounters with the spiritual realm of evil. We have understood that the Church can and should take authority over high-ranking spiritual powers in order to minister more effectively to the needs of people.

A STRANGE ORDER FROM GOD

The years 1989, 1990 and 1991 were years of great prosperity for our church. We had taken authority over the territorial spirit that Satan had assigned to Adrogue. We took authority once again when there was a change in strategy. We committed ourselves to grow, rejoicing in our one and only Lord. The church was growing in numbers, and everything seemed normal.

But, one thing disturbed us. God, through His Holy Spirit, did not allow us to extend our influence beyond the city. We wanted to plant churches in other cities, but time after time the voice of the Lord repeated to us, "Win Adrogue first, and the rest will be easy." We thought we had understood the word of the Lord, but the fact was we lacked an adequate vision of the Kingdom. We thought that winning the city simply meant that the church would grow, that we would help meet the social needs of the people and enjoy prestige in the eyes of the community. But God is not calling for our churches to grow until they are filled to capacity. The desire of His heart is for *whole cities* to believe and for us to fill everything in our cities with the gospel of Christ.

That is why, even as we grew, we were not completely satisfied nor happy. Something was missing. The idea that the new building was the "house of our growth" had been fulfilled. But we were in danger of being lulled to sleep by our success, believing that, because we were growing, we had achieved the fulfillment of God's purpose for us as a church. We had yet to learn some more very important lessons from our Lord.

One of the constant teachings throughout the Word of God is His people's need to depend entirely on Him. When God assigned to human beings the duty of being fruitful and multiplying, of subduing and ruling the earth (see Gen. 1:28), He was thinking well beyond the human race itself. The earth is the expression of three kingdoms: animal, vegetable and mineral, and all of these are influenced by the presence of human beings. People can bless their environment when their source of inspiration is God; they can curse and destroy their environment when their source is Satan. That is why creation is groaning waiting for the manifestation of the sons of God (see Rom. 8:22). Damage to the earth, even though it is by satanic design, is wrought by the hands of humanity. Consequently, the redemption and healing of our present world should be done through the new Adam, Jesus, the "life-giving spirit" (1 Cor. 15:45). The Church is His Body, so we are His instruments for redemption in dependence on the Spirit of God.

Facing the Red Sea, with the hosts of Pharaoh gaining from behind, the people of God received His order, "March on!" And when they marched on, the waters parted before them. Before the walled city of Jericho, the most absurd military order ever heard was given. Nevertheless, the walls fell. To the reduced army of Gideon (of 32,000 soldiers, only 300 remained!) the strangest weapons were given: a lit torch covered by an empty jar and a trumpet. Yet, the Midianite army was annihilated. This list of unusual and seemingly absurd divine orders could go on and on.

"BUY THE THEATER!"

To the ears of my church, a new God-given order sounded equally absurd: "Buy the theater!" There were two theaters in Adrogue. One was new, the Grand Adrogue Theater; the other was the old Argentine Theater. The word that God gave us indeed seemed very strange. The theaters were scarcely 13 blocks from the gymnasium where we had built our church, and the gymnasium had more seating capacity than both theaters combined. How could I encourage the congregation to purchase something like that? What kind of arguments could I use to convince my people to agree to such an odd proposal? How does one explain the inexplicable?

By that time, God had given me great favor and spiritual authority over the congregation. Nevertheless, the congregation continued to be very "Baptist." It was not customary for the people to accept the suggestions of the pastor without discussion. Finally, I had to announce to the congregation, "God wants us to buy the theater." Immediately, the people raised the obvious question, "Why?" And that was the easy question. Many more difficult ones followed. Nobody seemed to understand the sense or purpose of such a proposal. While we struggled with this issue, the day came when we learned one of the two theaters (the newest one) had already been sold. I was the saddest of all mortals. I felt as if I had disappointed the Lord.

That same evening, a resident of the city (an unbeliever) told us, in his opinion, the church should buy the older theater, because the place had a history. This word "history" moved us. That evening, after going and looking at it once more, we decided the building could be useful to us. The Lord said to me, "You made Me lose one, don't make Me lose the other." Buying that theater was truly an adventure in faith. Out of our own resources, without loans or donations from anywhere else, the congregation invested $540,000 to purchase the building and another $170,000 for the repairs necessary to make it useful—all in just one year! For our congregation, these amounts of money were astronomical. However, obedience, faith and generosity made possible this miracle from the Lord.

HISTORY LESSONS

Meanwhile, the word "history" drove us to research the history of the city. We looked into the city's layout, its origins, its founder, its social composition and the cultural characteristics of the city dwellers. We got into the historical memory of the community. We walked the streets of

Adrogue, asking the Holy Spirit for spiritual discernment and learning how to express spiritual truths in spiritual words (see 1 Cor. 2:13). It was an invigorating time of discovery. Every morning at 6:00, we would gather for prayer and ask for revelation from God. The Lord began to send us dreams and visions and forms of revelation totally new to us. The Holy Spirit would bring to mind quotations of biblical passages, texts which we had never memorized. The Lord then gave us clear pictures of the spiritual design of the city. These coincided with visions that we received and with the results of our historic research.

Astonished and enthusiastic, though hearing by faith, we slowly unveiled the deep spiritual secrets of the city. By this time, we were wondering if every city has a spiritual design. Many evangelical churches deny the existence of territorial spirits assigned by Satan to control their cities. Others recognize the possibility that such spiritual entities exist, but doubt that God has given the Church the authority to deal with them.

THE SPIRITUAL BLUEPRINT OF OUR CITY

Our unmasking of the spiritual principality over Adrogue set us on a collision course for an inevitable power encounter with the enemy. Nevertheless, we were encouraged that each step we took in that direction was accompanied by new revelations from God. Eventually the spiritual blueprint of the city became clear. A line of wickedness crossed the city from one end to the other. The geographical layout of this line appeared to our eyes as a huge serpent, which acted as the principal source of the evil spreading throughout our city.

We observed that the head of this diabolic serpent was clandestine gambling. Gambling had brought a great deal of corruption to the city from its inception. The person that controlled the city through the gambling industry lived in a great mansion, precisely in the place where we had located the head of the serpentine line of wickedness. Following the line, we discovered the presence of other sources of corruption and sin. An area of prostitution was followed by the presence of Freemasonry, then the business district. Crossing the railroad lines, we found strongholds of sorcery and the occult, followed by an area of wealth. At tailend of the line there lived a spirit of confusion or emptiness.

We divided up the 150 blocks that constituted the original city, and we assigned groups of believers to prayerwalk each of these blocks and engage the enemy in spiritual warfare. We have since covered the city in this way almost 20 times. As they prayed along the city streets, the brothers and sisters received new information that confirmed the earlier revelations given us from the Lord.

The Lord later revealed another line of evil. The old King's Highway of colonial days divided the city in two. Following scriptural analogies, we discovered that these two parts were Egypt, the scepter of power, and Assyria, the pride of riches (see Zech. 10:11). Looking at our city from this perspective, we saw that the analogy was most appropriate. The sector along the River Plate (Río de la Plata) was Egypt. The city hall, the Catholic church, the school, the police station and the old courthouse were all located there. On the other side of the line, Assyria held the businesses, banks and centers of wealth. These two parts of the city had long struggled in conflict with one another. Each time the municipal authority organized a public event in the richer part of the city, the people there felt they were being invaded.

AN ORDER OF WICKEDNESS

Through the Scriptures and through much observation, we have learned that the demonic powers over a city do not always act in harmony. We have come to understand that, even when there is a strong principality set over them, the kingdom of darkness does not stand with unity and authority, but lives in violence and conflict. The kingdom of darkness is truly darkness in all sense; it is a sordid, occult and violent reality.

When the Church ignores the devices of the enemy, it allows itself to be victimized by the destructive strategies of the devil. These strategies not only prevent the Church's growth and its testimony in the nation, but they also undermine the local church, destroying its harmony, breaking its unity and causing conflict among the brethren, while eroding the foundations of the congregation. Many times, this influence is so subtle, that churches are divided without considering for a moment that their division is the direct result of the enemy's action.

The devil attempts to establish his presence in the centers of power, right from the very moment of the foundation of the city. To do this, he uses people—their dreams, their ambitions and their influences. His purpose is to form social structures that later will allow him to control the development of the city and establish his wickedness in it. The Church is a hindrance to his plans, so one of his major objectives is to destroy the Church, or to keep it weak and ignorant of his devices.

> Only the Body of Christ can rise
> with enough power to oppose
> the forces of evil and neutralize
> their influence in your city.

It is easy to follow Satan's tracks, because they are tracks of destruction. Only the Body of Christ can rise with enough power to oppose these forces of evil and neutralize their influence in a city. When Paul advises Timothy (see 1 Tim. 2:1,2), he encourages all believers to raise a mantle of prayer over the whole city, including its authorities. According to Paul, the total environment of the city can change to such a point that it will be possible for its residents to live "a quiet and peaceable life in all godliness and reverence" (v. 2). In this way, the gospel will prosper in an atmosphere of peace and freedom. And this is precisely what God wants for each city, as He "desires all men to be saved and to come to the knowledge of the truth" (1 Tim. 2:4).

HOW SATAN CONTROLS CITIES

As we have learned, Satan sets his sights on controlling those individuals in positions of power, even from the very foundation of the city. He marks the territory of the city as his own and will attempt to keep the Church from establishing itself in that area. A city will normally preserve its basic structures through the years, and these can speak to us clearly of the presence of wickedness and its influence on the city.

In days of old, the great kings, emperors and officials of high rank kept as advisors a whole army of sorcerers, astrologers, seers, warlocks and wizards. These were persons, most of them demonized, who consciously or unconsciously were in the service of the devil. Remember the struggle of Moses in the court of Egypt against these diabolic agents. "Pharaoh then summoned wise men and sorcerers, and the Egyptian magicians also did the same things by their secret arts" (Exod. 7:11, *NIV*). Time after time, they intervened to twist Pharaoh's heart. But what the Scriptures state is true, "The light shines in the darkness" (John 1:5). That is why, on the occasion of the third plague, the Egyptian sorcerers, whose power was limited, had to admit, "This is the finger of God" (Exod. 8:19).

God has raised up the Church in a city so that, following Jesus' steps and example, it will do away with the works of the devil. With unmistakable clarity, Jesus said, "I give you the authority to trample on serpents and scorpions and over all the power of the enemy, and nothing shall by any means hurt you" (Luke 10:19).

When, on their first missionary journey, the apostles Barnabas and Paul went to the island of Cyprus, they had a very interesting encounter in the palace of the governor of the island (see Acts 13:4-12). Though Cyprus might not have been a territory of extraordinary strategic importance, this story illustrates the principle of satanic rule through the structures of human power.

The biblical text indicates that the apostles had the chance to come before the governor, Sergius Paulus. With him, there was a man who served as an attendant of the proconsul. The description that the Scriptures make of him eloquently reveals the mixture and confusion that Satan plots around those who are in authority. Bar-Jesus, or Elymas, was a Jewish sorcerer and false prophet. This agent of Satan opposed Barnabas and Saul, and he advised the governor not to listen to them. Paul took the offensive and, filled with the Holy Spirit, made a rapid and categorical analysis of the situation. As the light shines in the darkness, Paul immediately confronted the web of deceit and lies that Elymas had spun around the ruling seat of Cyprus. The voice of the apostle thundered, "You are a child of the devil and an enemy of everything that is right! You are full of all kinds of deceit and trickery. Will you never stop perverting the right ways of the Lord?" (Acts 13:10, *NIV*).

Paul then declared that God would place His hands on the issue and that, as a consequence, the false prophet would be blind for a while. The biblical testimony says that when the proconsul, who had observed this tremendous spiritual struggle, saw the results, he believed, being "amazed" at the teaching of the Lord (v. 12). Imagine what happened on the island from that moment on. The gospel went from person to person with freedom and fluidity.

In order to advance, the kingdom of God does not need the support of state officials, but it does need the conviction and courage of the believers in Jesus Christ. Believers like these, filled with the Holy Spirit, will convert even the most elevated government officials. In Adrogue, we have had many experiences just like this.

THE KING'S HIGHWAY

Esteban Adrogue, a prosperous businessman from Buenos Aires, was the founder of Adrogue. At that time, the whole region was open country. The beauty of the highlands attracted the attention of this rich and influential man, and he invested in them. He built there a large house for himself and his wife, and two more houses for his daughters. Although the main house was eventually torn down, the house of one of his daughters is today the House of Culture. The other house is today the Public Library, though for a while it was the City Hall.

Esteban Adrogue urged his family to use those houses as summer homes and to spend their weekends there, but the family refused because the area was too isolated. So Adrogue, to secure his investment, literally invented a city. He offered the railroad company free land in exchange for establishing a railroad station in that place. The railroad company named that railroad station Adrogue, to honor its founder.

Something curious then happened. Esteban Adrogue kept the land between the railroad and the King's Highway for himself, while he subdivided the lands that went eastward from the King's Highway (Egypt in our biblical analogy). As the city grew, this trend continued. The richest population was established to the west (Assyria in our biblical analogy) and the poorer population to the east (Egypt).

The city has honored its founder with a monument in Plaza Espora (Espora Square) on the King's Highway, which divides the city in two. Esteban Adrogue is in a sitting position. But it is interesting to note that Adrogue's eyes are looking towards the west, that is, towards that half of the city committed to business and wealth, while he turns his back on the area where the political power and the poorer residents of the city are located. This pattern of city life has persisted ever since.

PRAYER CHANGES THE CITY

Our church has prayed aggressively in this situation. With the knowledge we gained from our research and with the enlightenment provided by the Holy Spirit, we boldly called for change in this divided city. We continued until we saw tangible results: A growing business community was developed in the east zone (Egypt) and higher quality housing was built there. The city changed according to our prayers! Today there is greater harmony between the political powers and business community. In fact, the president of the Chamber of Commerce is now a politician!

These developments followed in the wake of aggressive spiritual warfare. We summoned all the church members who had vehicles to gather at the same place one morning to take part in a Jericho "drive," in which we would circle the city seven times. About 70 cars showed up, and each one was filled with people. Each car was given a cassette tape recorded for the occasion. The cassette guided the worship and intercession of the car's passengers so that we would all be praying in one accord.

By our third trip around the city, the first car had come up behind the last one, so that during the four remaining trips, a mobile ring of praise and prayer completely surrounded the city. Each trip around the city was three miles. When we completed our seventh trip around the perimeter of Adrogue, we then entered the city itself through the tail of the "serpent," the spiritual line of wickedness [many call this a "ley line"—ed.] in the city. When we arrived at the center of the city we began blowing our horns and shouting victory praises to the Lord. The people on the street greeted us and cheered us on. We prayed God's blessing on all the people we passed. From that moment, the spiritual environment of the city began to change.

Adrogue is a bedroom community. People live there, but they do not socialize or do their shopping there. We began to pray that the city would become a center of human relationships, a "Sought After" city (see Isa. 62:12, *NIV*). Previously there were only two places in the center of the city for people to come together for a cup of coffee or a snack. Today there are 16 such places, and they are always full of people having a wonderful time with each other. Restaurants have multiplied, even with the current national economic crisis in Argentina. Commerce in Adrogue has grown remarkably, with new banks opening in the area. God now wants the church to disciple the city and to bless it.

There were six discos in the city, two of them overtly demonic. They were painted in black and red, featuring grotesque masks and occult symbols, and lighted with dim, red lights. People with property near these discos came to us for help. The problem was not so much the intensity of the music (which was bad) as it was the atmosphere of spiritual oppression in the neighborhood. We took authority over the demonic spirits behind these two discos, until the discos were closed by their owners. We continued to pray, and both buildings were demolished. Today the residents of that neighborhood do their shopping at a modern plaza located on the very same site. We continued to pray God's blessing over our city, and the rest of the discos were also closed down. The property owners who asked for our help were not believers when they came to us. Today they are saved and are members of our church!

A MAJOR PROPHETIC ACT

One Saturday morning at six, the usual time for our Saturday prayer meeting, four groups of prayer warriors took up positions, two groups on each end of the city's spiritual line of wickedness. Simultaneously, they began to prayerwalk toward the theater we had purchased, which happens to be right in the middle of the city on that same line of occult power. Each prayerwalker had a group of intercessors praying for them in the theater itself, which was being remodeled at the time. The groups in the theater were separated from one another as they prayed continually for each one of the warriors that were on the street. A larger group of intercessors prayed for the whole city. At 8:30 A.M., the prayerwalkers arrived at the theater. As they began sharing with each other the revelation they had received during the walk, the atmosphere became electric. All those who had been prayerwalking and those praying for them in the theater had received the same revelation from the Lord. This could not be a coincidence. Only the Holy Spirit could be the mediator of such an experience.

THE GATES OF THE CITY

That day, God revealed to us seven gates of the city—and He clearly showed us how to open them to the King of Glory. The geographic, political, educational and traditional religious center of the city is Plaza Brown. This plaza is filled with Masonic symbols. Access to the plaza is surrounded by other small plazas that guard the heart of the city. One of the smaller plazas, Plaza Espora, was a particularly important symbol for the city because the remains of city founder Esteban Adrogue are buried there. God revealed to us that in each of these plazas, we were to position our prophetic intercessors. From there we were to enter the center of the city, proclaiming victory. We clearly felt we were to take authority over that spirit of wealth and business that was trying to impose death and decline on the eastern half of the city.

One Sunday morning, the congregation gathered for prayer in the gymnasium, while I led a group of intercessors and prayer warriors to the center of the city. There we engaged in some intense spiritual warfare, more difficult in some places than others. Suddenly, as we stood in the central plaza, we all felt an incredible sensation of victory and freedom, and we found ourselves engulfed by an atmosphere of joy and laughter. We walked to the gymnasium, where the congregation was waiting for us outside, greeting us with a loud song of victory. Now we call our city, "City of God!" We are confident in the Lord that people will love to live in this city, and "God bless you" will be a frequent greeting heard in its streets.

As time went by, God eventually showed us that the eastern part of the city, the part we had identified as Egypt, was like a great body of water. At first, we did not understand this vision, because nowhere in Almirante Brown County are there rivers or lakes. The county does, however, have a historical connection to the sea. The county is named for a famous Argentine admiral, William Brown (1777-1857). This seaman, born in Ireland, served our country in the wars for independence from Spain. The plazas of Adrogue carry the names of his principal lieutenants. Some historians say that the location of these plazas in the design of the city represented the position of the ships of the fleet commanded by Brown. God revealed to us in dreams and through His word (rhema), that the serpent which we had discerned in the line of wickedness through the city was, in fact, a Leviathan, the gliding serpent of the sea with seven heads (see Isa. 27:1; Ps. 74:13,14; Ezek. 29:3,4).

THE LUNATIC FRINGE?

We shared these new revelations with only a small group of experienced prophetic intercessors, since we did not feel that the whole congregation would be ready to receive them. Some in the congregation had been somewhat resistant to those things that had been revealed to us previously. Nevertheless, during one of the services, the Lord spoke to me and told me that I was to give this word to the whole congregation. I had no choice but to obey Him, but it was with a good deal of trepidation. Sure enough, one of the most influential members of the congregation went home with a deep concern, thinking that we had gone over the edge, and that we would all fall into extreme fanaticism and find ourselves on the lunatic fringe.

That night, however, the man could not sleep. This person adhered closely to the written Word, the Logos, but met the spoken word, the rhema, with skepticism. For about two hours in the night, the Lord showed him a long series of political and military battles in which he had no personal involvement. Then God told him he was to be personally involved in *this* war. God showed him that what I had communicated during the service that day was truly a revelation coming from Him. The Lord revealed to him the names of the seven heads of the Leviathan and made him write them down. With this information and the support of this influential brother, we went to battle against these seven heads. Most of them had mythological names, such as Thor, Mercury, Mammon, Minerva and others. In each of these battles we received immediate answers, and God gave us new influence and authority over many different aspects of the city.

It is necessary to overcome evil with good. This has an incredibly practical application. We have learned that the Church must sanctify itself, especially in those areas in which a particular demonic influence is being exerted over the city. Thus, for example, when we battled against drugs, the Lord gave us a program for the rehabilitation of drug addicts that gained national recognition. Through that ministry, we saw clearly that sins in the lives of believers can literally empower evil spirits. On the other hand, these same spirits are weakened to the degree that we live holy lives in obedience to God.

DEFEATING THE SPIRIT OF MAMMON

The church responded marvelously to the financial challenge of purchasing the theater. That in itself constituted a severe blow to the spirit of Mammon. At one point, the city council unanimously voted to expropriate our theater and to declare it a historical landmark. We fought this in prayer, knowing that the place belonged to God. The theater was like the saddle of the Leviathan that had been oppressing our city, and that is why the devil did not want the church to be seated there. We won the battle, however, and there has been no more trouble. Interestingly enough, the city councilman who promoted the action of expropriation is now a friend of the church.

Business interests, the city council and sometimes the weather were keeping our church from holding open-air activities. It seemed that any little thing we wanted to do met with opposition. Through prayer, we discovered that at the root of all these difficulties was Thor, the spirit of conflict and climate. So we immediately took authority and battled against the principality. As a result, we no longer hear any objections to our open-air presentations. We have the favor of the business community, the support of the city council, and even the weather seems to be on our side!

FOCUSING ON THE KINGDOM

We have now moved our congregation into the theater at the center of the city. The battle for Adrogue is not over by any means, but we have a renewed vision and unbridled optimism. Our focus is no longer primarily on the church, but is on spreading the kingdom of God to our entire city. The Holy Spirit is guiding us step by step, as we continue to take authority against any diabolic opposition that might arise. During weekdays, the public places of the city are seeded with brothers and sisters who know the needs of the people, who pray for them regularly and who lead them to the Lord. We are not concerned with filling our worship center with people, because we now realize that our mission is to fill the whole city and everything in it with the gospel of Christ. The kingdom of God matters much more to us than the local church. This is our reason for being on earth: so that the Kingdom can be extended, displacing the enemy and setting free those whom he has oppressed.

eight

ENGAGING THE ENEMY IN RESISTENCIA

BY JANE RUMPH

Jane Rumph is a freelance writer residing with her husband, David, in Pasadena, California. She has served as the chronicler of the activities of the International Spiritual Warfare Network, coordinated by C. Peter Wagner, since its inception in 1990, a responsibility which has taken her to many parts of the world. Jane accompanied Cindy Jacobs and Doris Wagner to Argentina several times during the Plan Resistencia. She is the author of Stories from the Front Lines, *a chief source for documentation of power ministries worldwide.*

What is a non-Argentine laywoman like me doing here among the illustrious contributors writing a chapter for a book like this?

As it happens, I was privileged to travel to Argentina four times during 1990 and 1991 at the climax of Harvest Evangelism's three-year city-reaching campaign in Resistencia. There I was an eyewitness to several turning-point episodes and, as a freelance writer and editor, I documented these events with extensive notes and interviewed several people for additional information. My file cabinet bulges with firsthand accounts and collected research from these visits.

On my first mind-boggling trip to this beautiful country in June 1990, however, I found myself asking this same question. *What am I doing here?* I had stepped into territory where God's Spirit was on the move as I had never experienced before. As a friend says, I made such a radical paradigm shift that I almost stripped the transmission gears.

Edgardo Silvoso, president of Harvest Evangelism and a brilliant Argentine strategist, had mapped out a plan to reach an entire city for Christ. Building on his years of experience organizing mass evangelism campaigns with his brother-in-law, Luis Palau, Edgardo and his team focused their efforts on Resistencia, capital of the northern Argentine province of Chaco.

In his book, *That None Should Perish* (Regal Books), Ed Silvoso tells the story of how Plan Resistencia (Spanish for an evangelistic strategy or plan for the city of Resistencia) came to birth and describes its principles. Despite the harvest of revival being reaped in many other cities in Argentina, Resistencia remained hard soil, with fewer than 6,000 believers among its 400,000 inhabitants. Disunity and division plagued the Christian community there. Of 70 congregations existing in 1988 when the plan began, 68 traced their origins to church splits. Moreover, witchcraft and a cult of death held sway there like nowhere else.

CALLED TO RESISTENCIA

A "faithful remnant" of pastors in Resistencia approached Chuck Starnes, a Harvest Evangelism team member, with an invitation to train the city's congregational leaders in effective church-planting strategies. The team recognized a God-ordained opportunity—a Macedonian call for help from a city with key influence among several northern Argentine provinces and a stronghold of spiritual darkness. If a city-reaching plan could work here, perhaps it could work anywhere!

Drawing heavily on Ed Silvoso's expertise, Chuck and the Resistencia council of pastors formed a three-year plan to evangelize their city. Key concepts included a network of hundreds of home prayer cells interceding for neighbors by name, mercy ministries meeting the city's practical needs, and celebrations of unity with churches coming together to reach out to the lost. The plan's goals focused not on the number of public decisions for Christ, but on the number of new believers incorporated into the churches.

As a prototype, Plan Resistencia emerged as progressive revelation. Rough-hewn ideas got refined as the team made mistakes, stumbled into successes and learned more about strategies of spiritual warfare. Then an eye-opening new panorama unfolded before us in early 1990 after Peter and Doris Wagner of Fuller Seminary took part in an April conference in Resistencia.

"Plan Resistencia is the best citywide evangelistic strategy I have ever seen," Peter declared. But its ambitious goals would be doomed without "a massive outpouring of the Spirit and power of God." Doris sensed from the Lord a key to unleashing this power: strategic-level intercession. All over Argentina, gifted intercessors and spiritual warriors were fighting skirmishes with the enemy's troops. But without communication or coordination, their efforts against the most powerful demonic strongholds of their cities and nation seemed to be scattering like shotgun pellets, rather than hitting the mark with the focused intensity of a laser beam.

ENTER CINDY JACOBS

Doris immediately thought of her friend, Cindy Jacobs, founder of Generals of Intercession and an international speaker with vast experience in strategic-level intercession for nations and cities. Ed Silvoso agreed that Cindy's insights could help multiply the effectiveness of prayers for Resistencia and the rest of Argentina, so upon the Wagners' return home in May they contacted her.

With the launch of the first massive outreach in Resistencia set for July, finding an opening in Cindy's schedule meant a race against time. But an unexpected cancellation freed her for the week of June 12-19. She agreed to both teach and model the kind of intercessory warfare that would target entrenched forces of evil.

Doris knew they would need special prayer covering for this trip. Of the rest of the Wagners' personal intercessors, my husband, Dave, and I felt led to join Cindy and Doris and help in whatever way needed, especially since we were not able to team up with one of the groups Harvest Evangelism was recruiting for their July campaign. In addition, we wanted to visit our friends, Sergio and Kathy Scataglini, ministering in the city of La Plata and on whose mission board we served. Glad to have both a porter-cum-gofer and note-taker, Doris and Cindy welcomed us along. Little did we know how much this trip would change our lives.

Information from Ed Silvoso, members of the Harvest Evangelism team and various secular sources armed us with considerable insight into the areas where we would pray—Buenos Aires, where we were to pray for the country as a whole, then in Resistencia. (The Harvest team believed that praying on a broad, national level would clear ground for a more successful assault in Resistencia.)

After a 15-hour journey from Los Angeles, Doris, Cindy, my husband and I landed at Ezeiza International Airport shortly after 9 A.M. on Wednesday, June 13. We were met by Mike Richardson, director of Harvest Evangelism's training ministry, and Bill Kennedy, head of Harvest's television outreach.

Over a light lunch at the Hotel Continental, Mike and Bill suggested places where the intercessors might need to pray. Later, Mike took us on a reconnaissance walk through the Plaza de Mayo, the central downtown square a couple of blocks from the hotel. As Mike related some Argentine history and culture, Cindy discerned a number of demonic principalities connected with buildings ringing the plaza, including the Metropolitan Cathedral, the National Bank and the Pink House (*Casa Rosada*), the presidential office building. Other spirits lurked at the Ministry of Economy, the Ministry of Social Welfare and the Cabildo, the historic town hall.

That evening Eduardo Lorenzo, Argentine national director of Harvest Evangelism, and his wife, Norma, hosted a dinner for the team. During animated discussion in two languages, we mapped out additional prayer strategies for both Buenos Aires and Resistencia. As we talked, the power of unseen realities gripped me with such force that I felt as though we had stepped into the pages of a Frank Peretti novel.

TRAINING AN ARMY

On Thursday Cindy Jacobs taught an all-day seminar at the Christian retreat center at Máximo Paz, an hour outside Buenos Aires. Advertised nationally in the interdenominational periodical *El Puente*, the seminar drew 450 pastors, lay leaders and intercessors who packed the facilities, sitting and standing in shifts. They eagerly soaked up Cindy's teaching.

Bill Kennedy videotaped each session as Cindy described the

ongoing war in the heavenlies, where the advancing kingdom of God confronted the forces of darkness controlling aspects of human society and culture. She explained to those gathered how to recognize and combat ruling spirits. She discussed the biblical basis of intercession for nations, the nature of corporate sin, the process of generational iniquity and the power of corporate and identificational repentance. Her listeners paid keen attention as she described the operation of witchcraft, the occult, familiar spirits, curses and blood sacrifice.

Cindy also explained that within every nation, city and people group God has placed a redemptive gift, a trait representing a facet of the Lord's character that He wants that group to display in order to bless others. "Have faith that your city and nation can be changed!" Cindy challenged the intercessors. "The only thing that limits God is unbelief. Nothing is impossible for God!"

Eduardo Lorenzo led everyone in response. We knelt and joined him in a prayer of repentance for unbelief, generational iniquity and personal and corporate sins. This was a holy moment, pregnant with destiny.

Then Cindy facilitated two reconciliations involving national traumas. These events had provided entrance for evil spirits to wreak havoc in Argentina. "Without repentance and forgiveness from each side," she explained, "Argentina will continue to be held in the grip of Satan over these wrongs."

The first involved the country's "dirty war" of 1976-1983. Ex-military men, a woman who had worked with the terrorists, and others who had lost relatives or close friends among the disappearances and murders of that period stood up. In an atmosphere charged with deep emotion, each group confessed and repented for their sins, released their hurt and extended forgiveness to the others.

Next, Cindy turned to the issue of the Falkland Islands/Malvinas war with Britain in 1982. An Argentine who had participated in the war, another who lost a family member, a woman with British heritage, and Cindy herself as a representative American all knelt and rendered prayers of repentance and forgiveness, as each in turn identified with their people and their role. Again tears flowed freely as the balm of Christ's healing flooded deep wounds.

BATTLING THE HOSTS OF
DARKNESS IN BUENOS AIRES

Early the next morning, after another strategy meeting, we and the Harvest Evangelism leaders joined forces with an army of 80 dedicated intercessors outside the Cabildo at the Plaza de Mayo in central Buenos Aires. Our mission: To do battle against spiritual hosts of wickedness in the heavenly places. Only those who had attended Cindy's seminar and felt a specific call of the Lord were invited to join this prayer assault team. All others were urged to pray at home or with their churches to provide intercessory covering.

In their discussions, Cindy and the Argentines had discerned three ruling spirits believed to hold sway over the entire nation: death and murder, greed (Mammon) and a religious spirit, including the stronghold of witchcraft and manifestations of the Queen of Heaven. Freemasonry was also recognized as a conduit for demonic influence throughout the nation. After prayers of praise and protection in the center of the plaza, we spent the next four hours moving from one building to another around the plaza's perimeter. At each one we identified spiritual powers, repented of wrongs committed, and interceded with intensity and authority until we sensed a change in the heavenly realm. Cindy and others received prophetic words and visions guiding and confirming the intercession. Moreover, several curious events took place that morning, which some interpreted as signs from God that something was indeed happening as a result of our prayers.

ON TO RESISTENCIA

Late Friday afternoon, the team flew to Resistencia, Chaco, to begin ministry there. David Thompson, head of Harvest Evangelism's outreach in Resistencia, and his wife, Sue, met us at the airport. Three churches held simultaneous praise, teaching and prayer meetings that evening, and we stopped by each one where Cindy spoke briefly.

Dinner came about 11 P.M. at Charly's, a favorite pasta restaurant near the center of town. As we ate, David shared with us additional historical background on Resistencia and the Chaco area. "Resistencia was founded as a base for military campaigns seeking to claim the Chaco and its resources, and specifically as protection for the city of

Corrientes, across the river," he reminded us. The city's name signified the white settlers' resistance against the hostile attacks of the region's original inhabitants, the indigenous Indians. This hostility, however, erupted in response to the settlers' own mistreatment of the Indians. Not surprisingly, hatred grew between the two groups.

We had already made note of one of Resistencia's most distinctive features. Its nickname, "the city of statues," reflects the abundance of public sculptures and other artwork erected on nearly every block. This characteristic would prove significant.

Resistencia, we learned, was the only place in Argentina with monuments specifically dedicated to San La Muerte, the spirit of death. The cult of this principality pervaded the whole area. "San La Muerte is both worshiped and feared," David told us. "The deceptive attraction is that he will give his followers a 'good death'—quick and painless."

Before our trip we had studied a paper written by Víctor Lorenzo, Eduardo's son, reflecting his substantial research into the folklore and religious beliefs of the local people. Using John Dawson's book, *Taking Our Cities for God* (Creation House), Víctor over recent months had mapped the spiritual history and condition of Resistencia, uncovering the roots of its demonic bondage. But after gathering the information, he sensed the Lord telling him to wait before taking action. Now, with Cindy's arrival, he knew the time had come to deal with these strongholds.

Early the next morning we rejoined members of the Harvest Evangelism team, including Víctor Lorenzo, for a briefing at our hotel. He shared much more about local spiritist beliefs and the origins of societal sins. Then, before Cindy began her seminar scheduled for that day, we walked a couple of blocks to the city's central plaza, site of Sunday's planned intercessory warfare. "Let me show you what I discovered in the plaza's public artwork," Víctor urged.

DEMONIC ARTWORK

Near one corner of the plaza stood three 10-foot-tall panels displaying modern art on each side. In the large central panel, about 16 feet wide, a thick snake was wrapped around figures holding a guitar and a harp. The tail of the snake entered a red sun on which a violinist played.

Cindy confirmed Víctor's observation. "The snake often symbolizes the python spirit—a spirit of divination or witchcraft," she said.

The smaller panel on the left, six-feet wide, showed a second snake intertwining two figures playing an accordion and another guitar. "It looks as though the python spirit is claiming control of these musical arts," Víctor noted.

> Artwork in the central plaza
> of Resistencia offered our
> intercessors a virtual map for
> planning their spiritual assault.

The 10-foot-square panel on the right featured a hideous image looming over another figure lying at its feet as though dead. The phases of the moon were portrayed, along with a plant with dead roots and stem. "This is San La Muerte," Cindy discerned.

Other images suggested a curse of poverty on the land, economic distress and the influence of religious spirits, including the Queen of Heaven. "About 80 percent of the art in Resistencia has some spiritual symbolism," Víctor stated. With his research, the panels in the central plaza seemed to offer the intercessors a virtual map for planning their spiritual assault.

SECRETS OF INTERCESSION

At 10:00 that Saturday morning, the Marconi Theater in downtown Resistencia pulsated with about 700 people clamoring for Cindy's all-day teaching on intercession and spiritual warfare. She followed the same outline as at Máximo Paz, with special insights for the city of Resistencia.

"I believe the redemptive gift of Resistencia is the gift of the Levite—those who sang in the temple, the worshipers, artists, craftsmen and musicians," Cindy declared. "Satan has tried to pervert and twist this gift to prevent people from seeing the image and glory of God."

As the seminar drew to a close, Cindy led her listeners into a time of prayer over past sins, as she had done at Máximo Paz. Different groups stood up in identificational repentance for the sins of the "dirty war," the wrongs inflicted on the Indians by the white settlers and other long-festering wounds.

Still more strongholds needed to be broken. "How many people have had any involvement in witchcraft, or feel that they have been cursed through witchcraft?" Cindy asked. "Please stand."

To her surprise, perhaps three-quarters of the people in the theater rose to their feet. Cindy led them through a prayer of repentance and renunciation, then followed up by addressing those struggling with other occult involvement or besetting sins. In each case, as God stirred people's hearts to repent, they got on their knees to confess and receive forgiveness.

That evening the Thompsons hosted tea at their home for us and the local Harvest Evangelism team. The meeting provided an opportunity to plot strategy for the next day's intercessory warfare. Víctor reviewed the primary strongholds he had discerned from his research: divination and witchcraft (the python spirit), San La Muerte (the spirit of death) and two kinds of legendary spirit beings. *Pomberos*, he explained, were seen as "little demons" spreading fear and division or disunity, with roots in the African slave trade. *Curupí*, on the other hand, was said to torment people through sexual sin and family dysfunction. All these evils were woven through the fabric of Resistencia society, past and present.

Others mentioned the pervasive influence of Freemasonry and the Queen of Heaven principality. These seemed to rule as territorial spirits for all of Argentina and beyond.

At 9:30 that night, Cindy Jacobs, Doris Wagner and a few key leaders joined a scheduled meeting of about 35 local pastors, while the rest of us interceded for this meeting and Sunday's spiritual warfare. The pastors, one by one, bared their hearts in response to Cindy's message at the seminar. As they knelt in prayer together, the Lord moved upon them with an anointing to confess sins of division, disunity, bitterness and unforgiveness. Barriers came crashing down as they prayed for God to cleanse and unite them.

The meeting ran longer than scheduled, but no one paid any attention to the time. The Lord, preparing His army, was bringing reconciliation as never before.

CASTING DOWN STRONGHOLDS

After another short night's sleep, we rose early Sunday morning, June 17, to join the intercessory troops. Some 70 pastors and laypeople—unified in the Spirit, working with pastoral approval and prepared by Cindy's teaching—came at the prompting of the Lord. In the cold morning air they waited for us near the central plaza's art panels. Between 7:30 A.M. and the warfare's conclusion nearly five hours later, the weather would warm up considerably for the first time all week.

The Lord had confirmed the major strongholds to be overthrown: San La Muerte, *Curupí*, the *pomberos*, Freemasonry and the Queen of Heaven. Ruling over these five spirits was the spirit of divination or witchcraft, represented by the python.

After pointing out the symbolism on the art panels, Cindy asked Eduardo Lorenzo to take authority in prayer to separate the evil spirits and cut them off from communication and cooperation. Then we turned to each stronghold, one at a time, to repent of the sins involved and come against them in the name of Jesus Christ.

Confronting the spirit of death, the prayer warriors repented on behalf of the people for their worship of San La Muerte. They confessed corporate sins and strongholds, including suicide, murder and extermination of the Indians. A gifted intercessor, Chabela Montiel, saw a vision of the word "liberty." Shortly afterwards, a bell began to chime. A few people stole quizzical glances at their watches—the time was not on the hour, half hour or quarter hour. Then Chabela interpreted the sign: "It is the liberty bell, ringing freedom from bondage!"

Turning to the legendary *Curupí*, intercessors old and young, male and female, stepped forward for identificational repentance. They stood as representatives to confess their society's sexual sins of all kinds, and to offer forgiveness and reconciliation. Then, addressing the spirit of the *pombero* that was feeding the root of division in families and churches, Víctor Lorenzo led prayers against this demon that brings terror, torment, deceit and disunity.

RENOUNCING THE SIN OF FREEMASONRY

The prayer warriors walked to the center of the plaza, dominated by a statue of General José de San Martín on horseback. "San Martín,

Argentina's national hero, was a high-ranking Mason," Cindy noted. We knelt in a circle facing each other and lifted our voices in concert, renouncing the sin of Freemasonry and then, in Jesus' name, binding the power behind this false religion.

On our way to the corner of the plaza across from the Cathedral, we spotted another set of three tall art panels. They showed a male and female teacher and two schoolchildren. A retired teacher and others felt impressed to pray to remit the sins of the educational system.

In front of the Cathedral, fervent prayers arose asking forgiveness for sinful attitudes towards the Catholics. Intercessors petitioned the Lord to raise up born-again priests and bring down the wall of partition between churches. They then repented for their people's idolatry of the Queen of Heaven as manifested through the local Virgin of Itatí.

Just then, David Thompson opened his eyes to see two workers removing the Argentine flag from the front of the Cathedral. What could it mean? The intercessors had prayed that false gods would have no more influence over the government of Argentina. Perhaps God was giving us yet another sign.

We walked past another long mural, perhaps 10x20 feet, depicting the lush Chaco forests before the white settlers stripped them of their wealth. More repentance and reconciliation followed, as intercessors confessed the exploitation of both the forest resources and the rural people, and prayed for revival of the land.

At another corner of the plaza stood a replica of the famous statue in Rome with twin babies Romulus and Remus suckling at the wolf's teats. Its plaque commemorated the first Italian families to populate the Chaco. Someone affirmed that the Italians had great influence over the local banking system, bringing corruption into both the banks and the churches. We noted, too, that the wolf's face looked directly across the street toward the National Bank branch. In response, intercessors repented for corruption, greed, the curse of poverty and other evils. They begged forgiveness and healing, then broke these curses in the name of Christ.

DIVINATION AND WITCHCRAFT

Finally, we returned to the original set of panels to deal with the ruling spirit of divination and witchcraft. Cindy described how the rod of God, which Aaron cast on the ground to become a snake, ate up the rods of the Egyptian magicians. "I believe the Lord is calling the pastors among us to walk around these three panels seven times in silence. We are going to plant the Word of God here, then shout and declare that the temple of the python spirit has been destroyed."

> The intercessors proclaimed an attribute of the kingdom of God to rule in the place of each bound principality.

Anticipation arose as about a dozen pastors circled the panels and the other prayer warriors. Afterward, we all planted our Bibles on the ground and knelt to pray. The intercessors then declared that with the rod of God cast onto the ground that had been cursed, the roots of wickedness would wither and die and the enemy would no longer possess this land.

We rose and let out a victory roar, then joined hands and ringed round the panels with a song of joy.

A final task remained. For each bound principality, the intercessors prayed and proclaimed an attribute of the kingdom of God to rule in its place. For San La Muerte, "Christ is life!" For *Curupí*, "Holiness!" For the *pombero*, "Christ is unity!" For Freemasonry, "Christ is peace!" For the Queen of Heaven, "Jesus is Lord!" Mike Richardson closed by reading Matthew 28:18-20 as a reminder of Christ's commission and the ultimate purpose of all spiritual warfare: making disciples of all nations.

BRINGING IN THE SHEAVES

Cindy preached at three churches that Sunday night. At breakfast Monday morning, she shared with intercessor Chabela Montiel several points of strategy for continuing an intercessory network for Resistencia, building on the hundreds of neighborhood prayer cells ("lighthouses") already established. Later in Buenos Aires, Cindy shared the same advice with Eduardo Lorenzo for the rest of the country. And, after confirmation from the Lord, Cindy agreed to return to

Argentina in September to teach a much longer conference.

With the fire of intercessory warfare lit, Plan Resistencia went into high gear six weeks later. Led by Ed Silvoso, nearly 150 North Americans and a like number of Argentines from all over the country descended on Resistencia for a massive evangelistic outreach campaign. During this two-week blitz, the gospel was spread through radio, television and literature distribution. Outreach teams shared the message through street meetings, neighborhood rallies and united rallies, as well as music, drama, mime, clowns, puppetry, sports and other means for all ages. Special presentations targeted the police, fire fighters, politicians, Rotary Club, university and medical community. In one day, all 63,000 homes in the city were visited with a "good news" packet of literature.

Simultaneously, media coverage featured social assistance projects carried out by Harvest Evangelism and the evangelical community. At the regional hospital, Ed presented a large gift of medical supplies and equipment. With money raised to build water cisterns in neighborhoods with no running water supply, the first two cisterns were completed and then dedicated during this campaign.

During these two weeks, local pastors reported hundreds of new decisions for Christ in their churches. But the climactic evangelistic phase was yet to come.

In September Dave and I joined Cindy Jacobs and Doris Wagner for another Argentine adventure, this time to Mar del Plata, where Cindy led a three-day seminar for leaders on strategic-level prayer and spiritual warfare. As attenders took the teaching back to their churches, Harvest Evangelism hoped to raise an army of intercessors from around the country to pray daily for Plan Resistencia. At the end of the conference, participants wanted to put the training into practice. Gathering in a public park, we experienced a powerful time of corporate prayer warfare against the city's sins and spiritual strongholds.

THE HARVEST

In October I joined other North Americans and Argentines for a nine-evening, citywide, open-air evangelistic campaign, which followed ten simultaneous week-long outreaches to designated areas of Resistencia. Ed Silvoso's book, *That None Should Perish*, describes the victories—and the demonic counterattacks—that ensued as the entire city heard the voice of God. Thousands of people came to faith in Christ. New converts met nightly with their new Christian fellowships to receive discipleship training and instruction in baptism. Pastors organized a mass baptism and communion service to demonstrate the unity of the evangelical churches.

By the close of the three-year Plan Resistencia in April 1991, the evangelical population of the city had grown by 102 percent, more than doubling! Over the next two years, unofficial estimates pegged cumulative church growth at over 500 percent, with 130 new congregations being established.

Lessons learned in Plan Resistencia have not been lost. This prototype city-reaching strategy has since became a model for effective evangelism in communities all over the country and throughout the world.

nine

INTERCESSION AND MIRACLES IN THE CHURCH

BY GUILLERMO PREIN

Guillermo Prein is pastor of the New Life Church, a new apostolic church in Buenos Aires. He entered evangelistic ministry when he was 16 years of age, and he has planted several churches. Prein is the founder of New Life Church where, through spiritual warfare and power evangelism, the congregation has grown to more than 5,000. He also founded Radio Parque Vida, a Christian FM radio station covering Buenos Aires 24 hours a day. Signs and wonders are so prominent in Prein's church that he has added a Minister of Miracles, an M.D., to his pastoral staff.

Sarah Sena was a happy woman who lived in the downtown area of Buenos Aires. She was leading a peaceful life, until one day, at the age of 43, she began to feel sick and weak. The vitamins prescribed by her doctor, which at first seemed to help, were ineffective after just a few days. The problem became worse, and she became weaker and weaker. Soon she began to lose her memory. She could no longer call to mind telephone numbers, names of persons, locations and such. Later, she suffered from urinary incontinence, and she had to wear diapers as if she were a baby. The doctors ordered a battery of advanced tests to diagnose the disease which was so pathetically destroying this relatively young woman. The outcome was frightening. Sarah was suffering from Alzheimer's disease.

The cause of this disease is unknown to the medical profession. Alzheimer's is an incurable sickness marked by irreversible physical deterioration. The disease progressively damages the intellectual, motor and neurological functions, leading inexorably to the death of the person affected. The only help medical science could offer Sarah was to slow down the process of deterioration, which, in her case, was rather advanced.

THE DAY SARAH LAUGHED

Two long years elapsed when, one day, a young businessman knocked at the door of her house. In his free time, this man would go out to his neighborhood to sow seeds of the Word of God into the hearts of all those who would listen and receive it. Sarah showed an interest, and the businessman invited her to a meeting in a luxurious hotel very close to her home. That night was the worst since her sickness began. She was overcome with dizziness, vomiting and severe headaches, keeping her awake through the night without rest. Nevertheless, she was determined to attend the meeting, so she asked a friend to take her to what she called "that evangelical service in the Sheraton Hotel." Upon arriving at the hotel, Sarah felt worse than ever. Staggering, and with great physical effort, she managed to get herself seated in a chair.

The meeting was already coming to an end when she arrived. However, when someone invited those who wanted prayer to come up front, she accepted the invitation and joined a group of persons who surrounded the platform. There she received prayer, with the laying on of hands, for the first time in her life. She fell to the floor, touched by the Holy Spirit. As she lay there, only half conscious, Sarah felt something wonderful. She felt as if someone were pulling something out of her head, like uprooting a plant from damp soil. It did not demand much effort. At that moment, an inexplicable happiness filled her heart and tears of joy poured down her gaunt and wrinkled face. When she stood up, she discovered she no longer felt any symptoms of her disease. She returned home, bursting with exultation and leaping with joy along the streets. She actually ran for part of the 10 blocks which separated her home from the hotel. Later, medical tests revealed a glorious diagnosis. Sara had been completely healed of that terrible, incurable disease!

A MINISTRY OF MIRACLES

This beautiful story stands in stark contrast to the pain that multitudes are experiencing in these days. Satan is successfully destroying the lives of millions of men and women. His hideous objective: to steal, kill and destroy. The diabolic forces of humanism, rationalism and relativism are implanting such strongholds in the lives of persons, that they are blinded to the truth and cannot come to know the Lord Jesus as the Savior of their lives.

In such times as these, one of the ministries of the Church most violently attacked by the forces of evil is that of miracles. This is so because a ministry of miracles is a powerful weapon that defeats the enemy and sets people free to live an abundant life. The devil desperately wants to suffocate the Church so that it cannot fulfill the commandment of God to minister miracles to humanity and, through this ministry, to impact the world.

In chapter 4 of the Gospel of Matthew, we see Jesus going to Capernaum to start His ministry, which would be characterized by miracles and wonders. "News about him spread all over Syria, and people brought to him all who were ill with various diseases, those suffering severe pain, the demon-possessed, those having seizures, and the paralyzed, and he healed them" (Matt. 4:24, *NIV*). Later, in His hometown of Nazareth, it was quite a different story. There Jesus was not warmly received, and, because of the hardness of their hearts, the Lord could not work miracles (see Mark 6:5). According to Matthew 13:58 (*NIV*), "He did not do many miracles there because of their lack of faith."

Compare Jesus' ministry in these two places, and you will discover a very important distinction. Here are two cities, similar in many respects, but with well-defined differences. The people in Capernaum were open people with much faith, ready to accept what God had for them. In their midst, the power of God was greatly manifested. The people of Nazareth rejected the works of Jesus, because they still thought of Him as the carpenter's son. With this satanic stronghold of unbelief, they hardened their hearts and failed to see the glory of God. Their lack of faith closed the heavens and they did not receive many miracles. For the few they saw, the people of Nazareth undoubtedly found a perfectly rational explanation.

FROM CAPERNAUM OR FROM NAZARETH?

In many of our cities and towns today, Christians are living like those people in Nazareth. Like them, we have closed heavens, with churches testifying and trying to advance the kingdom of God but without outward signs of success. In such places, we might hear Christians complaining, "These people are stubborn-hearted!" This is a common reaction among Christians in places where miracles do not flow. Others say, "The church lacks faith!" In this way, the church (which is probably trying the best it can to extend the kingdom of God) becomes burdened with guilt. In many cases, such congregations are so oppressed by demonic forces that they seem to be crying out, "Set us free!" Churches like this do not need critics; they need to be delivered!

The problem is not stubborn-hearted people. The Word of God teaches us that demonic forces are in operation throughout the world, using all the weapons at their command to keep the people blind to the truth. The apostle Paul said, "If our gospel is veiled, it is veiled to those who are perishing. The god of this age has blinded the minds of unbelievers, so that they cannot see the light of the gospel of the glory of Christ, who is the image of God" (2 Cor. 4:3,4, *NIV*).

The problem is that we too often choose to fight this battle in our own way. Usually the first thing we want to do is to refute the arguments unbelievers are using to deny the gospel, then to convince them of the truth we are preaching. Lastly we may set out to attack evil strongholds blinding these individuals. However, this is not the biblical design. The apostle Paul spoke from extensive experience in evangelism and spiritual warfare when he said, "For though we live in the world, we do not wage war as the world does. The weapons we fight with are not the weapons of the world. On the contrary, they have divine power to demolish strongholds. We demolish arguments and every pretension that sets itself up against the knowledge of God, and we take captive every thought to make it obedient to Christ" (2 Cor. 10:3-5, *NIV*).

The Word of God is very clear. If we attack the spiritual hosts of wickedness, they weaken or withdraw, enabling us to move forward against them. The strongholds that have formed in people's minds can then be demolished. Arrogance, pride, religiosity, humanism and unbelief disappear. What remains is fertile soil for the work of the Holy Spirit, so that the people come to know our Lord Jesus Christ in all His power. In the light of this teaching, it is easy to understand the significant place that Jesus gave to miracles during His ministry.

THE METHOD OF JESUS

Jesus used miracles as the most dramatic and expressive means for communicating His love to the people. Those who heard Jesus' message, after experiencing God's love by means of a powerful miracle, could surrender their lives to the Lord in a more complete way.

> Miracles are tools God has given us for opening hearts that they may come to know Christ as Savior.

This was the evangelistic method used by Jesus. Read it. It is in your Bible. It is a simple and striking method. It is a prescription which causes great impact. In most cases, Jesus worked miracles first and then preached the gospel to people. Why do we insist on doing just the opposite of what the Word of God has shown us?

There are those who would argue that miracles are contingent upon the individual's belief in Jesus. They seem to think that if a person does not first accept fully the Word of God, that person does not deserve a miracle. This position suggests that a miracle is some sort of prize for following Christ. What a terrible mistake!

Miracles are tools that God has given us for opening the hearts of human beings so that they may come to know the Savior (see Mark 16:20). Miracles confirm the content of the gospel. If we understand miracles in this light and use their power to awaken interest in Christ's message, there will be no time for debates about the validity of miracles. Our Christian witness will become more effective and powerful. We will discover that the evangelistic method of Jesus really works!

Experiences in Uruguay and Spain

We are using Jesus' method in our missionary work in Uruguay. This is one of the so-called "resistant" countries. Uruguay is the only nation in Latin America that has never experienced a spiritual awakening or revival of any kind. Protestant churches there struggle and struggle, but they are small churches and make little impact on society. The leaders are faithful, and they work hard. They are men and women who love the Kingdom and do their best, but they have seen few results.

God took our team to a small town in this country. In Uruguay, satanic *umbanda* rites and other occult practices stand in stark contrast to the high cultural level of the population in general. This country has almost no illiteracy. A full 80 percent of the population has graduated from high school, and 50 percent of those continue their studies at a university. However, though Uruguay maintains a high level of culture and education among its people, it is among the countries in the Southern Cone of South America where primitive *umbanda* rites are most popular. This Afro-Brazilian religion boasts from a million to a million and a half believers in Uruguay alone. This is impressive, especially when you take into account the total population of the country, which is slightly over 3 million.

Guided by the Holy Spirit and being conscious of these facts, we entered this small city in Uruguay and engaged the enemy in spiritual warfare in the name of Jesus. At that time, the local church was almost suffocated by the forces of evil. However, God cleaned up the spiritual atmosphere, and a revival came to this area, driving sorcerers, witches and fortune tellers out of the city and producing an avalanche of conversions. Even the local mayor entrusted his life to Christ.

Some months ago, a sister from our church visited her relatives in Uruguay. She had not seen them for a long time. She arrived at a town called Paso de Los Toros and began to speak about the Lord. The response to her testimony was positive. She suggested that we organize prayer groups in that town, and we did. During the first month,

40 persons accepted the Lord. By the second month, we had three homes open for the proclamation of the gospel. Today, after three months, there are five meeting places. People surrender to Christ in the streets. They come to us and ask us not to leave the town. They want us to stay and teach them more about Jesus. We also held a meeting in a nursing home. In this first meeting, of a total of 42 residents, 41 received the Lord. Miracles started to flow, and the people came to know the Savior.

On another mission field—the city of Granada, Spain—God showed us the spiritual nature of the area. Together with the pastor of the local church, Daniel Palma, we launched a prayer assault on the invisible world. Some days later, pastor Palma went to one of the near-by towns, Yllora, where another pastor belonging to the largest and strongest evangelical church in Spain had been evangelizing and hold-ing meetings every night for three months. The results had been frus-trating as virtually nobody ever attended the meetings. Pastor Palma preached in Yllora one night after having conducted spiritual warfare. In that meeting—without great effort—35 souls came to the Lord.

THE POWER OF MIRACLES

The method used by Jesus works. It is necessary to begin by removing the enemy from the air and then moving forward, coming against the kingdom of darkness with miracles. The enemy will resist in some places more than others, but in the end, if we fight with faith, he will always flee. Satan cannot resist a Church that actively engages in spiritual war-fare and trusts in the power of God to work supernatural miracles.

Miracles break the oppression of darkness. They are like battering rams that open the gates of hell, tearing down the strongholds of evil. Once this happens, when hearts start opening to the power of God, the Word can come with clarity. Jesus' answer to the doubts of John the Baptist was clear and striking. John, who was in prison, was ques-tioning whether Jesus was the one who would come. And Jesus replied, "Go back and report to John what you hear and see: The blind receive sight, the lame walk, those who have leprosy are cured, the deaf hear, the dead are raised, and the good news is preached to the poor" (Matt. 11:4,5, *NIV*). Notice once again the order of the actions as Jesus relates them: first miracles, then the preaching of the Word.

My Experience in Buenos Aires

Given this biblical knowledge and practical experience, I set about the daunting task of developing a ministry of miracles in Buenos Aires. Although there had been a flow of miracles when we ministered in other cities or towns in Argentina and in other countries, Buenos Aires had proved a difficult challenge for us. Whereas in other cities we would see people get healed even before the beginning of the service, we struggled to obtain the same results in Buenos Aires, even in the rare cases when we were able. Some of the testimonies of the power of God proved questionable, and they tended to cause more confusion. I made great efforts to come against this from the pulpit. Our congregation entered into intense intercession and warfare worship. We rebuked the enemy with all of our strength. We ended up exhausted and with scant results. What a despairing situation!

We had so many questions. What was happening to us? What was the matter with this place? How is it possible that in such a blessed city, where so many ministries have achieved a significant impact, we faced such great resistance? Why was it easier in other cities? Was it that we lacked faith? Were we doing something wrong? We cried out to the Lord, "Help us Lord! Speak to us!" Finally, as we prayed and fasted, the Holy Spirit revealed to us the spiritual reality of how the enemy was operating in the city. With the eyes of the Spirit, we saw where the spiritual strongholds of wickedness were located and how the enemy was working in believers and non-believers alike to destroy them. Along with this vision, we received from God a strategy to deal with the situation. The Lord showed us how to penetrate the kingdom of darkness and how to minister miracles so that people would draw near to Jesus.

Erika's Battle

It was on a Saturday in the winter of 1993 that our church in Buenos Aires began to hold what we call "miracle services." I was sick that day with a temperature of over 102° F. That morning, our six-year-old daughter, Erika Paula, began to feel pain in her chest. Her pain increased throughout the morning, becoming so intense that every time she breathed, she would cry out. The doctors arrived and ordered an X-ray. Their diagnosis was terrible: A large spot had covered one entire lung and was spreading to the other.

Eventually, I had to leave for church, though my fever had not diminished. As I said goodbye to my tearful daughter, the only words I could find to say were, "Resist, Honey. Resist in the Lord." When I arrived at the church, I showed the X-rays to one of our doctors, without telling him whose they were. This doctor later became a member of our pastoral staff and is now our Minister of Miracles. When he saw the X-rays, he said, "It is not possible to make a proper diagnosis by these pictures alone. But there is a strong possibility that this might be lung cancer." And he asked me, "Whose X-rays are they?" When I told him that they belonged to my daughter, Erika, he was beside himself. I tried to comfort him, because I realized this attack was part of the battle we were currently facing. I was convinced that the best answer to this situation would be tangible evidence of the power of Jesus. This is how we faced the challenge of our first miracle service!

We were not Nazareth-type doubters at the time. We have always believed in miracles, and our ministry included casting out demons, physical healing and miracles. However, this particular night presented a unique situation. This was now a very personal battle requiring us to engage the enemy in the invisible world. When I arrived at the church that night, I could barely stand on my feet. Very dizzy and still with a high fever, I ascended to the platform. However, by the middle of the service (I cannot remember the exact moment) my sickness and my fever had completely disappeared! It was then I knew that we had broken through and that it was time for God to work miracles in our midst. By persevering in faith and prayer, we had finally defeated the enemy. I began praying for the sick with great faith, and as the result of our very first miracle service, more than 120 persons subsequently gave testimony of how God had miraculously healed them!

But there was more. When I returned home, rejoicing in all that had happened at the service, I found my daughter was completely recovered. The following day, we repeated the medical tests and X-rays. To the doctors' surprise, my little girl's lungs were completely clean. Erika was healed!

CHILDREN MINISTERING MIRACLES!

Week after week, the miracles God worked in our church increased. God gave us strategies for interceding before and during the services. This is how, as a component of our church's intercessory ministry (which had already been well organized), we have integrated specific intercession for miracles. A team, made up of believers who themselves have received authentically verified miracles from God, carries out this very specialized form of intercession. They pray before the service, during the miracle ministry and after the miracles have happened.

> Every member of our congregation is equipped to go into the world to minister with power and authority, no matter what their age.

One day the children started to intercede, and suddenly God was working powerful miracles through them. God began speaking to us about getting the children of our congregation more regularly involved in intercession and spiritual warfare. So we organized what we call the "Children's Army." I have not yet heard of anything like it elsewhere in the world. One of its members, my daughter, Erika, knows suffering firsthand. She fought against the enemy until she was set free from her lung problem, and now she can free others through intercessory prayer.

In this way, little by little, our church has become a church known for miracles. Every member in the congregation is equipped to minister miracles, no matter what their age. Young people, children, adults and senior citizens have experienced the glory of God's power in their lives, and because of that, they can go out into the world to minister with power and authority.

CAREFUL VERIFICATION

Although we experience miracles on a regular basis, society in general does not believe such things can really be happening in a church.

The world looks at miracles with suspicion, at best considering them subjective impressions without serious proof. We have prayed about this matter, and we have received an answer.

Our church's miracle ministry office now compiles a file documenting each miracle testimony. Each file includes medical tests, conducted before and after the miracle, so that each disease and its healing is properly verified. In this way, the testimonies given in our church have come to enjoy some credibility in our city. Certain well-known television reporters have unsuccessfully attempted to discredit the reputation of God's work among us. Along with other non-Christian professionals, the reporters have had to admit publicly that God is indeed working these miracles. There was simply no other way to explain what they themselves had documented.

Our reputation has even spread to the hospitals in the city. We are currently working in every medical centers located in the southern area of Buenos Aires, serving those who are in need of a touch from God's powerful hand. Some of these hospitals allow us to hold miracle services right on their premises! It is amazing to see God's power at work.

FROM MIRACLE SERVICES
TO MIRACLE CAMPAIGNS

The attendance in our church services increased, requiring us to go to first two, then three services per day just to make room for those wanting to attend. Very soon, the Lord moved us to organize miracle campaigns in a local basketball stadium. And still we continued to grow. At this writing we are holding 23 weekly services in our church, apart from the miracle campaigns conducted in the stadium. Six weekly services are specifically focused on miracles. In addition, we send numerous groups out into the streets, the plazas, the hospitals and the prisons, where they minister God's power to the needy.

We try to use every available opportunity to share God's power and love. God has recently given us a new strategy which has proved very effective: prayer cells. These small cells are spread all over the city in homes, offices, factories, stores, hospitals, schools and universities. Our prayer cells are real altars raised up for God throughout the city. Their primary purpose is to evangelize, but we try to do it following Jesus' method. We invite the host's friends, relatives and neighbors to attend, and we pray for their needs. This method always works, and miracles start to occur.

In September 1996, we started out with 150 cells and some 500 persons involved in this project. After one year, we now have 340 groups, some of them outside Argentina, with approximately 2,200 attending weekly. Many of these persons do not yet attend our church, but they have already met the Lord of miracles, and they have experienced His miraculous touch on their lives.

THOUSANDS OF MIRACLES

What kinds of things have we seen in our miracle ministry? We have witnessed miraculous healings of paralysis, blindness, deafness, cancer, deformities, AIDS, hernias, tuberculosis, asthma, diabetes, bulimia, anorexia, mental disorders, cirrhosis, different blood diseases, ulcers, rheumatism, arthritis, myasthenia, heart and lung diseases, bone disease, eye problems, trauma in the optical nerve, homosexuality and a variety of addictions to such bindings as drugs, gambling, alcohol and smoking. We have also seen many cases of demonic deliverance, as well as creative miracles such as the replacement of missing bones.

Apart from physical healings, we have seen financial miracles in the midst of the severe economic crisis in Argentina. Many have prospered, receiving by miraculous provision houses, cars, businesses, factories, workshops, jobs, money to pay debts, etc. In the midst of a society bound by financial problems, the church is showing the way to deliverance by means of the provision and prosperity that only Jesus can give. We have ministered to many poor people and beggars who are now well off. Others had great debts and were on the brink of bankruptcy, but today they are solvent.

The miracles the Lord is working among us are so diverse. Some of them are surprising. Three persons were raised from the dead. Regretfully, we could not prove these miracles, because the doctors who had signed their death certificates tore them up when they saw these persons come back to life. Nevertheless, we have celebrated these miracles with great joy and thanksgiving to the Lord.

Today, we have documented thousands of wonderful miracles. Thousands of new testimonies of miracles are given each year. In the first half of 1996, the amount of documented testimonies actually exceeded the total number of miracles we experienced during all of 1995. Our God is great, and when the Church trusts Him and is determined to believe in the teachings of the Word of God, all promises are fulfilled.

TAKING THE CITY

Now we are in the process of taking and conquering our city for Christ. During the planning and execution of our continuing assault, we have learned the importance of two types of intercessory prayer, namely *defensive* prayer and *offensive* prayer. Defensive prayer means we keep our spiritual radar detectors permanently open, forewarning us of possible attacks from Satan and his hosts of darkness. In our church, we teach what we call "pastoral prayer" to all of our church members. The objective is to protect the whole congregation, from the pastor to the least member of the church. Pastoral prayer covers us all.

One of the goals of our church is to make sure that everyone is shepherded, so we feel it is essential to organize intercessory prayers for all the sheep. Our base is a strong pastoral structure, where nobody has more than ten persons under his or her care. In my capacity as senior pastor, I pray for the nine main elders and their families. These in turn pray for the other 40 elders of the church. Those 40 pray for our 450 prayer cell leaders, who in turn pray for the approximately 4,500 members of our congregation. This process of intercessory prayer simultaneously flows in the opposite direction. All the members of the church pray for their respective group leaders and their families. The group leaders pray for the 40 elders, who pray for the nine main elders, who pray for me and my family. This is done every day, three times each day! In this way, we cover and protect each other. Thus, even the newest convert in our church immediately practices defensive intercession.

HIGH-LEVEL INTERCESSION

Offensive intercession invades the enemy's territory. This type of intercession is more complex and cannot be explained in a few words. This type of prayer reveals the enemy's strongholds and maps their position in cities and towns. In our church, this strategic ministry is done by generals, intercessors, spiritual mappers, prayer warriors and evangelists. They expose the devil's work in a certain area and then they attack, first in the invisible world with prayer, then in the visible world through their personal witness. The results are wonderful, and we have documented numerous victories obtained through offensive intercession.

The spiritual stronghold over Buenos Aires is still in place, albeit weakened. This demonic force keeps on moving and causing spiritual damage among the people. But the Lord has shown us the position of the enemy in the battlefield and we also know the names of our chief spiritual adversaries. There is still a great work to be done, and we are growing into it step by step. God is teaching us more every day, forming our character through times of hard and intense discipline.

Day after day, the Lord reveals to us new strategies for attacking and defeating the forces of Satan. Intercession and miracles are two areas in which we are making significant progress, helping us to establish His kingdom on earth. As the multitudes come to Jesus' feet, our city will one day be conquered for Christ, and He will fill it with His glory. Filled with this hope, we continue growing and engaging the enemy in warfare. Remember, a war is not won with one battle, but through a succession of battles which undermine the plans of the enemy and assure us of victory. As one general and president in my country said, we move "without haste, but without pause." The Church must move with determination, believing in the teachings and methods of our Lord and doing the work He has entrusted to us, confident that we will gain the victory.

ten

GOD'S KINGDOM IN OLMOS PRISON

BY JUAN ZUCCARELLI

Juan Zuccarelli *is pastor of an Assemblies of God church in
La Plata, Argentina. He is a prison warden and the sergeant in charge
of Protestant religious groups in Unit No. 1, also known as Olmos
Prison, Argentina's largest maximum security prison. The results
of his ministry in Olmos have few, if any, parallels among
recorded prison ministries.*

I walked along a wet and stinking tunnel. A prison officer, an unbeliever, accompanied me. For the first time, I was entering the Penal Sector to meet the inmates of Olmos Prison face-to-face. I had walked only a few yards, when a powerful force of some kind came upon me, running along my body and choking me. The presence of the enemy was so strong that I couldn't go on. I told the warden who was accompanying me that I was feeling sick and needed to go to the restroom.

So we returned to the entrance, and I locked myself in a restroom to pray and cry out before the Lord. I pleaded with God, asking that I be free from any spiritual oppression in order to serve Him on this mission. Though I did not know at the time what was happening in the invisible world, that prayer proved important to the future of a church—the Christ the Only Hope Church inside Olmos Prison.

CALLED TO THE PRISON

One year earlier, in 1983, I received God's call to preach in the prisons of Argentina. To be honest, I did not want to preach to prisoners. My desire was to hold evangelistic campaigns; to win souls for the Lord, but not inside prisons. However, God's call grew stronger and stronger. So the day came when I set out to share the gospel at Olmos Prison, near Buenos Aires. But there had been a recent riot among the prisoners, and some had been killed. Therefore, I was not allowed to preach nor even enter the prison. I went home that day quite relieved. I said to my wife, "I obeyed. I tried to enter, but they did not let me in. Now it is no longer my problem, but God's!" But God insisted, speaking to me much louder than before. He then opened a new door for me.

God showed me the potential for getting into Olmos Prison as an employee of the Penitentiary Service. Still, I was not particularly concerned because I knew the application process for becoming a prison warden was extremely complicated. I knew it would take a minimum of several months, and perhaps by then, God would forget about my calling. So I filled out the papers with the help of a brother from my church who was working in the Penitentiary Service. A week later this brother called me and said, "Juan, God worked a miracle!" I thought that the Lord had healed someone in the church. But he replied, "No, this miracle has to do with you. What should have taken eight months took only seven days. You are accepted as a warden!" I replied, "Listen, God has so many miracles to do, why did He choose to do *this* one?"

There were two penitentiary positions open at the time. One was at Unit No. 9, the School of Cadets, located only six blocks from my house in the city of La Plata. The other was at Unit No. 1, Olmos Prison, located a few kilometers outside the city. There was not much time to think, so I told my friend I would be praying and asking the Lord to show me where I was to serve Him. It wasn't long before my friend came to my house telling me that the Lord had showed him that I should apply for the job at Olmos. I said, "Amen!" But I must admit that in my heart I was not too sure.

OLMOS PRISON

At that time, there was no school for new recruits of the penitentiary service, so training was provided at the prison itself. There were two instructors. One of them taught the applicants how to parade and how to handle the weapons; the other one taught us the rules and regulations of the institution. I had several questions regarding the rules, having served in the Argentine Navy for more than six years.

On my first day in Olmos, I raised my hand to ask a question of the officer in charge, Nestor Papa. I asked him if there would be a problem if I talked about religion in the Unit.

"What is your religion?" he asked.

I answered, "I am a Protestant."

"So, you are an Protestant!" he said. "I hate Protestants. You will have a lot of problems with me!"

"Well, God thinks differently," I said.

He looked hard at me and said, "For you, I *am* god."

He added emphatically that if I went on like this, I was in for lots of trouble. Nestor Papa really had a thing against Protestants. (Today he is one of the deacons of our prison church, and he serves as my private secretary.)

This was my first day in the prison.

Olmos is a high-security prison. Built in 1939 to lodge chronic inmates, the initial capacity of the facilities was 1,200 inmates. Later, it was enlarged to hold 1,728. The building consists of six floors. Each floor has 12 cell blocks designed to lodge 24 inmates each. At this writing the prison holds around 3,200 inmates—86 percent above capacity.

When I began working as a warden, Olmos housed only four or five inmates who claimed to be evangelicals. Though many outside pastors had made great efforts to evangelize them, there was little fruit. At that time, brother Jose Luis Tessi, an evangelist from our congregation, started to visit the prison. He is now pastoring a powerful church in the city of Tandil. Pastor Tessi began serving God in the prison, but with a fresh and powerful vision.

Because I was an officer at the Unit, prison authorities had forbidden me to preach to the inmates. One of the wardens even threatened to fire me if I were caught preaching to the prisoners. However, Pastor Tessi and I together made a good team. I made all the arrangements for him to come into the Unit, and he preached with the authority of the Lord. Of course, even in those days, I would find moments when I could pray for the inmates, even if I couldn't preach.

One day, one of the inmates fell sick, and I was called in to pray for him. We happened to be in an office attached to the prison school, and there was an office on either side. We closed the door and began to pray. Suddenly, the inmate fell to the floor, and we kept on praying for him. The person who was watching at the door, came in frightened, saying the warden on duty—the very one who wanted to fire me—was coming our way. I said to the others, "Let's pray that the angels of the Lord will protect us." The warden opened the door of one office, he opened the door of the other, but he could not open the door to the office where we were praying—now more fervently than ever before. The warden struggled and struggled, but although the door had no lock, he could not open it. We were certain that the angels of the Lord had protected us.

THE RADIO

Inside the prison was a small, inoperable radio station in need of repair. Tessi and I thought the radio could be useful for the Lord, so we proposed to pay for fixing the station if we would be given some time to preach over the air. The authorities agreed, and the station was repaired. At that time, the inmates had no TV sets. In each cell, there was a loudspeaker directly connected to the radio broadcasting system. It was impossible for the inmates to turn off the loudspeakers. That is to say, the inmates of the whole prison were forced to listen to anything that was broadcast.

When Tessi preached the gospel on the prison radio station, he would feel intense pain throughout his whole body, as if somebody were beating him with sticks. Many times when he got home, he would go straight to bed in order to recover. This was all-out spiritual warfare. Tessi's preaching was simple, but powerful. The messages were on God's love and mercy and our need for repentance and salvation. The demons that had been ruling the prison found themselves in a power encounter. Our home began fasting and praying for the work in Olmos.

THE EVANGELISTIC CAMPAIGN

By now we had a strong feeling from God that we were to win this prison for Christ. We knew this to be impossible through human efforts. Our only chance was to trust our lives completely to God and allow Him to work in us and through us. We were praying about holding an evangelistic campaign inside the prison, but this, too, seemed impossible. Nothing like this had ever been attempted in a prison in Argentina. The director of the prison feared that if the inmates from different floors (thieves, murderers, rapists, etc.) were allowed to congregate in one place, there could be fights and even deaths. I said we would be praying and asking God to prevent any such incidents. He said we could pray as much as we liked, but that he would never authorize such a meeting.

And so we did pray, and God moved sovereignly. After several days, the prison director called me into his office. "Now what was it you wanted to do?" he asked.

I explained the project once again. I told him we would bring musical instruments. We would sing, we would preach and at the end we would pray for all the inmates.

"OK," he said, "I agree. But if there is any trouble, I will have you beheaded!"

With great enthusiasm, I shouted, "All right!" However, inwardly I was praying, "Please Lord, help us so that everything turns out well. I don't want to lose my head!"

"ACTO Y CULTO!"

We planned to hold the meetings in the assembly hall of the school in the prison. The assembly hall was the place where different music groups and theater groups came to perform for the prisoners. These performances were given the generic name of "acto." A warden would go from floor to floor, announcing "Acto! Acto!" When they heard this, every inmate knew that they would be treated to a special show. On the other hand, when there were Christian meetings, the wardens would call out, "Culto! Culto!" meaning church service. In these cases, no more than 10 evangelical brothers would come downstairs.

But when we held our evangelistic campaign, the warden, most certainly guided by the Lord, went upstairs calling out, "Acto y Culto! Acto y Culto!" And he was right. It would be an "Acto" because there was going to be good music, and it would be a "Culto" because the Word of God would be preached.

Meanwhile, I gave instructions to the prison guards, saying that the director of the prison had given clear instructions that, once the inmates entered the assembly hall, they could not return to their cell blocks until the meeting was over. This meant that all the doors would remain locked until the end of the event. I knew that many inmates would come thinking that there would be a rock concert, and that when they saw us with our Bibles in our hands, they would attempt to return to their cell blocks quicker than they had come.

> We were a bit frightened
> when some of the prison
> guards, touched by the
> Lord, also fell to the floor.

A group of around 300 inmates showed up for the evangelistic meeting in the assembly hall. Indeed, when the inmates realized that we were evangelicals, many tried to leave. But the doors had been locked, so they had to stay. We literally had a "captive" audience. I knew that this might not be the best method to evangelize prison inmates, but I believe the Lord has already forgiven me for my brazenness, because it was the beginning of something wonderful for His kingdom.

We started by singing songs, aided by a group of men from our home church, and the Holy Spirit began to move in that place. The message given by Luis Tessi had a tremendous impact, and when he gave the invitation, about 100 of the 300 men present made decisions for Christ. After they prayed, asking forgiveness for their sins, they came to the front to have us pray for their personal needs. The Holy Spirit began to touch them, and one by one they fell to the floor under the power of God. The Lord delivered those who were demonized.

We did not have much experience with this kind of thing, so we found ourselves ministering in the midst of considerable confusion. Some of the prison guards watching over the inmates were also touched by the Lord. We were a bit frightened, especially when the guards fell to the floor and we went to minister deliverance to them. It was a wonderful experience. It showed us what God could do within a prison, when He is given the opportunity to move with freedom.

THE VISION EXPANDS

After this extraordinary experience, our vision expanded. Our faith grew accordingly, and we knew there were many things we could improve. Once or twice each week, visiting pastors came to preach, and this was very good. However, we soon realized what was needed in the prison was a true Christian church. The leaders of this church had to emerge from among the prison inmates themselves. So we began focusing our efforts on training the leaders of the future Christ the Only Hope Church of Olmos Prison.

A short time before all this happened, the city of La Plata awoke one morning to newspaper headlines screaming, "Evangelical Pastor Is a Thief!" One of the evangelical leaders of the city had robbed a store at gunpoint! He had been arrested and was later convicted of the crime. When I learned of the crime, I was furious. I admit that I felt like laying hands on that brother—but with a clenched fist!

But God dealt with me and my hateful attitude. When I finally did meet this man in Olmos Prison, I could lovingly talk to him about the Lord and invite him to repent of his sins. He sincerely did so, reconciling himself to the Lord and reconsecrating his life to Him. Both Luis Tessi and I wanted not only to minister to him, but to his family as well. The Lord, in His mercy, began to work. We saw significant changes in this man and the fruit of the Holy Spirit became evident in his life. He helped us with the radio programs and rapidly matured in Christ. When the time came to appoint the leaders of our new church, the Lord guided us to designate this "redeemed thief," Antonio Arcadio Garcia, as the first inmate pastor, fully recognized as such by all in the penitentiary.

Garcia discipled a small group of potential leaders in the church. One of the members of this group was "Chiquito" (Spanish for "Shorty") Delgado, a broad, giant of a man who stood 6'4" and had been in prison for more than 20 years. This man had experienced a marvelous change in his life, and he quickly grew in the Lord. When

Antonio Garcia was released from prison, Chiquito Delgado became the pastor. Other leaders followed, among them Hector Marquez, Jorge Kuris and Jose Cardozo.

EVANGELICAL CELL BLOCKS

Confession is a sign of weakness among prisoners, and the weak are always attacked by other inmates. Thus new Christians repenting and confessing their sins exposed themselves to real danger. To everyone's surprise, our petition requesting an evangelical cell block for Christians was granted! An area of the facility was opened to lodge 24 inmates under the leadership and responsibility of Hector Marquez. We considered this a real miracle, because in the Penitentiary Service of the province of Buenos Aires, inmates are grouped in the cell blocks according to the crimes they have committed. Thieves live with thieves, murderers are housed together, rapists occupy another sector, and so on. Thus, to get an exclusive cell block assigned for evangelical inmates was something unheard of.

Having an exclusive cell block was a great advantage. The brothers there could pray in peace, read and study their Bibles, fast and have all-night prayer meetings without being harassed or disturbed. This worked so well, we began to implement it in other parts of the jail. Jorge Kuris was the next to start an evangelical cell block on his floor, and before long we had a block on each floor.

THE STRONGMAN ON THE FOURTH FLOOR

We all knew the spiritual "strongman" was located on the fourth floor. The entire prison was informally ruled from there. So we felt we needed to do whatever was necessary to take the fourth floor for the Lord. We took authority in the name of Jesus, and the strongman was bound. The believers then began to pray to take the whole prison, cell block by cell block. An intense strategy of prayer and fasting was organized, and the kingdom of God began to grow inside Olmos Prison.

By 1988, the prison authorities decided to consolidate the evangelical cell blocks which, up to then, had been functioning on every floor. Their idea was to concentrate all the evangelical cell blocks on one floor. So this was done, and the believers occupied six of the twelve cell blocks located on the infamous fourth floor. By this time, Christ the Only Hope Church had 240 members.

We began to pay more attention to the internal organization of the church. Rules of faith, strict requirements for church membership and a permanent fasting and prayer program were implemented. We intensified our spiritual assaults against the demonic enemy in order to maintain our growth. In 1990 there were about 400 brothers in the church. By 1995 the members of the Christian community numbered more than 1,000. Not included in these figures are some 400 or 500 inmates who have made a decision for Christ, but who are not yet mature enough in their faith to fulfill the strict membership requirements of Christ the Only Hope Church. By the end of 1995, about 45 percent of the prison population had put their faith in Christ and were members of the church.

Once a year, large baptismals are held at Olmos, with 300 to 350 brothers giving public testimony of their faith in Christ each time. As of this writing in 1997, there are about 1,480 brothers in Christ the Only Hope Church. Keep in mind this has happened inside the highest security prison in the nation.

THE CHURCH IN THE PRISON

Christ the Only Hope Church is very different from other evangelical churches, not only because it is inside a prison, but because almost every day we lose a church member. Approximately 300 Christians leave the prison each year. Some are released, having served their sentences. Some are moved to other penal units, and others are paroled. This means that if we did not evangelize every day, the church would disappear in five years. So in order to simply maintain our present size, we must win about 10 percent of the prison population to Christ every year!

The Christian workers in our church are also quite different. Within the church, we recognize pastors, elders, evangelists, deacons and helpers. The training of these servants of the Lord is unique as they all live in the church, so to speak, 24 hours a day. For example, when anyone gets up in the morning, takes a shower, has breakfast, reads the Bible, prays, fasts or worships, he is surrounded by his brothers in Christ. There is no such thing as privacy, which means they are also surrounded by brothers in Christ when they do *not* read the Bible, or do *not* pray or fast, or do *not* take a shower, or when they are angry or in a bad mood. Because they are on display before the church every minute of their lives, it is not easy to be a leader. Nevertheless, we cannot stop training leaders, because so many of our leaders, including some of the best, are constantly being released.

Many converts testify, "I had to come to a prison to be set free!"

God has had to teach us daily what to do and how to do it. We had no textbook on how to win a whole prison for Christ. We were forced to write it ourselves as we went along. All we could see in the natural were battles, troubles and hardships, but our trust in the Lord was like that of a child.

My vision was to establish Christ the Only Hope Church in Olmos Prison, and this has been done. New leadership has been raised up in the congregation—Antonio Franco, Daniel Vazquez and Ramon Avalos—and they have worked very hard. A Bible institute was opened to train Christian workers, with a ministerial training program that lasts four years. A plan was implemented to evangelize the whole penitentiary for Christ, and large evangelistic campaigns have been carried out, with significant fruit. We had to begin holding our services in the sanctuary of the Roman Catholic Church in the prison, since all the meeting places we had been assigned were too small. God has given us the prison.

However, a serious problem still remained. The majority of our inmates' relatives were not Christians. We began to pray, seeking the Lord's guidance to find ways of evangelizing these lost souls seemingly beyond our reach. We asked permission for the church members to be allowed to meet their relatives in private, separated from the unbelievers. Permission was granted and Yard No. 1 was designated as the meeting place. Now before visiting hours are over, the leaders of the church hold a brief service in which they sing praise songs, read the Bible, preach and give an altar call. Many have been converted in these meetings, and later they testify, "I had to come to a prison in order to be set free!" Some have been healed, and others have been delivered from evil spirits that had tormented them. In all cases, we recommend that they look for an evangelical church close to their homes. In this way, the work of the Lord grows both inside and outside of the prison.

A DAY IN OLMOS

A day on the evangelical floor in Olmos Prison is very special. The inmates get up at six in the morning and commit the day to the Lord. Then, the wardens call the roll, counting them one by one. This is how we can give precise figures regarding the number of church members at any given time. After roll call, they have breakfast, take care of personal needs and study the Bible. At noon, they have lunch, then they have a free period and again they dedicate time to Bible study. After dinner every day, a church service is held in the cell blocks.

Most importantly, prayer vigils are held every single night in all the evangelical cell blocks. Six men from each cell block go to the dining room, which is located in the front part of the cell block. The prayer meeting is held in the dining room from midnight until six in the morning. During this time, two of the six members of the group share for two hours what they have learned from the Bible during the day. Two others kneel and intercede for a list of needs they receive beforehand. The remaining two go from bed to bed, praying for the inmates who are sleeping, for their families, their situation in the jail, and so forth. After two hours, they shift roles. Those who were sharing from the Bible kneel down, the ones who were kneeling go to pray for the ones asleep, and those who were praying in the dorm come to share the Word. Two hours later, another shift change takes place. In this way, during every night of the year, 132 brothers in Olmos Prison are on prayer duty.

INTERCESSORY CELL BLOCKS

Two prison cell blocks are designated as "entry-level cell blocks." New believers, those who are learning to take their first steps with the Lord, are housed and indoctrinated there. As they grow spiritually, they will be assigned to other cell blocks.

Until a few months ago, we also had five intercessory cell blocks in full operation. However, we sensed that God was telling us to select some brothers from these cell blocks and place them in a new intercessory cell block. We did so with excellent results. Our ordinary cell blocks fast twice a week, from 6:00 A.M. to 6:00 P.M. But the intercessory cell block fasts every day from 6:00 A.M. to 6:00 P.M., and someone there is praying 10 hours every day, apart from the all-night prayer meeting, which is mandatory. That is why, when we submit a prayer request to this cell block, we sleep in peace, because we know that God's answer will come soon.

Obviously, we put a great deal of emphasis on prayer and intercession. These two activities, together with fasting, are the fundamental columns for our church. Through them, God has worked extraordinary miracles among us. We also place a strong emphasis on holiness. Today, every prisoner in Olmos has a TV set. However, we do not allow church members to use them, due to the high pornographic content of most programs and movies. During a prisoner's years of confinement, watching TV will only further damage his moral and spiritual life.

The believers are very obedient. For example, they know that the Bible teaches to tithe. However, according to present regulations in the prisons of the Province of Buenos Aires, inmates are not allowed to have money. So they tithe out of the gifts brought by their relatives. What they collect is used to share with the inmates who do not receive visits, those in the prison hospital, poor relatives or even inmates in other prisons. Some time ago, for example, there was a great flood in our province, and the brothers in Olmos decided to gather the tithes of two months and send them to the flooded areas. The "least of society" was helping these cities in trouble. This made a great impression on the authorities.

AND TO THE ENDS OF THE EARTH

Within our prison system, Unit No. 10 in the city of Melchor Romero is a neuropsychiatric unit, where all inmates have serious mental disorders. When the director of this unit heard what was being done in Olmos, he called us to say he wanted an evangelical church in his prison, too. We visited this place and found that the inmates there were highly medicated. It was very difficult to talk with them for any length of time. We told the director we would pray about what we could do, because we did not have anyone in our ministry who had the training or the experience to start a church under those conditions.

While we were praying, the Lord reminded us that brother Ramon Avalos, who at the time was pastoring the church in Olmos, had once been confined in this neuropsychiatric unit. Later, he had been transferred to the Olmos Prison due to a clerical error. Diagnosed as schizophrenic, Avalos had been given 19 doses of drugs each day at Olmos, and he still was disturbing his fellow inmates. Things got so bad that his cell mates *forced* him to come to one of our services. The Lord worked instantaneously and miraculously, healing both his body and mind. When we prayed for him, he fell to the floor under the power of the Holy Spirit. When he got up after quite some time, he looked around and said, "Where am I?"

"At Olmos Prison," we said.

"This can't be!" he said, totally confused. He then innocently asked, "Why am I in prison?"

This man had committed more than 30 crimes, and he did not remember a single one of them! God had completely changed him!

EVANGELIZING THE INSANE

So we thought of Ramon Avalos as the person who could start a new work in Unit No. 10. When I suggested this to him, he said, "Amen, Pastor! You know that I am committed to your ministry." His answer was a blessing, as I had already put him in charge of 1,400 inmates in Olmos. Now I was sending him to evangelize the insane!

I talked to the authorities about the possibility of transferring Avalos to Unit No. 10. At first they did not agree. How could they officially justify sending an inmate from Olmos as an evangelist to the mentally ill in Unit No. 10? Truly, this was crazy! But we began to pray and to fast. After a few days, God moved and the authorities decided to accept our unusual proposal. Ramon Avalos was transferred to Unit No. 10.

At the beginning, Avalos's tasks consisted mainly of bathing the prisoners and looking after them. Then he started to preach. He lived with the inmates, ate with them and slept with them. He took every opportunity to show them the love of Jesus. So from Olmos we have now sent out our first inter-prison missionary!

When I later went to inspect the work there, I was amazed. The brothers were singing, praying and praising the Lord! Today in Unit No. 10, there is a church with more than 40 inmates—at a prison for the insane! At this writing, brother Avalos has been released from prison, and he is with his family once again.

By God's grace, we have now reached out to other prisons in the province of Buenos Aires. Our vision for each prison is the same: to establish a growing evangelical church in every one. The work is growing, and with the Lord's help, we are ready to win every prison in Argentina for Christ!

eleven

UNITY AS A SIGN OF REVIVAL

BY CARLOS MRAIDA

Carlos Mraida pastors, with Pablo Deiros, the Central Baptist Church of Buenos Aires. He holds a master's degree from the International Baptist Theological Seminary in Buenos Aires and a doctorate from the Catholic University of Argentina. Central Baptist Church has become an international training center for revival with many church leaders from other nations attending their frequent training events. Mraida is author, along with Pablo Deiros, of Latinoamerica en Llamas *(Latin America in Flames).*

The last moments of Jesus Christ on earth were marked by a deep concern. This concern surfaced in a prayer which came from the depth of His heart:

> I pray also for those who will believe in me through their message, that all of them may be one, Father, just as you are in me and I am in you. May they also be in us so that the world may believe that you have sent me. I have given them the glory that you gave me, that they may be one as we are one: I in them and you in me. May they be brought to complete unity to let the world know that you sent me (John 17:20-23, *NIV*).

Jesus' prayer expressed His innermost desire that His disciples would be one, and His wish was in agreement with His Father's will.

For several years now, the Holy Spirit has been producing a beautiful move of unity among pastors of all denominations here in Argentina. In each city, the fellowship among the Lord's servants of different denominations and ecclesiastical traditions has been growing. Ghosts of the past have faded away, mutual trust has increased and the spirit of unity is pervasive. This growth in unity goes hand in hand with the remarkable growth of the gospel in Argentina. That is to say, unity has been a cause of revival and, at the same time, it is a product of revival.

THE CHURCH OF THE CITY

The Church of Jesus Christ is defined, from a biblical perspective, in two dimensions: universal and local. Its universal character implies the Church is the people of God, through whom He is manifested on earth. This Church includes all believers in Jesus Christ, throughout time and in every place. This universal Church makes itself visible in local communities through the local church, which is essentially the incarnation of the gospel within a particular culture, people and geographical setting.

We in the modern Church need to recover the biblical meaning of *location*, in direct relationship to the strengthening of unity. In the Word of God, the concept of the church of the city is very clear. In each city there are not many churches, but only one. We hear about the church in Jerusalem (Acts 8:1; 15:4), the church in Antioch (Acts 13:1), the church of God in Corinth (1 Cor. 1:2; 2 Cor. 1:1) and the church of the Thessalonians (1 Thess. 1:1; 2 Thess. 1:1). The reference is always to one church in each city. When the addressees are the believers, not of a city but of a region, then the reference is plural— the churches in Macedonia (2 Cor. 8:1), the churches in Galatia (Gal. 1:2), the churches in Judea (Gal. 1:22), the seven churches in Asia (Rev. 1:4). But the singular is always used in connection with the church in a given city.

This does not necessarily mean structural unity or the existence of a local "superchurch." Nor does it imply that denominations are to be abolished. The emphasis is rather on one church, made up of diverse congregations with their respective traditions, convictions, shades and characteristics, but working together to further the same mission, share resources and leadership, and join forces to combat the enemy.

The city is the biblical environment that defines the local character of the church. What is set forth in the New Testament then is one church with one mission in each city.

THE PRESBYTERY OF THE CITY

If there is one church in each city, there is also one presbytery in each city. This is made up of all the pastors of the different congregations which form the only church of the city. This presbytery is made visible through what, in Argentina, has been called the Pastoral Council of the city. The different pastoral councils of each location are carrying out a task, which, in practice, aims at the recovery of the biblical concept of the church of the city. Unity in the leadership pulls down barriers of separation, creates an atmosphere of mutual trust and is projected to the whole Church and fundamentally to its mission.

The creation of Pastoral Councils in the majority of the cities of Argentina is a marvelous work of the Holy Spirit. At present there exist more than 200 Pastoral Councils throughout the nation, and several more are being added every year. This remarkable orientation toward unity in the church leadership is not the result of one person's vision, nor is it the work of a committee. Quite spontaneously, by the work of the Holy Spirit, these councils have been emerging independently in the cities and towns of Argentina.

The Pastoral Councils point in three directions: toward the pastors, toward the church and toward the city. As it relates to the pastors, the Pastoral Council aims to integrate all God's servants in the city into a tight and loving fellowship. The council shepherds the pastors, disciplines and restores those who need it and provides an environment of unity, communion and prayer, helping pastors to overcome the well-known phenomenon of ministerial isolation.

As it relates to churches, the Pastoral Council aims to make the different congregations in a city conscious of their identity as one church. Council programs help the local congregations enjoy the diversity and richness of the whole Body of Christ. Congregations are encouraged to share the multiplicity of resources with which God has blessed the church of the city. Congregations are exhorted to sit at the same communion table, celebrate together the presence of Christ in the city, and jointly announce His imminent return in glory.

As it interfaces with the city, the Pastoral Council assumes the authority and the spiritual government of the city. It acknowledges the problems of the city and searches for solutions. It exercises its prophetic voice in denouncing the injustices the city endures, and it assures that the announcement of the presence of the kingdom of God will be clearly heard. It prays and stands in the breach, interceding for the city and its people. It influences and permeates the different social and political structures of the city with the values of the Kingdom. And, above all, it seeks God's vision for the city as a whole and develops a missionary strategy common to all, truly impacting the city with the gospel of Jesus Christ.

THE APOSTOLIC NETWORKS

Through the work of the Holy Spirit, another biblical paradigm has reemerged in many parts of Argentina. It is the reaffirmation of an apostolic ministry and the exercise of the charismatic gift accompanying it. This is not the creation of a new denominational structure. Neither is the apostle an ecclesiastical official. What this *does* mean is that God is knitting together networks of ministers, ministries and churches starting from a common vision.

These networks are generally shaped through the personality of one or more "apostles." These are servants of the Lord in whom their peers recognize spiritual authority, ministerial backing and, above all, an unusual capacity for capturing God's vision for their time and communicating it to the rest. The apostles do not attempt to impose themselves through authoritarianism, but they are recognized for their spiritual authority. They are not self-appointed. They do not exert influence on others through the power of a structure or a legal position, but they are servants who build relationships with others, and to whom their coservants subject themselves voluntarily in spiritual matters.

Many servants of God in Argentina do not want to minister alone any longer. They are taking the initiative of looking for spiritual and pastoral covering from a coservant to whom they relate spiritually in order to receive advice, vision, accountability, correction, stimulus, prayer and ministry. This practice is highly meaningful because pastors are avoiding two dangerous extremes: forced dependence on a politically-placed denominational official, and the absolute autonomy of the church minister who moves independently and who is not accountable to anyone for his life and ministry. Meanwhile, each of these apostolic networks is relating positively to other networks, strengthening the Body of Christ in an incredible manner.

THE MISSION OF THE
CHURCH AS MEANS AND END

Regretfully, during these 2,000 years, it seems Christians have done anything and everything possible to avoid being "one" as a Church. We have long lived separated from one another, quarrelling, inventing new arguments and finding reasons to excuse ourselves for our sin of disunity. Knowing full well that the imperative to be one is as clear in the Scriptures as anything else, we have allowed the spirit of the world and of our times to mold us. In doing so, we have disobeyed the clear will of God.

Throughout history, the spirit of each epoch has suggested to Christians reasons to explain our divisions. We do not have space here to elaborate, but as an example, let us look at our own times. In the seventeenth and eighteenth centuries, a cultural movement emerged called *modernity*. According to this mind-set (which persists today) when reason governs human actions, humanity moves toward perfection. The Church absorbed this spirit of the times and adopted the paradigm of reason to define its unity, or rather, to justify its division. In favoring reason, all that was conceptual, doctrinal and dogmatic was given priority. As a result, Christians were driven further apart by different concepts and doctrines. If one was premillennial and another amillennial, this seemed to be reason enough to separate, leaving them unable to enjoy real and practical communion.

Today, the modernity paradigm is being seriously questioned as dysfunctional, giving way to so-called postmodernism. Today, there are fewer closed systems. The trend is not toward closing, but toward opening. Today, rigid and excluding dogmas are running out of strength. There is more softness in thinking, a loss of trust in stern ideologies. The postmodern era values experience over reason.

In Argentina, the Church is once again picking up the spirit of the times. We no longer like to quarrel over doctrinal or conceptual matters. Today, we are not as concerned as we once were whether or not we can lose our salvation or if the baptism of the Holy Spirit requires speaking in tongues. We are much more inclined to love and work with others, even if they might think differently on a few doctrinal issues.

POSITIONING EXPERIENCE ABOVE REASON

Ironically, now that reason has given way to experience, the Church has begun to position experience not only above reason, but also above God's will for unity! Now experiences are bringing their own brand of division to the Church! Those in favor of the anointing of the

> Discerning the signs of the
> times does not mean adapting
> to the shifting paradigms of
> the world's philosophy.

Holy Spirit (*la unción*), accompanied by external manifestations, oppose those who do not share this experience. Those who are being "slain in the Spirit" are ridiculed by those who cannot accept this experience as valid. Those who laugh in church meetings are walking different pathways than those who do not. Those who shout as buffaloes cannot get along with those who do not even open their mouths. Those who prayerwalk and do spiritual mapping clash with others who consider these activities to be crazy.

Thus, what seem to be tearing us apart in this postmodern era are not so much concepts or doctrines, but the experiences we live. Meanwhile, the will of God and Jesus' prayer for unity are still awaiting fulfillment.

The Bible teaches us about the need to discern the signs of the times. Discerning the signs does not mean adapting to the shifting paradigms of the world's philosophy. I believe that if we are capable of understanding the signs of the times in the light of the Holy Spirit, we will be able to develop a new paradigm to help us in the process of unification. I suggest we forget about the modernity and postmodern models. An important new paradigm is emerging, an eschatological paradigm. If we will only read the signs of the times and recognize that the return of the Lord is imminent, then the level of our unity will be determined neither by reason nor by experience.

The focal point of unity in the Church must be our mission. As long as either reason or experience remain the center around which our church life rotates, we will continue to come apart. But if we are consumed by the mission of the church, totally committed to carrying out the redeeming purposes of God in Christ, we will quickly realize that our enemy is not our brother or sister, but Satan and his devices. Only then can we come together and win the world for Christ. Because if we are one, the world will believe!

TOWARD A POSTDENOMINATIONAL CHRISTIANITY

It is necessary to make a distinction between Church and denomination.[1] The Church is part of the new wine of the gospel, but denominations are mere wineskins. While the essence of the Church is permanent, denominations are forms which the Church has historically structured itself for the fulfillment of its mission. The Church is God's creation, but denominations are a human creation.

The Church is a spiritual event, while denominations are a social event. The Church is cross-culturally valid, while denominations are culturally limited. The Church must be biblically understood and evaluated. Denominations are sociologically understood and evaluated. The Church manifests its relevance and validity for its spiritual qualities and its conformity to the Scriptures. The validity of denominations, because they are mere structures, resides in their functioning in relationship to the mission of the Church. The Church has an essential and eternal character, while denominations are transitory and temporal. The Church is the result of divine revelation, while denominations are the fruit of human tradition. The purpose of the Church is to glorify God, while that of denominations is to serve the Church.

As soon as we understand that denominations are not the Church, but are culturally determined structures, denominational controversies begin to lose their urgency. Denominational differences then occupy a secondary level, and we are free to give the top priority to that which unites, namely the affirmation that the Church is a people with a mission.

It is my personal conviction that we are moving toward a postdenominational Christianity. This does not mean the rejection of the richness of the denominational traditions, but it does open the possibility of fulfilling the mission together, using our particular traditions, but without barriers to separate us. The great issues that have divided us in the past are rapidly being set aside as we agree together to address the mission of the Church.

At least four phenomena have contributed to the almost daily homogenization of the Church in Argentina. The first is the evident "pentecostalization" of Christianity on our continent. Today, any congregation of any denomination is more Pentecostal than it was 20 years ago. The second phenomenon is a greater "formalization" of the Pentecostal churches in Argentina. Today, any Pentecostal-charismatic church is more evangelical-Protestant than it was 20 years ago. The third phenomenon is the displacement of the center of ecclesiastical activity from the formative—Sunday School or the Department of Christian Education or its denominational equivalent—to the cultic. The center is no longer placed on the doctrinal or conceptual, but on what can be experienced.

The fourth phenomenon has caused influential churches to thrive by combining denominational emphases. For example, an evangelical church in Argentina can support a Reformed Calvinistic theology, maintain a Pentecostal-charismatic profile, function with an Episcopal-type government, practice believers' baptism and move out in the world with a Methodist-type social concern. These churches, some of them independent and others belonging to specific denominational traditions, are the fastest-growing churches in Argentina, and, consequently, they are exerting the greatest influence over other congregations.

A CHURCH WITHOUT WALLS

According to Paul, the work carried out by Christ on the cross included pulling down "the dividing wall of hostility" (Eph. 2:14, *NIV*). The apostle had in mind the architectural structure of the Temple of Jerusalem. This Temple had three atria on the same level. There was the atrium of the priests, the atrium of the laymen and the atrium of the women. From the atrium of the Gentiles, the Gentiles could see the Temple as a whole, but they could not approach it. They were separated by a wall about five-feet thick. Along that wall were equidistant pillars with signs saying, among other things, that those who crossed the wall would be responsible for their own deaths since, in doing so, they would contaminate with their presence the Lord's Temple. A Gentile could definitely not step foot on the Temple's main area. But that wall was pulled down by Christ, who made Jew and Gentile one.

If we are honest, we will recognize that we have been building up walls of discrimination that divide us. When Zechariah speaks about the church of the revival, he says that a young man came to measure that church to see its dimensions, but an angel rushed after him to stop him. The angel told him not to measure, saying, "'Jerusalem will be a city without walls because of the great number of men....And I myself will be a wall of fire around it,' declares the Lord, 'and I will be its glory within'" (Zech. 2:4,5, *NIV*).

Zechariah indicates there will only be revival if in this Church there are no walls. If we are to live a powerful revival from God, the dividing walls must be pulled down. We must make a commitment that the only wall the Church of Christ must have is the wall of fire around it, the wall of the presence of the Lord.

In Argentina, we are beginning to experience this kind of Church without human walls. The Lord is using children, adolescents and young people for revival in unprecedented ways, for example. Massive youth attendance at congresses, encounters, Christian music recitals or worship concerts indicate they do not care much about matters like denominational identity or affiliation with a definite historical tradition.

UNITY IN DIVERSITY

Christ created only one people. Through Christ and in Christ, we are a new people. The Word of God assures us that in Christ, "there is neither Greek nor Jew, circumcised nor uncircumcised, barbarian, Scythian, slave nor free, but Christ is all and in all" (Col. 3:11). Galatians 3:28 says, "You are all one in Christ Jesus." This is not to say that differences have disappeared. Some of us have one vision for the

Church and others have a different one, but before Christ we are all together. We must not deny the differences. We do not attempt to abolish differences, because differences enrich us and give us value. But we do affirm unity in diversity. This evangelical assertion of unity in diversity is moving strongly into the collective conscience of Argentine evangelicals.

THE NATURE OF THE BOND

In his epistle to the Ephesians, Paul affirms that Christ made peace abolishing any enmity, because He is our peace (see Eph. 2:14,15). Later Paul says that we must make every effort "to keep the unity of the Spirit in the bond of peace" (Eph. 4:3). The unity of the Spirit can only be kept through the bond of peace. Notice that it does not say through the bond of *truth*. It is impossible to keep the unity of the

> The Church must make every effort to elevate our bond in Christ above any doctrine or experience that might divide us.

Spirit through the bond of truth, because what may seem like truth to me, may be seen differently by you. Our bond of unity cannot be our theology nor our dogma nor our practice. What binds us together as children of God is *peace*. What unites us is not that we all believe the same thing or that we all have the same spiritual experiences. What binds us is peace.

And who is this peace? Christ is our peace. He who binds us together is Christ; nothing can be stronger. We must make every effort to elevate the bond that is Christ above any concept or experience that might divide us. This does not mean that I give up my interpretation, my dogma, my experience, or what I believe to be correct truth. But it does mean that, believing what I believe, I can still love all those who believe differently. I am convinced that Christ in me and Christ in every other believer is more important than my hermeneutics, my theology or my ideology.

THE PRIORITY OF "ORTHOCARDIA"

Christ has given us all access to the Father through the same Spirit. The Holy Spirit dwelling in each of us says "Abba, Father!" He who dwells in me says, "Abba, Father!" The Spirit who dwells in a brother or sister of another congregation with concepts and practices different from mine, if he or she is a true child of God, says, "Abba, Father!" Thus, if they have the same Father as I, we are brothers and sisters.

As brothers and sisters, let us not grieve our Father's heart any longer! My wife and I have two children, Gabriel and Florencia. I would be devastated to see them apart, separated, divided when they grow up. I would be horribly sad to hear Gabriel denouncing or criticizing Florencia! What happens to God's heart when He hears us finding fault with those belonging to another congregation, or when He hears those of another denomination find fault with us?

Genesis 6:6 tells of the pain God feels in His heart as a result of our sin. Today we are more diligent than ever to minister healing to the hearts of individuals. But we must also minister healing to the heart of our heavenly Father, whom we have deeply injured with our divisions and conflicts. The only thing that can heal our Father's heart is the unity of His Church.

As Christians, we have long been preoccupied with *orthodoxy*, that is, supporting a sound doctrine. In the name of that doctrine, we have often wounded God's heart. More recently, our emphasis has shifted to *orthopraxis*, i.e., doing the right things as Christians. Yet, in the name of that orthopraxis, we have continued to engage our brothers and sisters in conflict, repeatedly wounding the heart of our Father. While sound orthodoxy and orthopraxis are important, we must move beyond these to an *orthocardia*. That is to say, we must try to live with a correct heart! A major step in this direction will entail a sincere effort to keep the bond of peace with all our brothers and sisters in Christ.

ONE LAST WORD

I want to close this chapter on unity in revival with some words of wisdom from John Stott.

The new society God has brought into being is nothing short of a new creation, a new human race, whose characteristic is no longer alienation, but reconciliation; no longer division and hostility, but unity and peace. This new society God rules and loves and lives in.

That is the vision. But when we turn from the ideal portrayed in Scripture to the concrete realities experienced in the church today, it is a very different and a very tragic story. For even in the church there is often alienation, disunity and discord. And Christians erect new barriers in place of the old which Christ has demolished, now a colour bar, now racism, nationalism or tribalism, now personal animosities engendered by pride, prejudice, jealousy and the unforgiving spirit, now a divisive system of caste or class, now a clericalism which sunders clergy from laity as if they were separate breeds of human being, and now a denominationalism which turns churches into sects and contradicts the unity and universality of Christ's church.

These things are doubly offensive. First, they are an offence to Jesus Christ. How dare we build walls of partition in the one and only human community in which he has destroyed them? Of course there are barriers of language and culture in the world outside, and of course new converts feel more comfortable among their own kind, who speak and dress and eat and drink and behave in the same way that they do and have always done. But deliberately to perpetuate these barriers in the church, and even to tolerate them without taking any active steps to overcome them in order to demonstrate the trans-cultural unity of God's new society, is to set ourselves against the reconciling work of Christ and even to try to undo it.

What is offensive to Christ is offensive also, though in a different way, to the world. It hinders the world from believing in Jesus. God intends his people to be a visual model of the gospel, to demonstrate before people's eyes the good news of reconciliation. But what is the good of gospel campaigns if they do not produce gospel churches? It is simply impossible, with any shred of Christian integrity, to go on proclaiming that Jesus by his cross has abolished the old divisions and created a single new humanity of love, while at the same time we are contradicting our message by tolerating racial or social or other barriers within our church fellowship. I am not saying that a church must be perfect before it can preach the gospel, but I am saying that it cannot preach the gospel while acquiescing in its imperfections.

We need to get the failures of the church on our conscience, to feel the offence to Christ and the world which these failures are, to weep over the credibility gap between the church's talk and the church's walk, to repent of our readiness to excuse and even condone our failures, and to determine to do something about it. I wonder if anything is more urgent today, for the honour of Christ and for the spread of the gospel, than that the church should be, and should be seen to be, what by God's purpose and Christ's achievement it already is—a single new humanity, a model of human community, a family of reconciled brothers and sisters who love their father and love each other, the evident dwelling place of God by his Spirit. Only then will the world believe in Christ as Peacemaker. Only then will God receive the glory due to his name.[2]

Many people debate whether there is truly a revival in Argentina. Those who say no would base their argument in part on *their* perception that the unity of pastors and of the Argentine church still falls below expectations. I personally believe this debate is foolish. We would do much better to focus our analysis of what God is doing in Argentina within its eschatological framework. When I speak of revival, I am not referring to the kind of local or short-term revival that has appeared from time to time through Church history. On the contrary, I am speaking of the last great revival, the latter rain of Joel, the great outpouring of the Spirit on all people.

When we understand what God is doing in Argentina as first fruits of what He will do throughout the world, our perspective changes. When we place these events within an eschatological framework, when we consider it as the last great revival in history before the triumphant return of Christ, then our vision is radically altered, making debate fruitless. But because it is eschatological, the movement has to do with something that "already is but not yet." In Argentina, there is already revival, because no one can deny the move of the Holy Spirit and its fruit. In Argentina, we still await the great revival, with its complete fulfillment. In Argentina, we do know remarkable unity as a result of the revival that God is sending us. In Argentina, we still need to achieve perfect unity.

Because of what God is already doing here, I personally rejoice and am bold enough to share these principles with the Body of Christ elsewhere. For what we have not yet attained in Argentina, I will be among the first to repent and humbly beseech God for more of His work and for greater unity, so that the world may believe.

Notes

1. Howard Snyder makes an excellent differentiation, and I will be using some of his concepts. See Howard A. Snyder, *The Community of the King* (Downers Grove, Ill.: InterVarsity Press, 1977), pp. 158-166.
2. John R.W. Stott, *God's New Society* (Downers Grove, Ill.: InterVarsity Press, 1979), pp. 110-112.

twelve

UNLEASHING THE HEADWATERS OF REVIVAL

BY ED SILVOSO

Ed Silvoso is president of Harvest Evangelism in San Jose, California, and serves as coordinator of the Prayer Evangelism Division of the A.D. 2000 United Prayer Track. His book, That None Should Perish, *has influenced Christian leaders on many continents. A native Argentine, Ed has furnished the principal bridge between the Argentine revival and North America and many other nations of the world. Furthermore, he has been one of the most sensitive prophets and keenest analysts of the revival since before its inception. His annual Harvest Evangelism International Institute has been the chief agency for allowing non-Argentines to see and participate in the revival firsthand.*

The Velez Sarsfield soccer stadium, one of the largest in Buenos Aires, is packed with 55,000 young people. The occasion is not a rock concert or a World Cup match, but rather a call to holiness. Yes! All those youngsters are on their knees asking forgiveness for their sins and promising before God and their friends that, from now on, they will live a pure life. The speaker is not Billy Graham or Benny Hinn, both of them well known for their ability to pack stadiums, but rather a virtually unknown young preacher in his twenties, Dante Gebel.

A few months later, the same stadium is packed by believers representing every denomination in Argentina. The reason: a praise and worship evening singing new songs that have become the "common language" for the Church in Argentina. The convener is a missionary kid from Mexico, Marcos Witt, whose music has taken Argentina by storm. Even though the 54,000 people present come from many different church traditions, the feeling of unity and common purpose is overwhelming. When the corporate praise reaches its peak, the whole stadium becomes a cathedral, and the audience becomes a living parable of what the Body of Christ is all about.

The foundation for both of these events is laid three years earlier when, at the same stadium, more than 50,000 believers representing a broad spectrum of the Church gather for a day in the presence of the Lord. His presence is such that multitudes fall on their knees to repent of secret sins. This is followed in many cases by public confession and costly restitution. The preacher—if there is one, as the Holy Spirit is in such total control—is a shy, young local pastor who just a few months earlier had contemplated quitting the ministry. His name is Claudio Freidzon. On this day, Claudio, now overflowing with joy, is leading the crowds to drink from Jesus.

In the city of San Justo, Buenos Aires, 70,000 people have gathered to hear a businessman-turned-preacher. Many of them have been delivered from satanic oppression, and quite a few have been miraculously healed of terminal conditions. This is not an isolated event, but one that is becoming almost routine in the cities of Argentina, where tens of thousands of people gather night after night, week after week to hear the gospel and enthusiastically respond to a call to a total surrender to Jesus Christ. The preacher, Carlos Annacondia, is not a televangelist, but the owner of a nuts and bolts factory in a suburb of Buenos Aires. He has no formal theological education, but he has led more than one million people to make a public decision for Christ, and many of those have become solid church members and leaders in their congregations.

A dynamic couple has just finished ministering at the old Federacion de Box stadium across from Plaza Once in Buenos Aires. Thousands of people have packed the facility, and many have publicly testified to experiencing extraordinary miracles. Some have been healed of cancer, some have had organs recreated, while others have been delivered from demonic oppression. This is 1988 and the couple,

Omar and Marfa Cabrera, are accustomed to such meetings. Every month they preach, face-to-face, to 145,000 people in more than 50 locations all over Argentina. To do so they travel over 3,000 kilometers a month by car and by plane. Most of these "church meetings" happen on weekdays since Omar and Marfa and their young band of associates can cover only a handful of cities on Sundays. It is not uncommon for members of the Vision of the Future Church to attend church on Tuesdays, Wednesdays or whatever day of the week the Cabreras are in their town.

In the winter of 1993, in a renovated, downtown theater, 13 services are held daily. The first service begins at 1 A.M., and the last one ends at midnight. For 23 hours people from all walks of life come and go. This theater-turned-church is now used by more people in one month than in the previous 10 years when it operated as a movie theater. Thousands of decisions are recorded every day. According to Hilario Wynarczyk, a Polish sociologist who studied the phenomenon, 14,000 each day "come to church" at this unusual church called Waves of Love and Peace.[1] The leader, Hector Anibal Gimenez, is a layman who used to be a drug addict, a bandit and a gunfighter. At the peak of his ministry, he is able to claim a congregation of 150,000 people, among whom are famous soccer players, movie actors and actresses, journalists and business people, as well as a multitude of poor and humble people from the slums.

SOLEMN ASSEMBLY AT THE OBELISK

It is October 30, 1991, and the inflation rate in Argentina is a devastating 1460% as the country stumbles from one crisis to another. At the Obelisk, an Argentine landmark in downtown Buenos Aires where the country was first established, 18,000 pastors, leaders and intercessors are participating in a Solemn Assembly. In plain view of their fellow Argentines and against the backdrop of a violent steel workers demonstration a few blocks away, these men and women, who have just marched through downtown Buenos Aires proclaiming the lordship of Jesus over the nation, are confessing their sins and the sins of their fathers as they seek God's forgiveness and pray for the eventual healing of the land.

It is a moving sight as pastor after pastor comes to the microphone

with hands held up by pastors from other denominations in a public display of unity and interdependency. For more than an hour, these leaders ask God's forgiveness in the spirit of 2 Chronicles 7:14. They specifically pray that the curse of inflation be lifted from the land. During the last 10 minutes, all 18,000 participants fall on their knees to ask forgiveness for Argentina's idolatry and to take the nation away from the Queen of Heaven, to whom it has been dedicated by the military dictators, and to place it at the feet of Jesus. It is a powerful moment. But the best is yet to come. Within a few weeks, the president's hand will be strengthened and he will be able to make radical changes in the political and social structure of the nation. A year later inflation falls to a "miraculous" 12 percent. Three years later it is down to three percent!

FROM ARGENTINA TO AUSTRALIA

A Baptist pastor from Australia has been studying at Fuller Theological Seminary, in Pasadena, California, in the United States. Even though his postgraduate studies are going very well, deep inside Rod Denton is very discouraged. He has an unsatisfied longing for the reality of God. He knows about Him, he knows about His book, the Bible, but Rod longs for a more personal manifestation of God. He is so discouraged, he decides that upon returning to Australia he will not go back to the ministry.

As a last-ditch effort he visits Argentina where, it has been said, God is doing great things. In La Plata he is invited to preach at Pastor Alberto Scataglini's church. He delivers a standard message. At the end he is asked to pray for the people. As he lays hands on the first person in line, Rod feels the power of God flowing through him and seconds later he sees its powerful effect, as the person for whom he is praying falls to the floor in the power of the Holy Spirit. This proves not to be an isolated case as person after person is touched by God through Rod's prayers. That night in his hotel room, he falls on his knees and thanks God for the reality of His presence and His power. Then and there, he vows not to leave the ministry but to dedicate his life to seeing his country reached for Christ. Rod Denton has since become a key player in the effort to reach Australian cities for Christ. Whatever he experienced in Argentina, it changed his life and, through him, the lives of many others.

FROM ARGENTINA TO JAPAN

Dr. Paul Ariga, a prominent Japanese Christian leader, is now a seminary president. He traveled to Argentina in 1993 because he had heard of "something" extraordinary happening there. During the Harvest Evangelism International Institute, he is exposed to the ministries of Carlos Annacondia, Eduardo Lorenzo, Omar Cabrera, Claudio Freidzon and many others. On the last day he falls on his face before God as he asks for the "Argentine anointing" to take back to Japan. The next day he boards a plane bound for Japan, pregnant with hope but harboring some questions.

Ariga concludes that he has been exposed to either the greatest lie ever preached or to the greatest truth ever missed by the Church. He decides to test the authenticity of what he saw and experienced on his journey. Since intercession was presented in Argentina as a key element, he spends almost one year recruiting 13,000 intercessors all over Japan. He then connects them by mail, by phone and by computer to track how many hours of prayer they are generating. His goal is 180,000 hours of prayer for Japan. While he waits for this goal to be reached, he leads public prayer and repentance meetings at hundreds of sites in Japan and neighboring countries. A few months later, he is delighted to discover that the number of hours prayed has surpassed 350,000. He feels the moment has come to test the principles learned in Argentina.

He rents a 60,000-seat stadium for three days in the city of Osaka, and enlists the help of child intercessors—something he was exposed to in Argentina—to pray for each one of the seats. The children spend 13 hours laying hands on each seat and asking God that someone will occupy it each day. They pray that those who sit there will hear the word of God and make a public decision for Christ.

Then Paul Ariga convenes the church in the area and publicly confronts the powers of evil "a la Annacondia," loudly commanding them to let go of those that God has prepared for salvation. A three-day campaign follows and 122,000 persons attend, of which 21,000 receive Christ. This is a staggering total, given the total number of born-again Christians in Japan in 1994 was only about 300,000. By 1997 the number of decisions through his "All Japan Revival Mission" has grown to 68,000. Paul Ariga declares confidently that what he experienced and received in Argentina has produced these results.

What *is* going on in Argentina? Obviously something extraordinary. Few countries have lay evangelists winning souls for Christ with the success of Annacondia. It is also uncommon in other parts of the world for tens of thousands of young people to pack stadiums to repent of their sins, or for local congregations to hold multiple services every day of the week in order to accommodate multitudes of inquirers and new believers.

THE HEADWATERS

Whatever it is, this Argentine movement has had a significant impact in the United States and Canada through two major, contemporary moves of the Spirit of God that many refer to as revivals: the "Toronto Blessing," instrumental in renewing and transforming the lives of tens of thousands of pastors and parishioners in the English-speaking world, and the "Pensacola Revival," which has touched hundreds of thousands and witnessed more than 120,000 decisions for Christ in a little over two years. Both movements upstream to what has been happening in Argentina during the last 15 years.

The city of Resistencia, in northern Argentina, has become synonymous with "city-taking" all over the world. More than 200 cities on five continents are involved in city-reaching plans "a la Resistencia." What could have happened in that marginal area of Argentina that would affect the entire world?

Furthermore, something extraordinary happened at a united public prayer meeting in the central plaza in La Plata in the fall of 1993 that built a bridge between Argentina and the United Kingdom. As a result, a network of leaders was launched in the United Kingdom for the purpose of reaching its cities for Christ. Only a powerful event of great significance could affect healing between these two nations that had, only a few years earlier, engaged in the unfortunate Falkland Islands war.

WHAT IS GOING ON?

What is going on in Argentina? More specifically, what has happened in the last 15 years to cause this nation to become synonymous with revival, intercession and city-taking?

To understand these events and the redemptive gift God has given to Argentina to pass on to the nations, we must take an in-depth look at the life of Argentina as a nation and the forces that have shaped the country's spiritual climate during the last 30 years, specifically the context in which the breakthrough occurred in 1982.

Argentina as a Nation

Three hopes had to be shattered before the proud Argentines would hear the voice of God. Nations, like persons, have a soul and as such a personality. It took three major crises for the Argentine pride to be broken.

First was the shattering of our political hope. In 1973 Juan Peron, who had dominated Argentina's political life since 1944, returned to the country after 18 years of forced political exile. His return coincided with a moment of deep political and social longing in the nation. The sad collection of puppet governments that followed the coup that brought down Peron in 1955 failed to fill the vacuum left by his absence and instead of erasing his memory, they created an uncontrollable appetite for his return.

As a result, when Peron returned and his political party won the elections hands down, almost every Argentine was expecting a political miracle. The hour for Argentina to take its place among the nations of the First World had finally arrived. However, Peron died within months of assuming the presidency for the third time. He was succeeded by his wife, Isabel, the elected vice president, who would then preside over a sad slide into chaos and ruin. *El Hombre* ("the Man"), as he was proudly called by millions of followers, failed to deliver, and with his death an extraordinary political hope was shattered.

A military junta replaced Mrs. Peron and, in an effort to gain the favor of the masses, tried to create "an economic miracle." At first they seemed to succeed. But within two years the country was teetering on the brink of bankruptcy, due mostly to mismanagement and rampant corruption. The fact that bankruptcy came on the heels of two years of artificial wealth made the pain all the more devastating. By late 1980, Argentina's economic hope was also shattered.

INVADING THE FALKLAND ISLANDS

In a desperate move to hold on to power, the military junta invaded the Falkland Islands. This was a shrewd move for two reasons. First, an external military conflict always causes the people, even dissidents, to rally behind the government, no matter how inefficient or evil the government. Hitler proved this to the extreme. Secondly, every child in Argentina, shortly after learning how to say Daddy and Mommy, is taught to say, *"Las Malvinas son Argentinas"* ("the Falkland Islands belong to Argentina"). Few issues touch the deep river of nationalism in Argentina as does the question of ownership of these islands. By invading them and promising to hang on to them, the de facto rulers created a "Military Hope."

> Those who today carry with joy the ripe sheaves of Argentina are standing on the shoulders of those who yesterday watered seeds with their own tears.

For a time every Argentine was united in the war against Great Britain. The military junta exercised absolute censorship over the news, and the Argentines were led to believe the most extraordinary reports. The flagship of the British Armada had been sunk. Prince Andrew had been taken captive. It was just a matter of days before British Prime Minister Margaret Thatcher would surrender the islands. All were lies, but very convenient lies to keep the masses behind a highly unpopular regime.

Then one day in June of 1981, the government called the people to the historic Plaza de Mayo, across from the president's palace, to make a sad announcement: "We have lost the war." This was so incredible at first and so shattering afterwards that the bulk of the people immediately broke with everything traditional. They threw up their arms saying, "Give us something new. We do not want any of the past traditions!"

A monumental vacuum in the Argentine psyche was created by the progressive shattering of these three hopes. It was as if the nation had lost its identity. With no firm political compass, no economic anchor and no military ballast, Argentina's confusion was similar to the one suffered by Japan in the aftermath of its surrender at the end of World War II. The past could no longer be trusted. The present was unacceptable, and the future was a mystery that by all means should be kept from remotely resembling the now-hated past.

It is at that particular point in time that the Argentine "revival" began. Most students of this phenomenon will identify its beginning with the emergence of Carlos Annacondia and his evangelistic campaigns of 1982.

However, no man is an island to himself, and no one person can produce a revival alone. The ones that today carry with joy the ripe sheaves are standing on the shoulders of those who yesterday watered seeds with their own tears. I believe that the headwaters of the river of God sweeping Argentina today are found many years back. Having considered the state of the nation at the time of the breakthrough, we now need to look at the progressive changes that shaped the spiritual climate of Argentina during the previous 30 years.

SHAPING THE SPIRITUAL CLIMATE OF ARGENTINA, 1954-1984

In my opinion there are 10 factors which decisively shaped the spiritual climate leading to the breakthrough in 1982: (1) the Tommy Hicks campaigns in 1954; (2) the arrival in Argentina of four American missionaries whose ministries powerfully impacted the Church; (3) the renewal among the youth in the Plymouth Brethren and other conservative groups; (4) an impromptu meeting of emerging leaders in Cordoba in 1981 at the height of the Falkland Islands War; (5) the impact of "The 700 Club" in Argentina through its network of regional offices; (6) the unorthodox launching of a myriad of Christian FM radio stations by a another businessman-turned-preacher; (7) the birth of *El Puente*, the first interdenominational newspaper with national coverage; (8) Dr. Yonggi Cho's visit to Buenos Aires in 1987; (9) the acceptance of Omar Cabrera and Vision of the Future by the Church in Argentina; and (10) the emergence of apostolic leaders at the local and national level.

Let's take a closer look at each of these factors.

1. The Tommy Hicks Campaigns

In 1954 the minuscule evangelical church in Argentina, numbering only a few thousand, received a tremendous boost when Tommy Hicks, a relatively unknown lay preacher from California, packed first one stadium and then a larger one with multitudes eager to hear the Word and to experience the power of God. It has been reported by reliable sources that 200,000 people attended each day during the closing week of the campaign. Large numbers received the Lord and an unusually high percentage joined the many congregations that sponsored the campaign.

The Tommy Hicks campaign set a benchmark with the intensity of the release of God's power surprising the Church with totally unexpected numbers. Among those who served during those historic days was a group of young leaders whose lives were enriched with a new dimension of faith. After Tommy Hicks left Argentina, these leaders saw the spiritual landscape of the nation gradually revert back to its pre-campaign state, but deep down in their hearts they knew that God was able to do something extraordinary and that, most likely, He would do it again.

Juan Passuelo, Omar Cabrera and Juan Terranova were three of those leaders, and 30 years later they would be in key positions of national leadership when God chose to surprise the Church again by using another unknown lay preacher by the name of Carlos Annacondia to touch the lives of unprecedented numbers of unbelievers. Juan Terranova was the president of the National Association of Evangelical Churches. Juan Passuello was the president of the National Association of Pentecostal Churches. Omar Cabrera presided over Vision of the Future, the most dynamic evangelistic movement in the nation.

God only knows how much the seed planted during the Tommy Hicks campaign influenced them to be open to the unorthodox ministry of Carlos Annacondia, especially in its uncharted beginnings. However, it is part of the public record that each of these men played key roles in affirming and confirming the ministry of Carlos Annacondia during those crucial early days.

2. Four Key American Missionaries

In the late 1950s and early '60s, four American rookie missionaries arrived in Argentina. These men—Keith Bentson, Orville Swindoll, Milton Pope and Ed Murphy—were to play key roles in the shaping of the spiritual climate prior to Annacondia's emergence. Keith Bentson was instrumental, with others, in ushering in the renewal movement of the 1960s. His impeccable and unimpeachable Christian character, along with his genuine humility, brought balance and stability to a very volatile movement. Others relied on his wisdom when the road appeared unclear. In addition, Keith Bentson was the one who spotted young Luis Palau, a clerk at a local bank, and invited him to be part of his evangelistic team. Keith and his team also organized Luis Palau's first campaign in the town of Oncativo, Cordoba.

Orville Swindoll became the pastor par excellence to the renewal movement of the 1960s. Teaming up with Keith Bentson and other national leaders, he brought the movement into the mainstream. One of the most solid denominations in Argentina today, "The Movement" has long been characterized by its strong biblical teaching. Jorge Himitian's revelational insights into the lordship and majestic nature of Christ shaped the lives of thousands, including my own, at a time when an overemphasis on experiences could have been devastating.

Milton Pope launched the best and largest theological-education-by-extension seminary. Reaching out to practically every church in the nation, Milton Pope and his associates trained tens of thousands of leaders. These leaders, endued with solid biblical reflection, brought stability to the local and regional churches. This stability proved crucial when the spiritual breakthrough came in the 1980s.

Ed Murphy returned to Argentina in 1985 to teach as only he can do it—with superb scholarship and passion for presenting the truth in a context of love that edifies rather than destroys. His was a most difficult subject: spiritual warfare and the demonization of believers. Ed Murphy's definitive teaching enabled Carlos Annacondia's then-controversial practice of casting demons out of believers to be accepted by many who had been taught that under no circumstances could demons affect believers.

Each one of these men is so humble that he will feel uncomfortable being credited with so much influence. However, in my opinion, without Bentson, Swindoll, Pope and Murphy and their impact, the Church in Argentina would have been unprepared for what was to come.

3. Renewal Among the Youth

In 1977 Luis Palau held an interdenominational campaign in Buenos Aires sponsored by a group of youth leaders, most of them from the Plymouth Brethren Assemblies in Buenos Aires. These leaders were struggling with the tension they felt between their rich denominational heritage and the need to further contextualize the gospel in order to reach the unchurched. Some of their elders understood how they felt. Others didn't. When Luis Palau accepted to be the preacher at "Juventud 77," he and his sponsors became the subject of great controversy.

"Juventud 77" turned out to be an excellent event. Many people came to the Lord. A breath of fresh air was added to the rich aroma of Brethren traditions and those of other conservative groups. There emerged a group of young leaders who, in a relatively short time, would be in key national positions. Following "Juventud 77," two of these young leaders, Juan Pablo Bongarra and Anibal Delutri, launched a unique national radio program at a secular station. Bongarra and Delutri brought so much dynamism and so much class and excellence to the program, *Compartiendo la Noticia*" (Sharing the News), that the Church as a whole identified with their program. For a season that radio program, and others they launched later, became flagships for the Church in the nation.

Also playing key roles were Ruben Proietti, a Baptist, and Bill Kennedy, a Plymouth Brethren. Along with Bongarra, Delutri and many others, they founded M.E.I., a parachurch ministry that during the late '70s and early '80s provided the best pastors' conferences in Argentina. Faculty for these national conferences were drawn from different theological and denominational streams, thus creating an initial platform for unity. Ruben Proietti became very active in the National Association of Evangelical Churches and also in Conela (Latin America W.E.F.) where he still serves as the executive director. Bill Kennedy was the bridge builder among these emerging leaders. His position as an elder in one of the most influential congregations in Buenos Aires and as the executive director of the largest retreat center on the outskirts of the city gave him great visibility and credibility which he wisely used for the kingdom of God. Bill was also bridge builder to groups and individuals outside the sphere of M.E.I.

With many others, these four men modeled a still imperfect but definitely better style of interdenominational and national leadership, giving the Church as a whole something to move toward as it slowly abandoned the fossilized forms of the past. The bonds established during the national pastors' conferences paid high dividends as city after city was shaken by Annacondia and the wave of spiritual power he was riding.

4. An Impromptu Meeting of National Leaders

In 1981, at the height of the Falklands War, many of the pastors in Argentina gathered in a retreat center in the town of Rio Tercero, Cordoba. Those were very difficult days and the military junta ruling the country had singled out the evangelical pastors as potential enemies of the state because of their historical connections to the United Kingdom.

At the end of one particular day, Eduardo Lorenzo, a highly respected Baptist pastor in Adrogue, a suburb of Buenos Aires, called a group of leaders together and asked them two questions. He first asked, "Can you think of someone who has done something good for you and you have not expressed your gratitude yet?" Lorenzo then asked, "Can you think of someone who has hurt you and you have not forgiven him or her yet?" These probing questions, by the power of the Spirit of God hovering over the meeting, produced a succession of confessions and repentance among those present as they became convicted by the Spirit of serious sins of omission and commission.

These public expressions of repentance and reconciliation set in motion a chain reaction that went beyond the walls of the retreat center and eventually touched, to varying degrees, most of the nation. That unexpected and spontaneous reconciliation reestablished relationships and resulted in a renewed commitment to praying together once the conference was over. As a result, a regular prayer meeting among leaders in downtown Buenos Aires became a clearing house for difficult issues. Those leaders would play a key constructive role when Annacondia exploded onto the national scene and his then-controversial style came under close scrutiny.

5. The Impact of "The 700 Club" in Argentina

Mario Bertolini was the national director for "The 700 Club" in Argentina. One of the key pieces in Bertolini's strategy to secure a national audience was to establish regional offices for "The 700

Club" in as many cities as possible in the interior of Argentina. He did that by putting those offices under the covering of a group of local pastors. At first these pastors were Pentecostal pastors who belonged mainly to the Assemblies of God, Bertolini's denomination. But soon the groups began to grow, and they became the seeds out of which grew local associations of pastors. When Carlos Annacondia's ministry went nationwide, these local groups were the ones that would bring him to town. Thus, Mario Bertolini and "The 700 Club" laid the tracks on which the breakthrough of the 1980s would travel.

6. The "Menoyo Radio Network"

Brother Menoyo was a businessman who, upon coming to Christ, received a special passion for the lost. As a businessman, Menoyo recognized the importance of the media and dreamed of a network of Christian radio stations all over Argentina. However, there was a problem: There were no broadcast licenses available and, even if there were, evangelicals could not own one because of the position of privilege granted to the Catholic church by the Argentine constitution.

Menoyo was not a man to be discouraged by mere "technicalities." He loaded several FM radio transmitters into the trunk of his car and drove to several cities where he distributed them to local pastors, encouraging each one to begin a *de facto* radio station. Menoyo continued until he had saturated the nation with these unofficial, unrecognized and unregistered radio stations. The military junta was perturbed, but the days of the dictatorship soon came to an abrupt end, and a truly democratic and liberal government was elected. Today there are more than 140 Christian FM radio stations in Argentina. None of them has been officially recognized by the government, but enough loopholes have been discovered in the existing legislation to guarantee their existence ad infinitum.

The emergence of this network of Christian radio stations has given the Church greater visibility in each city, and as the Church moves more and more toward unity, these stations become trumpets that herald to entire cities "what the Spirit is saying to the churches." Annacondia's radio program has become the leading program on most of these stations.

7. The Launching of *El Puente*

By late 1984 the changes discussed above were taking place in Argentina, but there was no national platform from which to address them. There was a felt need for a credible, middle-of-the-road means of communication. God raised up Marcelo Lafitte with a vision to launch a truly national interdenominational newspaper. He chose *El Puente* (The Bridge) as its name to illustrate its philosophy: to act as a bridge between two opposing shores on which people can meet to better understand each other, then return to their own shores, if they so desire.

El Puente is a guiding light which God has used to further establish His kingdom in Argentina.

From the first issue, *El Puente* became *the* newspaper for the Church in Argentina. During the difficult and sometimes confusing years when Annacondia was not totally accepted, when Omar Cabrera was still considered by some to be a charlatan, when the government was actively and deceitfully labeling the evangelical church as a sect in order to create the political climate to sanction restrictive legislation, *El Puente* was the voice of reason and objectivity. Marcelo Lafitte and his partner Daniel Puccio were successful from the beginning in offering its pages to the apostles of biblical unity in order to identify, validate and foster what the Spirit was saying to the churches.

Throughout the late 1980s and early '90s, *El Puente* proved consistent in rising above the dust stirred up by those who, willingly or unwillingly, opposed God's move in Argentina. Thus, the newspaper remains a guiding light which God has used to further establish His kingdom in this country.

8. The Inspiring Visit of Yonggi Cho

By early 1987 the move of God was almost five years old. Touches of institutionalization had begun to show up here and there. Some denominations felt satisfied with the extraordinary growth they had recently experienced and were ready to turn inward. David Hunt's infamous book, *The Seduction of Christianity*, with its unfair but piercing critique of the supernatural, had been translated into Spanish and was making the rounds among the leaders of the Church. Hunt made a special effort to criticize preachers who moved in the power of the Spirit, and the one he criticized most was Yonggi Cho.

When Cho called to tell me that God had told him to go to Argentina and to request that I organize his visit, I felt greatly honored. I felt that his message and his example as pastor of the largest church in the world would greatly benefit the Church in Argentina. However, except for Juan Terranova, the president of the Association of Christian Churches in Argentina, we received no institutional support. In fact many of the Christian radio and television programs turned against Cho and became advocates of David Hunt and his unbalanced and biased opinions.

Harvest Evangelism had just become established in Argentina and, as Cho's sponsors and organizers, our credibility was at stake. However, we pressed forward, keeping a tender attitude toward those who opposed us and trusting God to make all things work together for good. One hour before opening the gates of the Luna Park stadium, we had no idea if anyone was going to show up. But when the time came, 7,500 pastors and leaders packed the place to near capacity.

Cho's message was inspiring and empowering, but the most tangible fruit of his visit was the emergence of a new group of leaders who chose to examine the facts before reaching their conclusions. Many of today's key national and regional leaders in Argentina emerged for the first time during Cho's conference.

For us in Harvest Evangelism, it was a crucial moment as well, since as a result of our role we were given a national platform. Out of that came the exposure that allowed us to go to Resistencia to work alongside the local pastors in the now famous "Plan Resistencia." We were also left with enough credibility and visibility to organize an annual conference that has been imparting vision to a significant sector of the Church in Argentina for the last 10 years. As a result, today we are facilitating a plan for pastors to take each city in Argentina by the year 2000.

9. The Acceptance of Omar Cabrera and Vision of the Future
By 1987 Omar Cabrera was heading the most dynamic and fastest-growing Christian movement in Argentina. He founded Vision of the

Future in 1970 and, by 1987, was preaching face-to-face to 145,000 people every month! However, Cabrera had never been accepted as part of *the* Church in Argentina, even though he was a pioneer in city taking, power ministries, strategic-level spiritual warfare, intercession and highly contextualized evangelism.

After the Cho conference, Omar Cabrera gradually began to be accepted. As more and more of the emerging leaders talked to him for the first time, visited his headquarters in Santa Fe and attended his meetings, they found that everything he did had a biblical basis. And better yet, his work was producing great results!

This acceptance process reached its climax in October 1991 when first "The Movement" led by Swindoll, Bentson, Himitian and others, publicly asked Cabrera's forgiveness for the way it had treated him in the past. A week later, at our First Harvest Evangelism International Conference in Luna Park, Cabrera was acknowledged as a vital part of the Body of Christ in Argentina.

Why was this important? Because Cabrera had pioneered many of the practices that Annacondia had been popularizing, and these practices were still viewed by many as highly controversial. Adding Cabrera's solid theological reflection, not so much to Annacondia who is very solid himself, but to the myriad of younger preachers who began to imitate him, gave everybody a compass by which to keep the course and a very high standard against which to measure themselves.

10. The Emergence of Apostolic Leaders

Before the breakthrough, the Church in Argentina had a limited vision of the doctrine of spiritual gifts and their application. Spiritual gifts are discussed in three passages in the New Testament: Romans 12, 1 Corinthians 12 and Ephesians 4. The first two lists represent gifts given to people in the church. The third list describes gifted people given to the church. What is the difference? Well, a person with the gift of mercy or helps usually exercises his or her gift within the scope of a local congregation. On the other hand, Billy Graham could not exercise his gift of evangelism (at least not on a permanent basis) in the context of a local church. Why? Because Billy Graham himself is the gift to the church. The same could be said of such leaders as Bill Bright, Dick Eastman and Joe Aldrich. Rather than possessing a gift, these men are the gift themselves as described in Ephesians 4:11,12.

In the last five years, Ephesians 4 leaders have emerged all over Argentina. These men are recognized as a gift to the Church at large and, as such, they speak to the Church, even though the immediate setting may be a local church. Omar Cabrera is considered by many as the dean of them. Carlos Annacondia is another. Others include Eduardo Lorenzo, Omar Olier, Juan Calcagni, Pablo Deiros, Carlos Mraida, Pablo Bottari, Rino Bello, Jorge Gomelski, Juan Crudo, Tito Scataglini, Raul Belart, Norberto Carlini, Roberto Sorensen, David Thompson, Juan Passuelo, Ruben Proietti, Jose Vena, Pedro Ibarra, Juan Zuccarelli, Claudio Freidzon, Sergio Scataglini and Daniel Martinez. All of them have shared the same trench once the breakthrough began. All of them have touched and have been touched by Carlos Annacondia and his ministry.

This list is not exhaustive, and there are many more. The point I am trying to make here is that these men speak to the Church as a whole. They have the interest of the Church before their eyes, and everything they do aims at building the Church without partiality. In addition, they are good friends supporting and encouraging one another. This is a significant departure from the old days, when gatherings of leaders always produced their share of bloodletting due to seemingly unavoidable divisions caused by jealously of the worst kind. Those were days when the power of the leader emanated from his political position and the purse he controlled, whereas now the influence of these leaders is a result of the vision and anointing entrusted to them by the Holy Spirit for the benefit of the Church.

As stated earlier, many observers of the Argentine phenomenon trace its beginning to the emergence of Carlos Annacondia as a national evangelist. I agree with this position, and this is why I have sought to connect each of the preceding ten elements to the breakthrough with Annacondia's ministry. However, in order to fully understand that breakthrough, we must look at the precise moment when it occurred and at the circumstances then enveloping the nation and the Church.

What was Argentina like in 1982? The "dirty war" had just claimed the lives of thousands of Argentines (estimates run from 30,000 to 80,000), mostly young people who had "disappeared" in the middle of the night as they were detained by members of the army or the police. Army bases had been turned into detention camps, and many of them became slaughtering grounds where suspected terrorists were first brutally tortured and then killed in cold blood.

THE CURSE OF JOSE LOPEZ REGA

During the government of Juan Domingo Peron that preceded the military dictatorship, a leading priest in the Macumba religion, Jose Lopez Rega, had used his influence over Peron, his wife Isabel and the presidential cabinet to propagate witchcraft all over Argentina. First he infiltrated the media and the entertainment world, always ripe fields for the occult. Then he moved on to the captive audiences in the welfare and public school systems. In the 1970s and '80s, there was so much witchcraft in Argentina that the population was exposed daily to witches and warlocks, many of them prominent national figures, "testifying" on television and radio shows.

The Macumba leaders in Brazil (probably encouraged by Lopez Rega) got into the tourist business and began to organize "affordable tours of Brazil" for unsuspecting Argentines who, once in Brazil, were introduced to Macumba practices under the guise of exposure to the local culture. Thousands of tourists returned demonized without knowing exactly how it had happened.

A specific group targeted by the *Macumberos* was surgeons. Once initiated in the Macumba, surgeons were able to sew fetishes into the bodies of their patients while under general anesthesia. I personally was asked to help in a case where a lady under demonic control kept in check the elders of the Baptist church who tried to minister to her. They called me, totally puzzled by the inefficiency of their efforts. However, once the main demon was put under the direct authority of Jesus Christ he confessed that the key to their power over the lady was a fetish planted in her body by one of the leading surgeons in town. As the administrator of one of the local hospitals, I happened to know him and was able to verify his Macumba status.

Local churches were regularly targeted by witches' covens, and some of them suffered serious damage. I remember one particular church in San Justo where, all of a sudden, the church, known for its brotherly love and strong spiritual ties, began to experience the exact opposite. The elders, most of them lifelong friends, bitterly fought each other. The congregation took sides, and the church began to wither. When we visited the pastor, we felt that witchcraft was involved. We encouraged the elders to declare a truce and to come to our training center for prayer and intercession. As we shared with them basic principles of spiritual warfare, the elders took authority over the evil one and, as a corollary of their new found spiritual authority, they decided to put a specific area of town under spiritual authority. That meant that they prayerwalked that area and constantly showered it with prayers and intercession for its inhabitants.

THE WITCH CONFESSES

Soon afterwards a witch came to the Lord who "happened" to live in the area that had been put under spiritual authority. Immediately she confessed that she had been part of a conspiracy involving 29 other witches who had been cursing the church for the specific purpose of destroying it through division and strife among its elders.

The elders immediately redoubled their prayers; they also made the 29 remaining witches the object of their intercession. Many people from the area placed under authority began to come to the Lord. Less than a year later, this particular church played a key role in bringing Annacondia to town and seeing 70,000 people publicly receive Christ as described earlier in this chapter.

I could go on and on with examples like this. But this should be enough to show that the spiritual climate over Argentina was controlled by the evil one and that witchcraft had become an appealing alternative.

When the Argentine defeat in the Falkland Islands became known, a monumental vacuum developed, ready to be filled by something. What was there ready to fill it? Witchcraft! Organized Macumba! At that particular moment, the Church was largely unaware of the weapons available to confront such dimensions of evil. It is at that precise moment that God raised up Carlos Annacondia, a leader who did know what to do.

DEMONSTRATING GOD'S POWER OVER DARKNESS

Annacondia introduced the Church in Argentina to the reality of the heavenly places, to the imminence and transcendence of the spirit world and particularly the immediate presence and activity of demons. He proved and demonstrated beyond the shadow of a doubt the efficacy of the power available to the Church for its battle against the forces of darkness. He did not do it by teaching on it, but rather by demonstrating it through dramatic confrontations and power encounters that invariably produced powerful deliverance of the captives.

> Millions in Argentina struggled under the oppression of demonic powers. God used Carlos Annacondia to prepare the Church to set them free.

His campaigns became field laboratories and training grounds for the use of the divinely powerful weapons. The extraordinary number of converts bought him goodwill with pastors and leaders who might otherwise have been skeptical of his approach. The new converts, pouring into local churches in record numbers, immediately affected the spiritual climate of those churches. Through their dramatic testimonies they became living proof of the power of God over the power of the devil. The nation was already demonized to a degree. God used Annacondia to prepare the Church to deal with it.

Annacondia's ministry came at just the right moment to meet a felt need in the Church and in the nation. Even in the Church, many people had been under the influence of supernatural evil, as it was prevalent all over the country. Millions all over Argentina were struggling under the oppression of demonic powers. By meeting this felt need, Annacondia became accepted as the leader of something that at first had no name but was later called "God's visitation," "the Argentine revival" or "the move of God." Without a doubt, the majority of people in the Church could not get enough of it. The timing of Annacondia's arrival on the national scene plus the visible results of his message made him irresistible.

When a dam cracks, at first there is just a trickle of water. When it breaks completely, a lot of water rushes through and then a steady flow follows. This is also true of the spiritual breakthrough in

Argentina. The dramatic deliverances from demonic oppression were accompanied by signs and wonders such as tooth cavities being miraculously filled. Also, missing (or surgically removed) organs were re-created in answer to prayer. Angelic apparitions became almost common in the context of frontline evangelism. Children intercessors were sovereignly raised up by God in congregations all over Argentina. Spiritual mapping was pioneered, first in Resistencia, then in La Plata as God disclosed to the Church, mainly through Víctor Lorenzo, revelational insights into the devices of Satan in those cities.

CONFRONTATION IN THE PLAZA DE MAYO

Strategic-level spiritual warfare was done in downtown Buenos Aires on and around Plaza de Mayo, the site of so many evil deeds. Identificational repentance took place between Christians who used to be members of the police and the army during the "dirty war" and relatives of the disappeared ones. This eventually resulted in the government acknowledging the evil deeds committed by the security forces during the "dirty war." I have already described how the economy of Argentina was healed in response to public repentance at the Obelisk.

Resistencia, Azul and now San Nicolas have become cities reached for Christ. Another 20 cities are in process of being reached for Christ. Thousands of overseas visitors have come to Argentina to seek inspiration and insights to help them take their cities for Christ.

Furthermore, the first wave of anointing entrusted to Annacondia was followed by a new refreshment, given initially to Claudio Freidzon. Now an impartation for holiness has been deposited in Sergio Scataglini, who is faithfully dispensing it all over the country and beyond. Dante Gebel seems to be the depository of a special anointing to minister to youth.

As one can see, the picture of what is going on in Argentina is rich and complex. And even though everything I have mentioned or described up to this point is exciting, unique and extraordinary, I believe that God's redemptive gift for Argentina is none of the above. Please, allow me to close by discussing it.

God's Redemptive Gift to Argentina

Nations are created by God and their limits are established by the Almighty (see Acts 17:26). God allows a nation to come into being for a redemptive purpose. That divine purpose is always the target of the devil who tries everything in his power to obscure it and, if possible, to eliminate it.

This is why spiritual mapping should not be confined to simply discovering what the devil has and is doing in a city, but rather it must have as its final objective the uncovering of God's original purpose for that city.

One of the easiest ways to learn that purpose is to look for what the devil has done in the city. Usually it is the opposite of what God intended for that city. For instance, a city consumed with strife and division is usually a city called to brotherly love like Philadelphia in the United States. A city known for its greed like Minneapolis, Minnesota, is a city whose original purpose is generosity for the work of God.

The Stronghold of Pride

To identify Argentina's redemptive gift, we must examine what the evil one has been doing there. Argentines are known for their pride and for their self-centeredness. Our people have been constantly bombarded with statements to the effect that we are the best, that we are world leaders, that other countries should follow our lead.

Before the spiritual breakthrough of the 1980s, believers in Argentina were absorbed in developing the best-quality church, with little or no attention given to the lost. In fact, so few people were coming to the Lord that the Church, generally speaking, embraced (at least in practice if not in belief) a hyperdispensational approach to evangelism. Many leaders found comfort in the fact that each dispensation is supposed to end in failure. This belief told them that they were right on target since hardly anyone was responding to the gospel in the present dispensation of grace.

For instance, one of the most common criticisms of Cabrera when he was an outsider was that the mere size of his congregation proved he did not care for quality, since such quantity could not sustain quality.

The same was said of Annacondia's unusually large number of decisions at the beginning of his ministry. Something so big, it was thought, cannot be that good.

THE OPPOSITE SPIRIT: HUMILITY

If pride, self-centeredness and lack of concern for the lost is what characterized Argentina before the breakthrough, I believe that it is fair to say that God's redemptive purpose for Argentina involves the opposite of those three negatives:

1. Humility in the midst of successful public ministry
2. A servant heart toward other nations
3. A passion for the lost

Those that have met Annacondia, Lorenzo, Cabrera, Scataglini, Freidzon or any of the key players in the Argentine church are always impressed by their true humility. Carlos Annacondia's pastor, Pedro Ibarra, is one of the most humble men I have ever met. Even though leaders struggle with pride, there is a constant striving for true humility. Annacondia and Scataglini always ask those they had just prayed for to pray for them, and to that effect they kneel down in their midst.

In the last 15 years, key leaders from every continent have traveled to Argentina to receive a spiritual deposit. Thousands have come to our own conferences (which are held in eight languages) seeking inspiration and empowerment to go back and take their cities for Christ. God chose a humble town, Resistencia, in a very poor province, Chaco, to entrust Argentina with a principle to pass on to the whole world: how to reach a city for Christ.

When Alejandro Juszczuk, president of the Plan Resistencia committee, visited other countries in Latin and North America three years after the conclusion of the plan, he was deeply moved by the testimonies he heard everywhere of how blessed people have been by the principles behind Plan Resistencia. By that time, the pastors in Resistencia had fallen once again into disunity, and there was no agreement among them as to whether the plan had been a good thing. Upon returning to Resistencia, Juszczuk gathered the pastors together and explained to them, "What we thought was for us in reality was for the world. We need to pass it on." That declaration marked the beginning of better days for Resistencia.

PASSION FOR THE LOST

I would say the distinctive feature of the Argentine church is its new-found passion for the lost in stark contrast to the days when it could not have cared less about them. When one asks an Argentine pastor about his ultimate objective in life, whether he pastors a group of 50 or 5,000, the answer always describes the same objective: to reach the nation for Christ.

It is this passion for the lost that has steadily pushed the Church into the terrain where the forces of evil are deeply entrenched, and strong spiritual warfare is constantly required. By continually battling the forces of evil, the Church in Argentina is working to keep itself in shape. Let us keep in mind that the revival began in an evangelistic campaign in the context of intense spiritual warfare, and that the key player was a relatively new believer who had more in common with the multitude of sinners around him than with the Church he had just joined.

I believe this commitment to the lost is the main reason why the Argentine revival has lasted so long. As long as the Church continues to reach out to the lost, God will sustain the revival. As long as the Church enters territory held by the devil, it will have to keep its weapons cleaned, oiled and loaded. One of the unfortunate by-products of contemporary revivals in other lands is a lack of spiritual discernment regarding demonic activity as a result of a sterile focus on the saved at the expense of the lost.

In Acts 1:6 the disciples, upon hearing of the upcoming outpouring of the Holy Spirit upon their lives, asked if such thing would mark the return of the Kingdom to Israel. Jesus corrected them, saying that such was not going to be the case. Rather they would receive power through the Holy Spirit and as a result they would be His witnesses in Jerusalem, Judea, Samaria and the uttermost parts of the earth.

Notice that the lowest level of power Jesus promised was power to reach the city in which we live. For the original disciples it was Jerusalem; for you it is your own city. The next level up is power to reach our region, in this case, Judea. The following one is power to reach our nation. Finally, the maximum amount of power available to us is power for those determined to reach such countries as those inside the 10/40 Window.

When I first understood this, I came under tremendous conviction of sin because all my prayers for power have had to do with personal needs; none of them were concerned with the needs of the lost in my city, much less those in the 10/40 Window. Let the Spirit of God speak to you now. Do you want power? If so, for what? To expand your kingdom? God will only give us power for the purpose of reaching the lost, first in our city and from there, all the way to the ends of the earth.

ARGENTINA FOR THE NATIONS

As long as the Church in Argentina remembers that the power entrusted to it is not for itself but for the nations, the move of God will continue. As soon as you make reaching the lost in your city the all-consuming objective of your life, you, too, will begin to experience the power of God.

Is there a revival in Argentina? Would that those who do not believe there is revival in Argentina be proven right! Why? Because if what we have now—so extraordinary, so powerful, so contagious—is not revival, then there must still be much, much more to come! If so, I want to see it and be a part of it!

Note
1. Hilario H. Wynarczyk, "Tres Evangelistas Carismaticos: Omar Cabrera, Carlos Annacondia, Hector Gimenez," unpublished manuscript, Buenos Aires, 1989, p. 65.

INDEX